Timberlake

PLAYS TWO

Timberlake Wertenbaker's plays include *New Anatomies* (ICA, London, 1982), *Abel's Sister* (Royal Court Theatre Upstairs, 1984), *The Grace of Mary Traverse* (Royal Court), which won the Plays and Players Most Promising Playwright Award in 1985, *Our Country's Good* (Royal Court and Broadway), winner of the Laurence Olivier Play of the Years Award in 1988 and the New York Drama Critics' Circle Award for Best New Foreign Play in 1991, *The Love of the Nightingale* (RSC's Other Place), which won the 1989 Eileen Anderson Central TV Drama Award, *Three Birds Alighting on a Field* (Royal Court), which won the Susan Smith Blackburn Award, Writers Guild Award and London Critics' Circle Award in 1992, *The Break of Day* (Out of Joint production, Royal Court and tour, in 1995), *After Darwin* (Hampstead Theatre, 1998), *The Ash Girl* (Birmingham Rep, 2000), *Credible Witness* (Royal Court, 2001), *Galileo's Daughter* (Theatre Royal, Bath, 2004), *Arden City* (NT Connections, 2008) and *The Line* (Arcola Theatre, 2009). She has written the screenplay of *The Children*, based on the novel by Edith Wharton, and a BBC2 film entitled *Do Not Disturb*. Translations and adaptations include Marivaux's *La Dispute*, Jean Anouilh's *Leocadia*, Maurice Maeterlinck's *Pelleas and Melisande* for BBC Radio, Ariane Mnouchkine's *Mephisto*, adapted for the RSC in 1986, Sophocles's *The Theban Plays* (RSC, 1991), Euripides' *Hecuba* (ACT, San Francisco, 1995; BBC Radio 3, 2001) and *Hippolytus* (Riverside Studios, 2009), Eduardo de Filippo's *Filumena* (Peter Hall Company at the Piccadilly Theatre, 1998), Pirandello's *Come tu mi vuoi* and Gabriela Preissova's *Jenufa (Arcola Theatre, 2008)*

TIMBERLAKE WERTENBAKER

Plays Two

The Break of Day

After Darwin

Credible Witness

The Ash Girl

Dianeira

Introduced
by the author

faber and faber

This collection first published in 2002
by Faber and Faber Limited
74–77 Great Russell Street, London, WC1B 3DA
Published in the United States by Faber and Faber Inc.
an affiliate of Farrar, Straus and Giroux LLC, New York

Typeset by Country Setting, Kingsdown, Kent CT14 8ES
Printed in England by CPI Antony Rowe, Chippenham, Wiltshire

The Break of Day first published in 1995 by Faber and Faber Limited
© Timberlake Wertenbaker, 1995. Lyrics © Jeremy Sams, 1995

After Darwin first published in 1998 by Faber and Faber Limited
© Timberlake Wertenbaker, 1998

Credible Witness first published in 2001 by Faber and Faber Limited
© Timberlake Wertenbaker, 2001

The Ash Girl first published in 2000 by Faber and Faber Limited
© Timberlake Wertenbaker, 2000

Dianeira © Timberlake Wertenbaker, 2002

A CIP record for this book is available from the British Library

ISBN 978-0-571-21253-8

2 4 6 8 10 9 7 5 3 1

Contents

Introduction

If the plays in Volume One were mostly about discovery, discovery of language, of self, of art, the plays in this volume are essentially about identity. In a fluid and rapidly changing world, who are we? Who am I? In *The Break of Day*, gender identity is questioned and suffered. Is female identity ultimately bound up with having children? Three women face different options in an uncomfortable setting. Even *After Darwin* is about identity. The Captain of *The Beagle*, Robert FitzRoy, feels his identity threatened by Darwin's discoveries, and the play questions the possibility of moral certainty in a world that lives with the uncertainty of evolution. *The Ash Girl* is a fairy tale, the Cinderella story, but Ashgirl has to discover and affirm her own identity before she can find the Prince; and finally, *Credible Witness* is totally about identity: national identity and one's freedom within that identity. Every one of the eleven characters struggles with this troubling question and its emotional consequences.

Only *Dianeira,* originally a radio play inspired by the *Trachiniae* of Sophocles, does not quite fit and is more about anger than identity, although I think the two are linked.

Threatened identity or even troubled identity easily leads to anger. We long for certainty. The feeling of uncertainty is deeply uncomfortable. When not only the outside world but the inside world seem insubstantial, unreliable, that sense of discomfort is acute. All of these plays were written as one century and one millennium moved into the next. There is a sense of general trepidation, of fear. I felt a sense of discomfort myself, a feeling that the world was trying to redefine itself, no one really knew who they were and even basic assumptions about human beings were coming into question. It's been a curiously uneasy time for Britain, not knowing whether to place itself in Europe or in an Anglo-American paradigm. I felt this acutely, having been educated in France as a European but being of Anglo-American origin. And as I write this, we are in a very different and shifting world marked by 11 September and its consequences.

I feel, then, that I haven't finished writing about identity, the area is not totally explored. It does not, however, make for easy plays None of the plays in this volume has easy answers, none had an easy reception, and they are permeated with sadness: the sadness I have felt that in this twenty-first century, in this third millennium, human beings are in trouble in some way. They have lost their certainty. Perhaps it was never really there, but if you look at much of our literature you find periods of confidence and a kind of certainty, you find optimism, a sense of progress even. Perhaps this was lost with Darwin, then lost more profoundly in the twentieth century, partly through an awareness of the limits of science, its own uncertainty; and partly because of the savagery of the wars; then lost again with the fall of political ideologies in 1989; and now with 11 September, when even the rules of hostility have changed. Indeed, when there seem to be no rules.

What does the theatre do in all this? Well, you can batten down the hatches and go domestic. This is interesting and perhaps necessary. Or you can go out into the storm.

It's more solitary and scary and there may be fewer with you. When I talk to actors or other practitioners, I find there is a sense of identity crisis in the theatre itself and I have tried to reflect this in a couple of the plays. Too many plays have shown actors as charming, selfish children – I've done it myself. I wanted to show some of the questioning they themselves go through both with their work and their relations to the world.

I still believe the theatre is like some kind of cultural skin. It is the edge between the interior world we inhabit of poetry, language, music, and the exterior public world of other people, a crowd, a group, a *polis*. That edge, that skin is the point of contact between the audience and the play, it is a totally different experience from reading a book or a poem alone. It is more exposed, often more uncomfortable; one's identity can be put in question. I've noticed a tendency in the theatre to try to target audiences, gay plays for gay men, women's plays for women, black plays for the black community. If this succeeds, it will be a great shame. Perhaps, after all, it is not the best thing to have a solid, immutable and unquestioned identity, maybe it's more interesting to shed these skins occasionally, maybe it's more human to be uncomfortable. And finally, maybe it is more consoling, maybe even more hopeful to be uncomfortable in a diverse group, in an audience.

Most of the plays in this volume have large casts. One of my greatest sadnesses is that, to date, each has only had one production. In the past, I have honed my plays through the first two or three productions, maybe a few line changes, sometimes dropping entire scenes. All of these plays, I feel, would have benefited from second productions – some just to be seen by a wider audience. In the present climate, this is almost impossible. Nevertheless, here they are. Reader: I hope you will accept the uncomfortable edges of this work and find interest, even pleasure, in the shifting ground.

Timberlake Wertenbaker
27 November 2001

THE BREAK OF DAY

For D.

The Break of Day was first performed by the Out of Joint company at the Haymarket Theatre, Leicester, on 26 October 1995, and in London at the Royal Court Theatre on 22 November 1995 The cast in order of appearance was as follows:

Nina Maria Friedman
Tess Catherine Russell
Hugh Brian Protheroe
Paul Lloyd Hutchinson
April Anita Dobson
Natasha Madlena Nedeva
Jamie David Fielder
Robert Nigel Terry
Nick Barnaby Kay
Marisa Kate Ashfield
Mr Hardacre Jerome Willis
Mihail Bernard Gallagher
Dr Glad Lloyd Hutchinson
Eva Madlena Nedeva
Boian James Goode
Dr Attanasov David Fielder
Mr Statelov Jerome Willis
Dr Romanova Anita Dobson
Victor James Goode

Other characters played by members of the company

Director Max Stafford-Clark
Designer Julian McGowan
Lighting Designer Johanna Town

Sound Designer John A. Leonard
Musical Director Steven Edis
Dialect Coach Jeannette Nelson

Characters

Nina
Tess
Hugh
Paul
April
Natasha
Jamie
Robert
Nick
Marisa
Mr Hardacre
Mihail
Dr Glad
Eva
Boian
Dr Attanasov
Mr Statelov
Dr Romanova
Victor

When I was a little girl,
'Bout seven years old,
I hadn't got a petticoat
To keep me from cold.

So I went into Darlington,
That pretty little town,
And there I bought a petticoat,
A cloak and a gown.

Hark to me,
Listen what I say,
Little girls are important
At the break of day.

I went into the woods,
And built me a kirk,
And all the birds of the air,
They helped me to work.

The hawk with his long claws
Pulled down the stone,
The dove with her rough bill
Brought me them home.

Hark to me . . .

The parrot was the clergyman
The peacock the clerk,
The bullfinch played the organ,
And we made merry work.

Hark to me . . .

Hark to me . . .

Act One

The garden of a small country house in the middle of summer. Lawn, some flowers. Nothing grand, but beautiful and peaceful. It is early morning. Tess Warner is sitting with a huge pile of newspapers, which she is scanning very fast. She cuts out one small item. Nina Sehn comes out in a dressing gown. The women kiss on the cheeks.

Nina You're working.

Tess I wanted to get this done before breakfast.

Nina Can I help?

Tess Scan. Anything to do with women. Something individual. It'll be buried in the back pages.

Nina looks.

Nina Here: 'Fertility begins at forty.' It's about gardening.

Tess Here's one: 'Many of the motorway protesters who live for months in trees are women.' 'Women who live in trees,' that's a good title. Or, as my old paper would put it: 'The passions of a tree girlie.'

Nina I could do that –

Tess Nina, they don't have bathtubs up there.

Nina More than eighty per cent of England is within hearing distance of a busy road. It drives me mad.

Tess Does it disturb the music in your head?

Nina It disturbs the silence in my head.

Tess You could write a song about it.

Nina Joni Mitchell did it twenty years ago: 'They've paved paradise and put up a parking lot.' You can't write that song now.

Tess When we first met you were writing those types of songs. You'd formed your band.

Nina That's right . . . you came to interview us.

Tess I remember every moment of that night, don't you?

Nina I never think about the past.

Tess I felt so powerful. There you were, an all-female band, and I was the only woman reporter on a rock magazine. Women were exploding everywhere, with their anger, hunger, confidence, all those possibilities. We talked all night, you must remember.

Nina I must have met Hugh then. He was sent by his record company.

Tess That was because they realised women even had the power to sell albums. It was almost exactly twenty years ago – a week after my twentieth birthday.

Nina Your birthday, why didn't you say?

Tess I'm celebrating it this weekend.

Nina Now I understand. That's why April is coming.

Tess I can't believe she sang with you.

Nina Her voice was wonderful, but she only wanted the money to get her through university.

Tess Our formidable Professor of Classics.

Nina I hope she doesn't terrify everyone.

Tess I'll keep her under control. We'll have a great weekend. We'll send the men off to play tennis and we'll commemorate.

Nina I don't like to remember.

Tess That's because you're so secretive. I remember those consciousness-raising sessions, we'd all be describing our orgasms or lack of them in great detail and you'd say you had to protect the identity of your lover.

Nina Hugh was married at the time.

Tess As if orgasms have anything to do with the identity of the male. You were better once you were with Robert. Actually, I have a confession to make . . . It was the way you described Robert that made me decide I wanted him.

Nina I see.

Tess I felt I had a right to what I wanted. It goes with the empowerment I felt all my life. Born into this heroic empire – that's what they taught us – educated, national-healthed. Then the sixties when all you had to do was be very young. Being a woman in the seventies, then being in London and clever in the eighties, making money despite myself, buying this house. And now –

Nina Now?

Tess That's why you're here.

Nina I'm the last person who should be here.

Tess You succeeded where you wanted to – like me.

Nina I'm not doing anything, I'm a kind of traitor.

Tess Hugh says you've been working on new songs.

Nina What?

Tess I want to hear them. April will analyse our lives for us and then, then – I'll feel empowered again. We all will.

Nina Tess: I don't have any new songs.

Hugh comes in.

Tess Aren't you planning another album?

Nina (*to Hugh*) Is that what you're saying?

Hugh What a perfect morning. Clear, green, English.
I still love this country – although it's not as green as it
used to be: look at your grass.

Tess You need someone to play tennis. Where's Robert?
He's just been offered two jobs at once, after a year not
working.

Nina (*to Hugh*) Why are you saying I'm working on a
new album?

Hugh (*to Tess*) Isn't that good for Robert?

Tess One of them is a Chekhov in a tiny company for no
money, the other is a television. Poor Robert. It's going
to be a weekend of agonised indecision, he's probably
still in bed with the duvet over his head, I'll go and get
him for you.

Hugh You're the perfect hostess.

Tess I've looked forward to this weekend – I want to
celebrate, remake old friendships. When Jamie comes
you can have a powerful foursome.

Tess leaves.

Nina Why are you saying I'm working on a new album?

Hugh Because you are. You may not know it.

Nina There's nothing in my head.

Hugh It's not there yet.

Nina You need the successful album.

Hugh Yes, but so do you. I have other artists.

Nina So why are you pushing me?

Hugh I'm trying to help you, I think you'll be happier if you get some songs out –

Nina I tell you, they're not there.

Hugh Does that make you happy?

Nina No.

Hugh Then make an effort!

Nina You know it's not that simple. Anyway, I have other things on my mind.

Hugh I know, Nina, but you also have your work, it's under your control. That's what you do best.

Nina How can I know? I haven't tried anything else. I should get dressed. (*She doesn't move.*)

Hugh I love you. I want you to be happy. What's wrong with a happy marriage? Is it oppressive or something?

Nina Sometimes I feel I have to redeem you because you made your first wife so unhappy.

Hugh All I want is to enjoy this weekend, play tennis, get you to write one song.

Nina Tess is raking up the past – how we stood in front of life with all those possibilities – not because we were young but because it was that moment. I don't feel powerful at all, is that because of this moment?

Hugh There you are. Work it out.

Nina I can't, that's the point. I'll get dressed.

Hugh Will you wake Nick up?

Nina He's your son.

Hugh Nina –

Nina All right. I'll knock on his door. If he growls at me?

Hugh Growl back.

Nina goes off. Hugh is alone. Paul, the gardener, comes on.

Paul The question of happiness. Men never ask themselves if they are happy, they just have heart attacks. I'm Paul, I do Tess's garden. I remember your wife's first album. Sensational.

Hugh Don't tell her that.

Paul I have a girlfriend now, she says she'll only be happy if I marry her. I think to myself, at least this is an unhappiness we both understand. I want to keep it that way. If it doesn't rain soon, this lawn is going to die, all the lawns of England will die, all the gardens will wither. We'll have to do what they do in California and create desert gardens, but California is yellow anyway, whereas England is deep green. That would make me unhappy, if England became yellow. I've never understood how people can leave England for Greece and Spain.

He goes off. April comes on.

Hugh April. You look well.

April I'm exhausted.

Hugh Is it Sappho?

April Sweet of you to remember. Jamie always asks which Greek lady I'm writing about. No, it's the government. I used to teach. You know, talk to students, share learning. Now I fill in forms. I won't bore you with it.

Hugh It interests me.

April You Americans are always so courteous. This is a country where you don't need to act any more, you only need to describe actions on paper. My students don't ask me questions, they assess me. Was this teacher (a) very good, (b) mediocre, (c) unspeakable? What kind of dialogue is that? The easier I make things for them, that is, the less I teach them, the more they like me. Stop me. I've already ruined the morning. I wanted to have a romantic drive down with Jamie, I went on and on, he's now escaped to his mobile. How is Nina?

Hugh Inactive. Give her some lines of Sappho.

Natasha comes on and brings them coffee.

April They're only fragments. Fragments every generation fills.

Hugh That's what songs are. Fragments of a generation. Tell me more about Sappho.

Natasha leaves.

April There's your American politeness again. Who's that?

Hugh I'm Jewish, April, I like to know everything that's going on. I like to know about my musicians' lives. I'm not creative, I facilitate, mix, edit, but I'm always fascinated by what my artists pick up from the world. Why are young people returning to lyricism in music, why Sappho for you?

Natasha comes back on with croissants.

April A mystery. A woman about whom we know nothing, revered as the best among the best Greek poets. Thank you.

Natasha bows and goes.

Who is she?

Hugh One of Tess's servants it seems. Please talk to Nina about Sappho. Inspire her.

April To what?

Hugh Her third album. She has to do it.

April Why?

Hugh That's what she is.

April Are you sure?

Hugh I know these artists. They all get mesmerised by this idea of silence, because they're angry or they want to punish themselves. It's no good. You've seen Nina in front of an audience, you know it's the closest she comes to happiness.

April I'd like to find someone who loved me that much.

Hugh It's a burden I place on her.

April I could take it. Will you help me in exchange?

Hugh It's a deal.

April Talk to Jamie. It's been a year. He can't commit himself to living with me. He's even nervous about spending a night together in his sister's house. You can talk sense to him. There must be something that can be unlocked. We have a great time together then suddenly – tell me, am I frightening?

Hugh Not to me.

April Convince him.

Jamie comes on, distraught.

Jamie How do you start a revolution?

Hugh Hi, Jamie.

Jamie Apparently there's an article in the papers. (*He tears through the papers.*) It must have been something like this that led to the Peasants' Revolt, the Russian Revolution. One day, you say, I've had enough, how dare you do this, to me, to us?

April What's happened?

Jamie We'll have to organise a sit-in.

April Jamie, I left you five minutes ago with your mobile checking up on a little girl whose hand you'd saved.

Jamie is still tearing through the papers.

Jamie Here it is. I was good in chemistry.

Tess comes on with Nina. They kiss April. Jamie ignores them.

I know how to make a bomb.

Tess What's going on?

April We're trying to find out.

Hugh Jamie seems to want to join the Baader-Meinhof.

Tess Have you told him he's thirty years too late? What's wrong?

Jamie We've got to stop it. Tess, you've stopped things in your time. Greenham Common, all that.

Tess You can't become political overnight.

Jamie I just have.

Tess If I said I'd become a surgeon overnight, I wouldn't be allowed near a hospital. Stay away. You'll look silly. Tell us what's upset you and then let's forget about it.

Jamie Forget about it? They want to close down the whole hospital. It's in here! My hospital, the oldest, the best. I've worked all my life to become a consultant in a big NHS hospital. There's been nowhere better to be. Yesterday I saved a girl's hand. It took twelve hours. Finger by finger, vein by vein, one millimetre at a time. You get one finger sewn back in three hours and you ask yourself, Why are there so many damn fingers to a hand? But I did it. Not just me. My team. Together for ten years. I need to make five hundred different requests during such an operation. My theatre sister knows what I want before I ask. I hold out my hand, the instrument is there. The child will be able to move all her fingers. They want to close us down. I don't understand. It can't be the country that wants this: when I was only a junior doctor in Wales, they dressed up to see me, they called me Sir.

April They tried to close the Classics Department at my university. We fought.

Jamie Did you win?

April We compromised. We no longer teach Greek and Latin. It's classics in translation, without the bone, the beauty of the original language. And the classes trebled. We thought we'd won, but I suppose really we lost. Now they want us to make the degrees easier. We take weak students, we give them a good degree, they haven't learned anything but the university looks good.

Jamie I won't accept that.

April Dictatorships use force. Democracies convince you you are wrong.

Nina Or make you feel there's no value in speaking.

16

Robert comes on with an old-fashioned racket in its press.

Robert I'm a terrible host, I'm sorry. I was reading all night. Natasha's bringing more coffee and croissants for the women and I understand the men are playing tennis.

Jamie I'm not playing.

Tess You have to play.

Robert We have to do what Tess wants, we're celebrating her birthday.

Jamie It was last week.

Tess If you remembered, why didn't you send me a card?

Jamie I'm your brother, why should I send you a card?

April I remembered, I brought you a fabulous new translation of Marcus Aurelius, you know, the Stoic, my students love it.

Robert We're celebrating this weekend. We're playing tennis.

Tess I thought you'd all enjoy a good men's game. It's what you like doing together, isn't it, sport?

Robert I spent the whole night reading Chekhov's stories. The men never play sports, they talk. They talk endlessly. I envy civilisations where talking itself is a sport. I'd like to come to you now and ask you all to help me make a decision. I can play Vershinin or I can play in a television series about hospitals. It's badly written and the subject's been done many times before. But it's money. I feel embarrassed even saying this, the decision must seem unimportant. Being an actor is unimportant.

Tess Robert, this isn't talk, it's a melancholic soliloquy.

Robert I'm sorry.

Jamie People used to watch *Dynasty* and *Dallas* to escape. Now it seems the summit of people's fantasies in England is to be treated in an NHS hospital by a consultant like me.

Robert I shouldn't do the series.

Tess He didn't say that.

Nina You shouldn't do the series.

Robert I haven't worked for a year. It's well paid. I can't let Tess have all the responsibility – although – have you told them?

Tess No . . .

Robert Why not?

Tess It's not definite.

Nina What?

Robert It looks like Tess is going to be made the Editor of her magazine.

Nina You mean you're going to run it, that's wonderful!

April You can make some changes.

Tess Why?

April I was reading it last night and there are aspects I find unacceptable.

Robert I am so proud of Tess. Her own magazine.

April Yes, but she has to make it a worthwhile magazine.

Nina April, we can't all read the *TLS*.

Hugh That's a wonderful racket, Robert.

Robert I got it from a series. That was a good series, I had a small part but I was pleased to be in it.

Tess You don't have to do it.

Robert How can I tour for nine months for no money with a tiny theatre company no one will watch? And yet, last night, I opened the door on a whole world. Those three sisters suspended in an odd paralysis at the end of their century, with a cataclysm already in formation. There's something familiar about that paralysis, feeling outside history, I wanted to explore it – well – (*Pause.*) Even learn Russian. I didn't go to university like Tess, sometimes I get to learn on the job. I could if I did the part – but it's not responsible. Being an actor isn't responsible. It might be if it were valued. I keep reading articles on why no one wants to go to the theatre. I'm convinced.

April You see: democracy. You'll soon be convinced no one needs medicine: if people looked after themselves better, they wouldn't get sick in the first place.

Hugh I think you're forgetting you can also change things in a democracy.

Nina Not if you can't see them clearly. I walk out in the streets. I see a blur of misery, but I don't know where to focus. In this country, you're not encouraged to look.

Tess You mean look at the negative –

Robert Chekhov makes you look, but what's the point if nobody goes to look at him? Even Tess doesn't go to the theatre, except to mega-openings.

Tess I have to be seen. I don't always like it.

Robert I'm not complaining. Certainly one isn't seen on the opening night of a small touring company in Worthing. Let's play tennis.

Jamie Chekhov was a doctor, wasn't he? Why did he give it up?

Robert He didn't. That's what's so extraordinary. He – never mind.

Nina You should do what you want.

Tess That's what I say.

Robert But you don't mean it.

Nina Hugh says that to me, he says he'll produce any song I write, but he really wants me to sing something that will be a hit single.

Hugh That's a complete lie: I've always let you follow your caprices –

Nina Caprice.

Hugh Even you admit that feminist collective of yours was a caprice.

April You're not talking about our band!

Hugh No, that was fresh, it wasn't even that feminist.

April We disguised it.

Hugh After Nina's first album she decided to rebel and got mixed up with these women who spent all their time discussing whether they could allow a male producer and a capitalistic record company to interfere. It was a complete disaster, of course –

Nina Nobody promoted it.

Hugh Every interview was vetoed if it was a male interviewer. We couldn't find a cover, nobody would

dress as anything. We said to you, Be really masculine
if you want, be really feminine, just be something – men
in the music business usually make themselves really
feminine and they look great. OK, they don't have
thousands of years of exploitation behind them, but we
had a record to sell. Then there was your rustic phase,
playing to yourself in the back of remote pubs, bringing
poetry to rural areas or whatever you were doing –

Nina That was a great time. I took up riding.

Hugh But the music was bad.

Nina Does anybody care?

Hugh I did and so did your record company. Then total
silence from you.

Nina You said yourself no one was interested in songs
any more, kids were mixing the sounds themselves –

Hugh That's changed. The record company wants a
third album from you, it's in your contract, what can
I do to make her do it, what?

April You can't push her.

Tess I'd do an interview with you.

Nina I hate publicity.

Tess That's not integrity, Nina, that's suicide.

Nina I have a right to silence.

Hugh No, you don't!

Nina And then, England . . . it sort of makes you silent.

Hugh It's the government's fault now, is it?

Nina You treat me like a perverse childe. You have no
idea what it's like, day after day, trawling for the phrase,

the feeling, that'll catch the song. But when I get a glimpse, I think, No, it's not important.

April That's the discomfort of democracy. Everyone can speak, so all words have equal value, or none at all.

Tess I've loved every song you've written.

April So have I. Well, most.

Nina I was reading about Eastern Europe the other day, and the writer says culture is what allows society to understand itself. What struck me most was his confidence in using that word. I used to love that title: singer-songwriter. It feels meaningless. Using words, it's called chatter. Music, it's called sounds.

Robert I can understand that sense of worthlessness. I used to think I could change the world.

April I lecture to seventy students at a time, I'm already telling these kids they're worthless, there are too many of them for me even to remember their names. At Oxbridge, they would have one so-called eminent tutor, looking after them, one to one, valued –

Jamie I have this young patient who was born with a terrible face tumour. I've done seventeen operations on her. The last one would have restored her ear, but apparently some ear quota had been filled. I watched this withdrawn miserable child turn into an increasingly confident girl, but finally some manager decided her future happiness was too expensive.

Hugh Americans have always overcome their feelings of worthlessness by being in love with the future. Once you lose that, the rot really sets in.

Robert Chekhov seems to love the future, I'm not sure I do.

Jamie Does anyone in this country even believe in the future any more?

April I still do. I know that at least one of my nameless students will come into contact with an ancient, wise and passionate mind and ignite.

Nina To sing, you have to believe someone will be there to listen to you, not only now – in the future.

Robert If there is a future, by that I mean a future with language – I should speak the lines of Chekhov. If there isn't – it doesn't matter what I do.

Pause.

Tess It's not even lunchtime and we're all depressed sitting talking around a cafetière.

Robert The Russians sat around their samovar, talking –

Tess Look what happened to them.

Robert Time to play tennis.

Nick comes on.

There's our fourth.

Tess Did you sleep well?

Hugh What do you think about England, Nick?

Nick Not much, I mean, I don't think about it. Dad, listen . . .

Hugh Aren't students concerned?

Nick They're worried about money, Dad . . .

Tess What do they think about the world?

Nick Yeah. Dad, listen, what's happened is, look, Marisa's here.

Hugh Marisa?

Nick Remember? I told you, my girlfriend.

Hugh The beautiful blonde one?

Nick No, that was ages ago. You haven't met her. She's – well, she hasn't wanted – but look, she's here.

Nina You didn't invite her!

Nick No, I don't know how she found me, I mean, anyway, she's waiting, at the station, she's been travelling all night, she's just called –

Nina Aren't you going back to college on Monday?

Nick It's – she says it's important, she's waiting, Dad . . .

Hugh All right, we'll go and get her. Is she as nice as the last one?

Nick No, I mean, she's different, she's not like – I mean, she doesn't come from a family like this, you know, arty-farty, she's more – she's political too.

Nina We like that.

Nick Not like you, I mean, Nina, you and Dad, you'd drive two cars to an anti-traffic demo. Marisa doesn't even wear leather –

Tess We're having roast lamb for lunch.

Nick Maybe there's a vegetarian caff, we can stop on the way –

Tess This is the countryside, Nick, there's one pub, it'll be serving roast beef. She can have lots of birthday cake.

Nick She, you see, she doesn't believe in birthdays –

Tess I thought a birthday only oppressed the one who was having it.

Nick It's not that – well, she'll tell you herself, she's very together about it – I don't believe in birthdays either. Dad, you always forget mine.

Nina He forgets his own, Nick, he doesn't want to get old.

Nick Dad . . . Please –

Hugh and Nick go out.

Tess I'll see what I have in the kitchen. Robert, if you find Paul you could ask him if we have any vegetables, or herbs, or flowers she can eat –

Nina I'll come with you, I'm good on herbs.

Tess, Robert and Nina leave. April and Jamie are left alone. Pause.

Jamie I should go and ring some colleagues.

April If you want to mount a campaign for your hospital I can help you. There's a way of going about these things, using the press, everyone you know who knows somebody, getting to the Prime Minister for five minutes, it's quite disgusting in some ways, but you can win. (*Pause.*) What's wrong? You're giving me that look again.

Jamie What?

April I can't accept the keep-off-this-grass look. Why do you always make me feel I'm invading your territory?

Jamie This is such a shock for me.

April And I want to help you.

Jamie I know, but –

April Accepting my help would be some kind of commitment and you can't – I'm tired of being at the edge of your life. You should decide – now.

Jamie This isn't the right place, the right time –

April It is. Tess and Nina have men in their lives, what I call daytime men, they're there, in broad daylight, I have a twilight man –

Jamie Thanks.

April There for the evening, dinner, the first half of the night –

Jamie I operate in the mornings.

April You know what I'm saying –

Jamie All Tess, Robert, Hugh and Nina do is argue and complain about each other in public –

April I'll even accept that, it's part of the daytime man. I don't have to have it now, but I have to know it's going to happen.

Jamie I don't even know what's going to happen to my hospital.

April You can't wait for a new government to make an emotional commitment.

Jamie April, I have to ring my colleagues –

April I want an answer.

Jamie If you want an answer right now –

April I can wait until tonight, even tomorrow if we spend the night here. This is so humiliating . . .

Jamie I'm sorry . . .

He leaves. April is alone. She slaps herself. Natasha comes on. She sits next to April and touches her hand.

April I'm sorry?

Natasha Sappho.

April Are you Greek? Are you from Lesbos?

Natasha Lesbos. Sappho.

She lunges at April and kisses her.

April What are you doing!

Natasha Sappho.

Tess comes on.

Tess Natasha! What's going on?

April I think we're having a cultural misunderstanding.

Natasha Sappho, you say: Sappho.

April That's the point of my book. She wasn't gay, at least not in the way we understand the word, it's a historical misunderstanding –

Tess I'll have to fire her, she's mad.

April Baffled, lonely, in a foreign country. In America once, I was very flattered by the attentions of a male student, until I realised he wanted me to pay him. That was supposedly the same language.

Tess She knocked on the door looking for work, I assumed she was from Bosnia. She's probably from Cardiff.

April You can't be gay and a war victim?

Tess Where are you from?

Natasha Kitchen. I go –

She goes. Robert and Nina come in.

Robert Paul gave us some dandelions, some nasturtiums, every herb in *Hamlet* and he said he'd ask our neighbour

Mr Hardacre for tomatoes. He's doing wonderful things in the garden, how much do we pay him?

Tess You mean how much do I pay him –

Robert Fine. I'll take the telly.

Tess I didn't – I'm sorry, April's almost been raped by a Bosnian. I don't know what to do about lunch – I wanted this to be such a good day.

April I'll go and apologise to the poor woman, she should really apologise to me. Have you noticed we're the most arrogant nation on earth but we always apologise? But no, I should apologise –

Tess Why?

April Because we don't know where she's from, and her life has ceased to interest us, although we cry for her on television, because our imagination has been depleted by this terrible century – because words like compassion and humanity have cracked in the last fifteen years and we've let it happen –

Tess It's Jamie, isn't it? Do you want me to talk to him?

April What can you say?

Tess I'll tell him how odd and wonderful you are.

April He knows that, it's not the problem.

Tess and April leave.

Robert In *Three Sisters* the characters contemplate the end of their century with that same sense of waste, of being outside history, but Vershinin intoxicates himself with a vision of a better future. I don't believe Chekhov intends to mock that. He kept building schools: humanity could become better.

Nina My grandmother started life like one of those sisters, but then she found herself in St Petersburg during the famine. She often told me how she went in search of bread to bring back to her son, my father, but ate it all on the way back. I don't think she was a very good mother. My father said she kept him in short trousers so she would seem younger and remarry and get out. A lot of those Russians went around missing their estates, but I think she enjoyed it: migration, husbands, lovers, history. Even when she was old she kept moving house. I have her restlessness and I envy her experience of history.

Robert Ninotchka, you never told me about her.

Nina You weren't playing Vershinin.

Robert I'm not playing him now. How can I? Tess and I want children, did she tell you? Aren't you still her best friend?

Nina Friendship is like marriage, there are Siberian wastes you don't cross.

Robert She'd sort of forgotten about it in the heady eighties, I reminded her we ought to start. I think she thought it would be like everything else and she would have two perfect children there and then. She went to the women's magazine to have more time – you can't really have a child if you're on a daily. That was three years ago. We don't talk about it. I study the calendar secretly. It's beginning to feel like Lorca's *Yerma*. All last year I was thinking how nice it would be to take my children to the park, but I wasn't working. If there's going to be a child, I ought to do the telly, otherwise . . . I would love to do Vershinin . . . Did they ever find out what was wrong? I'm sorry, is it painful for you?

Nina I keep hoping. And there are other ways . . .

Robert Tell me . . .

Nina Is that why you left me?

Robert I left you because you did nothing to keep me.

Nina There were so many men, so many possibilities. Some of my friends solved the problem by sampling a lot of men at once, I could only do it serially. You were better than most because you were an actor so you paraded a lot of different men in my life, but then I never had you . . .

Robert I never had myself . . . In Chekhov there's one moment when two people might come together and find happiness, but one hesitates, or makes a wrong move, and those people's chance is over, for ever . . .

Nina We felt we had an infinite number of chances . . .

Robert Will you stay faithful to Hugh?

Nina Yes. It's less tiring mentally. But whenever I think I'm happy, I begin to feel this gnawing in my stomach and that worm eating out the black hole that women can never fill. I tried to write a song about it once, this void inside us, insatiable, unfillable. You don't have it.

Robert We work, we think about the future.

Nina We work. It's still there. It's worse because we can no longer say it's because we have nothing to do.

Robert Children . . .

Nina . . . not to fill the void.

Robert But to fill the future . . .

Nina I compose lullabies in my head. I can't tell Hugh.

Robert Nina, I miss you.

Nina Don't.

They embrace. Tess comes on.

We were remembering.

Tess I've been remembering all weekend. Is this my retribution?

Nina I never really forgave you.

Tess What's feminism for if we still hate each other?

Nina It's a peace treaty, not a love feast.

Nina and Tess go off.

Robert 'How can I put it? It seems to me that everything in the world must gradually change – two hundred years hence, three hundred years . . . eventually a new and happy life will dawn.'

Robert shakes his head. Marisa rushes through.

Marisa I'm going to be sick.

She comes back and looks at Robert and screams.

You're that rapist. On the television.

Robert I played a rapist. I'm an actor.

Marisa Yeah. And you're that father.

Robert No . . .

Marisa In that film, the one who sleeps with this girl but doesn't know she's his daughter, that could have been me, I mean, I don't know who my father is.

Robert I'm sure it's not me.

Marisa Where were you in October 1973?

Robert I can't remember, probably on tour in the north of England.

Marisa There you are. My mother was in the north of England. She can't remember. She was drunk. I'd know if I was sleeping with my father. How come she didn't know?

Robert I don't know, I didn't ask her.

Marisa You were sleeping with her!

Robert Only in the film. We did what the director told us.

Marisa It's terrible not to know who your father is, how could he have done that, my dad? I think men should take responsibility, don't you?

Robert Yes.

Marisa I'm going to be sick again. No. It's gone.

Robert I think you want to speak to Nick about this.

Marisa How can you know what I want?

Robert It's my job as an actor, finding out what someone wants. I'll call him.

Marisa I wanted to tell them in the car but his dad kept talking about raves. Weird. I guess he wanted to be friendly, but I like opera. My favourite video is *Bluebeard's Castle,* by Bartok, do you know it? I could have been a musician. In my last foster home, they had a piano, but it was too late. I suppose Nick told you I was in care. I'm not ashamed of it, it wasn't my fault, people look at you as if it was. I was lucky, I wasn't abused, but two of the families were struck off. The one with the piano, they loved me, but I was already sixteen, they couldn't keep me.

Nick comes on.

Nick Lunch is almost ready, Nina's made a nasturtium salad, it looks great, come and meet everybody.

Robert Marisa has something to say to you. I'll tell Tess and send her out. (*to Marisa*) I think it's good news. (*He goes.*)

Nick What?

Marisa He's nice for a duvvie –

Nick A what?

Marisa Isn't that what you're supposed to call arteestes?

Nick Don't mention those words in this house. Also, look, don't tell jokes about, you know, racist, using those words. I never told you, but Dad's Jewish.

Marisa You never told me he was American. That accent's so oppressive.

Nick What's the good news?

Marisa I haven't slept. I had to take three different trains.

Nick How did you find me?

Marisa I called your mum.

Nick You called my mum!

Marisa I wanted to see you.

Nick Well.

Marisa Can't you guess?

Pause.

Nick No.

Marisa The surgery called yesterday, it's definite.

33

Nick But –

Marisa Didn't you say your dad and Nina couldn't have children. Now they can have a grandchild.

Pause.

Nick Don't tell Dad. (*Pause.*) Look, I'm not sure – I have to finish my degree, then I want to go to America, do a postgraduate. Dad doesn't have any money any more, I mean, you don't have to have it.

Nina comes on.

I need a walk. I'll – I'll – I don't – I don't want it. (*He goes.*)

Marisa You must be Nick's stepmother. Nick says the divorce was very painful for him, maybe that's why he can't be responsible now.

Nina Don't you kids learn sex education in schools?

Marisa Yeah, Nick and I both had an AIDS test.

Tess comes on.

Nina Didn't you take precautions?

Marisa I was sure I couldn't have children. My mother couldn't.

Nina She had you.

Marisa She always said that was a miracle, except she didn't want me.

Nina Wouldn't that suggest –

Marisa I took risks before, nothing happened.

Nina I can't believe this.

Tess It doesn't matter, women make mistakes. I can help you. I know a good clinic. I can make an appointment for you.

April comes on.

Marisa Thanks.

Tess Shall I make one for next week?

Marisa There's plenty of time.

Tess Not that much, you should go soon.

Marisa I know what to do. I'm taking lots of vitamins.

Tess Wait – you're not planning to have it?

Marisa It's a baby.

Tess It's not a baby yet, Marisa.

Nina What did Nick say?

Marisa I don't care. It's not his. I mean it is, but it's mine.

Nina He has years of study ahead of him. On a tiny student grant. You can't expect him to quit and work in a supermarket.

Marisa The state helps you.

Nina Not any more.

Marisa I'd like to work on a magazine. I like writing.

Tess What are your qualifications?

Marisa I have a GCSE, I can learn to type.

Tess I have girls with firsts from Oxbridge desperate to work as secretaries. They're whizzes at computers.

Marisa I'll work in a pub.

Tess Who's going to look after the baby? Your mother? Didn't you tell Robert she was an alcoholic?

April What are you two trying to do?

Tess Don't meddle, April.

April I'm ashamed of you.

Nina We're trying to look at facts.

April Isn't the reason you haven't had children, Nina, because of an abortion that went septic?

Nina It was a back-street one, you and I marched to make them safe.

April But not to force young women to have them if they don't want to.

Tess April, shut up.

Marisa She's right. You're trying to make me kill my baby, you're child murderers – animal murderers – and –

Nina We're trying to get you to make a sensible decision.

Marisa So I can end up like you, married to ambition, bitter and childless –

Tess We've waited until we could look after our children –

Marisa Looks like you've left it too late –

Tess I don't think so – and at least we won't bring them up on a council estate with a succession of violent men.

Marisa Nick isn't violent.

Nina What makes you think he'll stay with you?

Marisa runs off, crying. Pause.

April I hope you're proud of yourselves.

Nina She can't ruin Nick's life.

April Do you remember Tony? He made me have an abortion, wait until he was divorced for us to have a child. Then his wife got pregnant. I should hate him for ten years of false promises, but I hate her. She was only trying to survive. You're not trying to help Marisa, you simply hate her.

Nina What if Marisa did it on purpose? We fought against that behaviour too.

Tess I don't hate her, I hate stupidity.

April So she has no right to children? I can understand you betraying feminism in your public life but you could at least apply some of it privately.

Tess Who's betrayed feminism? I'm on one of the best magazines around.

April Women's shlock.

Nina I have fun reading it.

Tess It has serious articles.

April Sandwiched between adverts for lipsticks and orgasms.

Tess Orgasms went out of fashion In the eighties –
I think the idea was they took too much time –

April Filofaxes, whatever.

Tess They went out of fashion in the nineties, reminded people of the eighties.

April All right, whatever it is.

Tess New Labour. No ideology. Going with the flow. Being gay is stylish. Trees. No cars.

Nina I'm for that.

37

April (*over*) I remember what you used to write, the analysis, it was astounding.

Tess *Eve's Pear.* Read by twenty-five people.

April You had one of the best minds – your deconstruction of just the kind of magazine you're editing. How it held up an image of happiness that was unattainable.

Nina Happiness is unattainable, April.

Tess We've had twenty years to discover women don't like serious magazines, they like the ads.

April What can you decide in twenty years? You wanted money, you succumbed to a designer version of yourself – just as you have a designer version of mothers.

Nina You've read the statistics about those mothers, they're frightening.

April The answer isn't forbidding them to have children.

Nina I didn't say that! Or did I? I hope I didn't.

Tess Anyway, we don't say designer, we say label.

April Let me say what I mean: you were corrupted –

Tess Who wasn't?

April You were the standard-bearer – not Nina with her songs, not me stuck in my classics, not a lot of other women – you, with your sense of the moment. Listen to you now.

　Short pause.

Tess I want a child. I was horrible to Marisa because I was envious, because she has what I want. I could bring it up, I could give it love, and nature goes for an irresponsible girl who only wants a doll. I've been trying for three years, I'm forty years old. I'm in biological recession. I want a child. I've never wanted anything so badly.

Pause.

April Having a child isn't the only purpose of a woman's life. That was our credo.

Tess We were wrong.

April Don't say that.

Tess I don't want that conclusion, April. I organised this weekend to avoid it. That's why I asked you. Not just my oldest friends, but my only friends who don't have children. We'd validate each other. Get back some of the passion of our early days when that was the last thing we wanted. Then *she* comes.

Nina There are so many children in the world. Lost. Waiting. Why don't you look into that? I have lots of information.

Tess I couldn't cope with a child who's been abused in different foster homes for years. You have to know your strengths. I want my own child, in here, like her. Lunch must be ready. We have to celebrate.

April Tess, you will get over it. You accept the consequences of your choices. You grieve. You go on.

Tess I wasn't trained for grief. None of our generation was.

Tess and Nina go. April stays. Paul comes on.

Paul I've read a lot about the sixties generation.

April We came later. We were the women of the seventies, no one talks much about it.

Paul I'm a child of the eighties.

April leaves as he speaks. Paul follows. Nick and Marisa come on.

Nick There won't be any trains.

39

Marisa I'll walk.

Nick In your condition?

Marisa Who cares?

Nick I do.

Marisa You don't. You're just like them –

Nick I'm not.

Marisa Always thinking, talking, telling others what to do, you can't feel anything.

Nick I haven't got used to the idea . . .

Marisa See: idea. It has a heart, it wants love.

Nick Yeah . . .

Marisa It's a miracle, I was really sure I couldn't. You have to give in to life.

Nick Yeah. But now you know you can, maybe later – in a few years –

Marisa You see, just like them, escaping into the future. This is my family. Now.

Nick Yeah, but what about the – well, for it, the future.

Marisa I hate that word. I'm going.

Nick Marisa, stay.

Marisa Why? You don't care.

Nick I do. It's part of me.

Marisa Only if you want it to be.

Nick I do.

Marisa You do?

Nick Yes.

Jamie and Hugh come on.

Jamie We haven't met, I'm a doctor, Tess sent – are you all right?

Marisa I don't believe in doctors, I do herbs.

Jamie That sounds sensible. I heard you weren't feeling well –

Marisa I'm fine. I wouldn't listen to you anyway because I don't trust authority, but I'm fine.

Nick Dad, we're going to make it work together.

Hugh Ah – well, if that's what you want.

Marisa Yeah. Would you like us to call it anything? I mean, I thought if it's a boy, maybe Yehudi –

Hugh Mm – I don't know . . .

April comes on.

Marisa If you don't feel strongly about, about the fact that you're a – I mean, if it's a girl maybe she could have an Indian name, like Sunrise.

Hugh You have a long time to think about that –

April Aurora means sunrise in Latin, that might be better –

Marisa That's good. Is Latin very difficult to learn? Maybe I could become a Latin teacher in my spare time.

April (*to Jamie*) You brought my bag to the guest room, but not yours.

Jamie I left it in the car.

April I'll unpack it for you.

Jamie I called most of my colleagues, the ones who aren't playing golf or tennis. Two of them are leaving the NHS, one's leaving medicine altogether. One of them kept going on about this Shop-a-Doc idea, said we were being turned into a medical Securitate, everybody spying on everybody else.

April You're already giving up. Why don't you get your bag?

Jamie No one seems to know how to fight.

Hugh The trouble with these campaigns is that they exhaust you. Even if you win, it's usually only for a while, then you have to start again. You need support while you're doing it.

Jamie Yes.

Hugh You need a wife, someone intelligent, who knows about these things, like Tess, or April.

Jamie I don't want a family in these circumstances.

April I don't want a family.

Jamie Later, I'd like one.

Hugh Anyway, you need a wife.

April (*to Hugh*) It's too late. The moment's passed.

Beat. April turns away.

Nick Marisa and I don't agree with campaigns. We think that if you lead your life properly as an individual, that pervades the world.

Marisa I've refused to learn to drive.

Hugh You could be right. Maybe progress is the last ideology and that too needs to be exploded. But that would be painful, you're asking for a future where there's no more expansion. You stop with what you have. Zero growth. That's what you young people are into. It's great.

Nick Dad, you're off again.

Marisa I haven't understood a word either, but I'm going to like having you as a father-in-law.

Nick Marisa!

Robert comes on.

Robert I've prepared a surprise for Tess. Nina is going to sing a song she's composed –

Hugh You've got Nina to sing?

Robert Natasha is lighting the candles. Where's Tess?

April She was looking for her mobile.

Robert I've made the decision. It's a kind of small political gesture. I'm going to play Vershinin. I called the director earlier. He didn't even sound surprised. I'd forgotten how arrogant people are in the theatre, I'm agreeing to starve for a year and he seems to think I should be pleased to have the part. Where has he been in the last fifteen years?

Tess comes on and kisses Robert.

Come and celebrate.

Nina comes on, followed by Natasha with a cake. Nina is singing her song, leading into 'Happy Birthday', which they all sing. Paul comes on with a mobile, which is ringing; he hands it over to Tess with distaste.

Paul I was hoping to bury it.

Marisa You can be seriously damaged by passive mobile phone use.

Tess (*answering the mobile*) Who? Miss Sehn. Nina, it's for you.

Nina For me? Ah – (*answering the mobile*) Yes? What? A little girl . . . I see. How old is she? Yes, yes, we have everything.

Hugh has begun to listen.

Hugh A little girl . . .

Nina clicks the phone off.

Nina She's there. She's waiting for us.

Robert Who? Where?

Hugh Our little girl . . .

Tess No . . .

Nina She's in Eastern Europe. She's not well.

Tess No.

Nina I enquired a year ago. It didn't look possible.

Tess You didn't even say anything.

Nina I couldn't talk about it. I tried, earlier.

Tess And now, on my telephone, no.

April Tess – be generous.

Nina Come with me, Tess, there are so many children.

Tess I don't want some stolen Romanian baby with AIDS. We ran articles on them.

Nina All media stories about adoption are negative. I've done my own research.

Jamie We have had some very sick children from Romania.

Nina It's not Romania.

Robert It's very exciting.

Nina Tess, I mean it, come with us.

Tess I won't, Nina, but I do wish you well, I do. I've decided to go to a fertility clinic. I know of a very good one. I'll call on Monday. I don't want to waste any more time.

Jamie Tess, do you know what you're getting into?

Tess Yes. Now I want to drink to Nina and Hugh. There's some elderflower water for Marisa.

Nick Dad, does this mean you're going to be a dad again?

Hugh So it seems.

Nick I hope you do a better job this time. Look, I'll give you advice.

Marisa I think it's great news. Weird. But great.

Jamie My hospital has the best paediatric department – well, used to. It may be open for a few months –

April I'll advise you on schools.

Paul I'll plant a tree.

Mr Hardacre, a man of eighty, comes on with a suitcase.

Mr Hardacre Good day. Paul said you needed some tomatoes for the intruder. (*He opens his suitcase and carefully brings out the home-grown tomatoes.*)

Robert Thank you, Mr Hardacre, will you join us?

Mr Hardacre I'm going on my march with my suitcase.

Nick A march? Where?

Mr Hardacre It's my wife. I was born the year the First World War started. My dad survived, but three of my

45

uncles died. Look at this tomato, isn't it beautiful? My wife's father was a Jew from Macedonia, he had a good business in France. When they were rounding up the Jews, this is 1943 now, I was in the RAF, she and her mother escaped. This was her suitcase. I met her in 1949. She taught at the village school here and to this day old pupils come looking for her, I think because she brought an air of history with her. She was such a good teacher, she had a temperament, the children loved it, she used words like art, truth, beauty, not very English, you might say. She always kept her suitcase. She died three years ago just when the war in Eastern Europe started. I watch the television all the time now. And I see them. I think I see her. People with suitcases, walking, walking with their suitcases. I thought we'd never see those images again. Do you remember in Denmark how everybody wore a Star of David as a protest against the Nazis? To say we are all one. This suitcase is my Star of David. I'm going to march with my suitcase every day for the rest of my life. I'm going to protest against history.

He goes. Pause.

Nina Natasha, where are you from?

Natasha Madame, quick, your candles. (*She points to the candles on the birthday cake, burning low.*)

Tess Yes. My candles.

Fade.

Act Two

The airport of an Eastern European country. Hugh, Nina and various airport scroungers.

Nina We've been waiting for an hour and forty-five minutes.

A Man approaches them.

Maybe he won't come. Maybe it's a hoax.

Man Taxi? Very good car.

Hugh (*to the Man*) We've told you: we're waiting for someone.

Man Maybe he not come.

Hugh (*to Nina*) I spoke to him on the telephone from London – he'll come.

A Woman approaches.

Woman Hotel? Very good room.

Hugh (*to Woman*) We have somewhere, thank you. (*to Nina*) Are you sure you want to go through with this?

Woman Where? Where you stay?

Hugh We don't know, it's been arranged –

Nina I suppose you don't.

Woman Best room in the city. Best view of demonstrations.

Hugh No!

The Woman goes.

If it's what you want.

Nina What's the point if you don't?

Hugh I have a son. I know it's not the answer to every thing.

A Man approaches.

Man Currency? Very good terms.

Nina You don't think it's going to work. Fine. Let's go back. There must be flights tonight.

Man Better than bank, better than black market.

Hugh This is Eastern Europe, there is probably only one plane and it's gone. We may need currency, I couldn't get any in London. Let's see it through. (*to the Man*) What's the exchange rate?

Man Very good terms.

A Woman comes on.

Nina It's not a record contract, you have to want it to happen.

Woman Icon? Very good saint.

Hugh I want it to happen for you. (*to the Man*) OK, here's fifty dollars, what do I get?

Nina That's not good enough.

The Man grabs the money.

Man Much. Much. I come back. (*He goes.*)

Hugh Wait!

Man Taxi?

48

Hugh (*to Nina*) I think I've just lost fifty dollars.

Man Taxi?

Woman Saint, makes miracles.

Hugh I'm supposed to be producing three tracks for one of my favourite singers. I've delayed for two weeks to come here, isn't that enough?

A Gypsy comes on, begging, with something wrapped like a baby.

Nina Not if you don't want it.

Hugh I said I would help you even if it's a completely crazy idea.

Nina That's a useless attitude.

Hugh (*to the Gypsy*) We don't have any local money.

Gypsy I take dollars.

The woman selling icons spits at the Gypsy and sends her away.

Woman You need saint protection in this country. Here.

Hugh All right. It's a wonderful adventure. Where is this man?

Two Students come on with flowers and hand them to Nina and Hugh. They take them, astounded.

Girl Student Welcome.

Boy Student We come every evening and now you are here!

Hugh Wait.

Boy Student Our director is here too, he is very tired but the joy of seeing you will make him better. I run to get him.

Nina I think there's a mistake.

Girl Student Dahvid, Kyril?

A Bookseller approaches.

Bookseller Books.

Hugh We are Hugh and Nina.

Girl Student You are not Dahvid Edgahr and Kyril Churchill, not delegation of United Kingdom theatre?

Hugh My wife's a singer.

Girl Student Oh, this is terrible.

Girl takes back the flowers.

Every day for week we come with flowers. With fax and telephone broken at our drama academy we do not know arrival.

The Boy Student comes on with a very effete, well-wrapped, fatigued Director.

Director C'est avec plaisir que jour après jour nous vous attendons. (*He holds out a delicate hand.*)

Nina Nous ne sommes pas – Je suis une chanteuse.

Director Quel dommage. Ça ne fait rien. Venez voir notre théâtre. C'est au milieu de la ville. *Les Trois Soeurs.*

They lead the Director out. He waves in a kind of blessing.

Bookseller (*taking out his books*) Agatha Christie. Guide to this country. Greek myths.

Hugh Can I see the guide? (*looking at the book*) It was written in 1968.

Bookseller Classic.

The money-changer comes back on.

Man Here. You count?

Hugh I'm sure it's fine.

Hugh buys the guidebook. A Prostitute comes by.

Prostitute Massage?

Nina No thank you.

Prostitute Men only.

Woman Saint. Buy saint.

An Old Man comes on.

Old Man Medals? Uniforms?

Nina What are we going to do?

Man Taxi?

Other Man I am also guide. This country is not – (*gestures width*), but it is – (*gestures depth*). Ancients, Greeks, Romans, Khans, Byzantium, Turkish Yoke, Russian Yoke, now West. I show you ancient monuments and new monument by American democracy.

Woman You cannot sleep in airport, I take you to hotel.

Other Woman Saint, you have saint.

Man Taxi! I take luggage now.

Mihail comes on, breathless. He rushes to Hugh and Nina, shakes their hands as everyone else disperses. He is formally dressed.

Mihail Hugh, Nina, you are so welcome. I spent all last night in a petrol queue. Two hours before your plane is to land in this country they run out. I abandon the car, I rush to the bus, the bus does not come. Such is our life in the new chaos, but your hotel is booked, we will take a taxi, eat supper, and tomorrow we look for your child.

Nina Where is she?

Mihail That is what we do not yet know.

Hugh We understood she was in a hospital here in the capital.

Mihail She was. But she is now out of hospital. That is good news, no?

Nina Yes, but where is she?

Mihail I think she is not in the capital. This happens.

Nina What's happened?

Mihail Nothing has happened. It can happen a child is here and then somewhere else. Or that we have not understood where she is. I have a good friend at the Ministry of Health, he will find. And tomorrow you will meet my wife, Eva. Now let us go to the hotel and then to dinner.

Hugh My wife would like to rest.

Mihail We have very good restaurants in this city.

Hugh Thank you, Mihail, but we're both very tired.

Mihail And then the wine is not expensive although it is more expensive than it was. I have arranged a table.

Nina Of course, we'd be delighted. Mihail, I can't stop thinking about the child.

Mihail We will find her.

Nina Tomorrow?

Hugh I have to get back in a few days.

Mihail Do not book your ticket yet. This is a beautiful country. Perhaps tomorrow we go to the mountains.

Song.

A London clinic. Dr Glad, Tess, Robert.

Dr Glad We can do anything. Have you seen those
strange fertility goddesses in the British Museum? Now
women have us. You seem to have what we call reduced
fertility. Nothing is wrong, but nothing is right. It may
be that naughty biological clock for you, Tess. And the
twentieth century isn't kind to men with their sperm
count. First we'll jolly up your eggs with two weeks of
hormones, given to us by nice menopausal women,
mostly Italian nuns, that's why it's quite expensive. Then
in about two weeks, a little operation. On that day, we'll
cream off the best of your sperm, give it a good spin
and presto. A nurse will go over all the details with you.
You'll have to be examined every other day, so we advise
you to give up work. I don't like to give interviews,
but you can see me on the television tonight on the six
o'clock news, we've performed another miracle. Best of
luck. You pay as you go out.

Robert Luck?

Dr Glad Attitude is important. Think positive.

*Inside a church. Hugh, Nina, Eva. Also some people
doing what people do in Eastern churches: crossing
themselves, kissing icons, muttering.*

Eva (*to Nina*) What a beautiful face you are, the face of
someone who suffer too much. I, too, suffer. You cannot
have a child from this country.

53

Nina We were told we could have a child who was ill. Eva, I want to see her.

Eva My husband says someone from the ministry come, but he cannot. My husband, he is old. His power is – thrown over. And this man, he is gypsy. But I pray and maybe God listens to me.

Mihail comes on.

Mihail I call, he is not there. He must come soon.

Hugh We've been here an hour and a half.

Mihail I am a Marxist but I am proud of our churches. We respected them. It was always a good place for meetings. (*He indicates that no one can listen.*)

Nina It's very beautiful.

Hugh Are you sure this man is coming?

Mihail The church across from your hotel was built by the Russians to remember our help for liberation from the Turkish Yoke. And you will see our monasteries – he lends me an obligation –

Hugh Owes me a favour –

Mihail Hugh, you will help me with my English.

Eva He will not come.

Mihail He come maybe by a circular road, not to be seen.

Hugh Are we doing anything illegal?

Mihail I am a lawyer, I do not allow that.

Boian comes on. Eva rushes to him and shakes his hand.

Eva You are man of honour, I will light a candle for your good health.

Boian I didn't want to be seen leaving the ministry. Things are difficult, there are so many rumours.

Eva Do not say, see how this poor girl suffers.

Nina What rumours?

Boian People are now so confused and suspicious, they are saying foreigners come to this country to get organs for babies.

Nina How horrible!

Boian This might happen in Romania, not here, but the West lumps all Balkans together. The minister is disturbed and the people are ignorant. And when there are such rumours – I am a gypsy, the only one in the ministry, the only gypsy ever educated abroad – because of Mihail –

Eva It is impossible, I always say.

Mihail This is a difficulty but Boian, is it not surmountable?

Eva No, it is the end.

Nina Do you know where she is?

Boian Not yet. She left hospital three days ago. I will find out where she was sent. And when you visit, you will say you are a delegation from the Red Cross.

Hugh It's not true!

Mihail To prevent rumours. Of course everyone will know the truth.

Nina I can do that. I'll wear glasses.

Boian I will come back in three days, I cannot say the time.

Hugh Listen, in three days –

Mihail (*over*) Boian, we will be here.

Nina Yes.

Boian Three days is very soon.

Nina Do you have a photograph of her?

Boian I saw her when she was in the hospital, she is very beautiful.

Nina What does she look like?

Boian A baby. Now I have to get back.

Eva We brought a little thing, English.

She fetches a carrier bag full of clinking bottles. Boian takes them without a word and leaves.

God hears me. Even under communism, I pray, so I have special relationship.

London. Tess in a hospital gown. She is depressed. Dr Glad comes on.

Tess Doctor, I've been waiting for you.

Dr Glad Feeling a little sore? It's the air pumped into the body and the cutting, of course. You know the drill: phone us in two weeks and ask to speak to the nurse.

Tess What do you think?

Dr Glad We found one viable egg. I would have preferred more, but it only takes one. And your husband's sperm looked a little depressed, but I live in hope. Now I have to go and induce one of my babies, we didn't think that would work either.

Tess I've read the statistics, ten per cent, going down to six. That's not very good, is it?

Dr Glad But you could be the lucky one, Tess.

The church. Nina, Hugh.

Nina We've been waiting a week. It's freezing in here. It's a beautiful church, but it wasn't meant to be lived in. I need a cup of coffee.

Hugh Do you want to give up?

Nina I suppose you do.

Hugh Let's give it another day. If we don't, you won't forgive yourself. Worse, you won't forgive me.

Nina The songs I could write about waiting –

Hugh We don't have a bad life, Nina. And having a child is a lot of work.

Nina You really don't want this to happen.

Hugh What am I doing here?

Nina How do I know? Maybe you want to sign up the church choir.

Hugh All I'm saying is, you won't be able to moon around being selfish.

Nina I see.

Hugh You're self-absorbed, like most artists. I don't mind, I'm used to it, you're not the worst.

Nina I'm not an artist any more. The product's gone, but I'm stuck with the temperament. Or rather you are. What are we doing together in this crazy country? Why did you come?

Hugh Because you decided this was your happiness and when you love someone you follow their zigzags.

Nina It's not me you love, it's my first album.

Hugh If you're going to behave like this, I will go back to London.

Nina Hugh, I want to see her. She's there, somewhere, all alone, herself. I feel her presence, but I don't have a face.

Hugh I think it's going to work.

Nina You think God is on our side? Or because it's you? Even Americans don't always get what they want.

Hugh No, but they're better at it. They try harder.

Boian comes on.

Nina Boian!

Boian Have you seen the demonstrations? We think government might have to resign. This would complicate everything.

Hugh Any news?

Boian I have good news.

Nina She's here!

Boian Not here, but you can drive in a day. Here is the address. Remember you are from the Red Cross. Please do not get me into trouble. This is a bad time.

Boian leaves. Hugh and Nina look at the writing.

Nina We must learn the alphabet.

Eva comes on.

Eva I pray to all the saints, but they look sad.

Nina We have the address!

Eva looks at the paper.

Eva Holy Mother of God, it is a terrible town. The people are black. Small. My husband has a heart attack in that town. I was here, in the capital, I took bus, all night, bumping, turning, I came to hospital room and there was other woman. How I suffer. But my husband was dying. I forgive. I prayed, he lived. But he has weak heart. If he goes back to that town, he can have other heart attack. It is too much, he is old, I know you suffer, you want child, but this town can attack my husband's heart. Please, perhaps tomorrow you go back to London?

Hugh, Nina.

Hugh We drove west to east on an empty road. Soft mountains, rich plains, sudden pollution, a valley of roses, then emptiness. When we tell her the story we will say this: We did our best to play the part of Red Cross officials well. We looked at every baby in the room, we checked the cots, all very clean, and then Mihail whispered to us, There, there, and thrust a baby in Nina's arms.

Nina Light, thin. I felt delicate bones through my fingers. Another baby was quickly thrust in the other arm and Hugh took a picture. The other baby vanished and I looked at her. I will say to her: It was not like the fairy tales. You did not look up and smile. Faces meant nothing to you: food came from white coats and I wasn't wearing one. But I held you. So light. I held you.

Mihail We leave now. Give her to me.

Nina No.

Mihail They will suspect, Nina. You have to.

Nina No.

Mihail We have to go.

Nina Please. No. (*She bursts into tears.*)

Mihail (*points to the baby*) She is crying too.

The hotel room. Hugh, Nina, Mihail and Eva are singing. They have been drinking a lot.

Eva And the words are – how to say, a girl, a girl, she will go, Mihail –

Mihail A girl went out early one morning for water, a young man said to her, Stay and talk, they sat and talked, dusk fell and the moon smiled.

Nina And my child came into being . . .

Mihail We have many great poets too –

Eva Listen: Mother how I misses you now I goes far away. It is better in our language.

Mihail The communists preserved all the poets' houses, one day we go and see –

Hugh How soon can we get her transferred to a home in the capital? Tomorrow?

Mihail Maybe . . . Maybe the day after . . .

Nina We need to get her back to England.

Mihail Patience, Nina, there are many horse jumps.

Hugh Hurdles.

Mihail You are decided? I know it was only five minutes –

Hugh We're decided.

Nina Yes.

Mihail This is a beautiful child –

Nina Isn't she?

Eva She is too thin. And her nose.

Nina It's a baby nose, it's beautiful.

Eva And her ear –

Hugh You're sure you can get her transferred?

Eva And her legs – very thin –

Nina I need to get her back, get her on a proper diet immediately.

Mihail He who goes slowly goes fast, as we say. First we get her to the capital, where I know people.

Eva You did, Mihail, now they don't know you.

Mihail We did many good things, Eva, universal education, health, people do not forget – and later bad things, but we wished to do right.

Eva I do not like politics.

Mihail Eva came from a rich family, I was very poor.

Eva He was youngest lawyer ever. I was teener, sixteen.

Mihail I have been a happy man.

Eva They confiscate everything of my family.

Mihail Now you get it back and I help some children –

Eva You like power, Mihail, like alcohol.

Mihail Eva, do not say these things –

Eva It is the truth.

Mihail We communists thought we had the truth. Now I know truth is not fixed, it is not Platonic ideogram, it moves with history. I will not let them make me believe I am evil because that is the new truth. (*He bangs his fist.*) No one will tell me capitalism is truth.

Eva You see, politics is bad for heart.

Mihail In the capital, every taxi driver charges different fare. In front of your hotel, Hugh, the most expensive. They beat up any driver who does not belong to hotel mafia.

Eva You had mafia too.

Mihail It was mafia with ideals. I told the government when they were bad.

Eva That was very stupid. We had terrible times.

London. Tess, Robert.

Robert It's one minute to twelve, we can call.

Tess Ready? (*She dials on her phone.*) Hello, it's Tess Warner. (*Pause.*) I see. Yes. Well, it's not your fault.

Robert It didn't work.

Tess shakes her head.

I'm sorry.

Tess That's not good enough.

Robert goes to her.

Don't touch me.

Robert Tess . . .

Tess We'll have to do it again, that's all.

Robert We've just spent five thousand pounds. It's not even that, I can't stand to see you doing this to yourself.

Tess I'm giving myself a chance for happiness.

Robert Tess, the drugs, the anaesthetic, this waiting. I don't want to make love to two tubes at once, so they can split off the cream or whatever they do – with a porn magazine in front of me. You need to go back to work.

Tess I'm not interested.

Robert Life goes on.

Tess Not mine.

Robert I fell in love with an independent, intelligent woman. Only two months ago I'd call you and hardly get past your secretary.

Tess You have your revenge.

Robert I'm proud of you. I don't want a mother for my children.

Tess You can always find one when you do.

Robert I have to go back to rehearsals. I got the afternoon off, but I was asked to be back this evening. I'm sorry.

Tess You'll have to take a television, we're out of money.

Robert My contract is for the year.

Tess Break it.

Robert It's the first time in years I've enjoyed myself. It's difficult, precise, strange and also familiar. What you want in a part. It's terribly sad, and yet, the acceptance of life, the slit of hope – read it, Tess.

Tess I can't concentrate. Can't you do some ads?

Robert You know I won't.

Tess What's the difference between an ad and a drama anyway? It's all the selling of dreams.

Robert If you no longer know that, you –

Tess What? Go on.

Robert I have to go to rehearsals.

Tess It's easy for you. You can escape into your romantic Vershinin, not think about anything –

Robert It's my work. I'm already late. I do understand.

Tess No, you don't.

Robert No, I don't. Come to rehearsals, you can sit in the coffee room.

Tess Just what I need: a grimy room full of obsessed actors.

Robert Call an old friend, Nina, April, someone at work.

Tess Nina's still out of the country, April thinks IVF is a male conspiracy to sell women drugs, the women at work have children, I have no one – it should be you –

Robert Tess, acting may be a useless profession, but people work hard at it. I can't ring and say I'm not coming.

Tess You'll be all right, you can always play King Lear.

Robert I won't be asked if –

Tess But what am I going to do for the next twenty years?

Pause.

I'm making an appointment for next week.

Robert I won't do it.

Tess You have to. I'll sell the house in the country. One more time. Otherwise – we're nothing.

Robert How can you say that?

Eastern Europe. The hotel. Hugh and Nina are packing. Nina looks at a few items of baby clothes. They are both dejected.

Nina I'll leave them in the room. A cleaner will find them.

Hugh We can try somewhere else.

Nina I'm not going through this again.

Hugh looks out the window.

Hugh Look, another demonstration.

Nina ignores this.

Nina I don't understand. First it was the next day, then a week's delay, then another week, now they don't even bother to say.

Hugh Eva said she would come and say goodbye.

Nina I don't want to see her.

Pause.

You didn't hold her.

Hugh There are other children.

Nina I don't want another child. I want the child I held.

Hugh takes a photograph out of his pocket and looks at it.

Nina You'll never understand.

Hugh is keeping himself from tears. Nina notices this.

Hugh . . .

Hugh When it was an abstraction, I didn't – I thought it was a pretty loopy idea. Then there's a child . . . and she even looks like you . . .

He is really crying now. Nina holds him.

Nina Don't cry. I can't bear it. Somebody has to hold the world firm. How can I be saying this? I'm going to get us some vodka.

Nina rushes out. Hugh puts the picture back in his pocket. Eva comes on.

Eva You pack, I am so truly sorry, where is Nina? I know you think we cheat and lie, but it is Mihail. He thinks he can do things but he is nobody now and everyone, how do you say, overflow with fear. Before we were afeared but we knew of what. Now . . . You come at wrong political time. Look out there, politicians cannot agree government. The Turks hold balance, but if they hold power, we have war. I would like to come to England. A ticket, is not expensive? I clean houses. And the snows come. Even if baby will come to capital you cannot do anything when snows are here. And my husband, he is more fragile of heart. Maybe I die of cold.

Mihail comes on, out of breath, sinks down.

Mihail I did not want to telephone. (*He pauses for breath.*)

Eva He is dying.

Mihail I have run.

Eva Call ambulance!

Mihail Hugh –

Eva Water. Quick. Do not speak, Mihail, you will die.

Eva covers Mihail's mouth with her hand; he manages to take it away.

Mihail I am so happy.

Eva He is seeing paradise. He is a good man, God will forgive the communism.

Mihail She is here.

Eva Yes, I pray to Mother of God. Now she take him.

Eva crosses herself. Mihail catches his breath.

Mihail Nina. Where is Nina?

Eva Always the younger woman, but I forgive. Hugh, call ambulance.

Mihail The little girl is here. She came last night.

Short pause.

Eva You see, I pray, and now God takes pity.

Mihail We can see her. I even told big capitalist mafia taxi downstairs to wait.

Eva Where is Nina? Maybe she commit suicide.

Mihail Today we celebrate, tomorrow real work. You have passports, police records, medical records, accountant letter, good character certification, letter from psychologist, then the social report, I get all translated – yes and marriage certificate, birth certificate, your divorce permit, you have? Photographs of house, name and birth of parents, you have.

Eva Mihail, stop, you get brain tumour.

Hugh It's all here.

Mihail This is good, I am impressed.

Hugh I studied law before becoming a record producer.

Mihail You never said.

Eva Hugh is modest American and all your life you say terrible things about Americans.

Hugh It's all right, so do I.

Nina comes on. She is carrying a bottle one-quarter-full of vodka and is very drunk.

Nina I seem to have drunk most of this. I was talking to the prostitutes in the foyer –

Mihail Nina, Nina. Your little girl is waiting for you.

Nina takes it in.

Nina She's here?

Eva We stop at church and thank God.

Mihail Afterwards, Eva –

Nina I'm so drunk, what will she think?

London. Dr Glad, Tess.

Dr Glad Nature is cruel: you were born with a finite number of eggs and now they're used up or old. I would say try one more time, twice, you might twist my arm and try three times, four, even five, but after that we need to take the next step.

Tess What's that?

Dr Glad We use a younger woman's eggs. The success rate zooms up. And we can still use your partner's sperm, we like to include the chaps in all this.

Tess The child won't have my genes . . .

Dr Glad No, but you'll breastfeed, it'll have your antibodies. I'll put your name down, there's a two-year waiting list –

Tess Two years!

Dr Glad You can jump the queue if you find your own donor. You might have a friend –

Tess There all in the same position I'm in.

Dr Glad Someone at work . . .

Tess It's a lot to ask . . .

Dr Glad It is such an altruistic gesture, many women might enjoy it if they knew about it.

Tess Is it expensive?

Dr Glad Double the trouble, double the cost, my secretary can go over that with you, she's been with me for fifteen years, she knows more than I do. No money must be exchanged between the women.

Tess It's dangerous for them?

Dr Glad No more than for you, high doses of hormones, some danger of overstimulation, we monitor very closely. We like to match hair colour and skin.

Tess What about –

Dr Glad Intelligence? That must be left to your husband's genes. Now I must give evidence to an ethics committee, they are so rigid. We're at the forefront of science. You ought to write an article.

Tess And what if that doesn't – work?

Dr Glad A very nice woman the other day had some extra embryos she was willing to give, and there you go, a happy couple were able to adopt an embryo. Before we get to that we would suggest different sperm, we have very nice donors, all nationalities, Jewish, anything you need. And once we don't have to deal with your eggs, Tess, there's no age limit. We can go on for years.

The hotel. Nina.

Nina I know only one myth that sings of a mother's love for her daughter. The goddess of the earth, Demeter, loses her daughter to Hades, god of the underworld. In her grief, she blights the crops, famine descends on earth. Diplomatic shuttle on Olympus, a deal is struck: Demeter is allowed her daughter back for two-thirds of the year, but for one-third, Persephone deserts her for the underworld. Demeter mourns her absence by covering the earth with the bleakness of winter.

    We don't have the daughter's version. We only know of Demeter's joy when her daughter is by her side, her grief when she's absent. Do I think of this myth because my daughter was absent for the first six months of her life? Because I see her for only one-third of the day? I know how fragile is the gift of her presence. And when I cannot hold her, the world goes dark, wintry.

Hugh comes on.

Hugh How did it go?

Nina I held her. I walked up and down in that little office and talked to her. I told her we would be in England soon. She still won't meet my gaze, but she seemed comfortable, almost happy. And so am I. You?

Hugh We picked up the papers from the translators, queued for hours to get every single page stamped. Bureaucracy must make them feel they still have government. I had to call London again. I think I've lost the job.

Nina I'm sorry.

Hugh It's not just the job, it's my reputation. How will we bring up this child?

Nina All right. I'll do the album. As soon as we get back.

Hugh That, Nina, makes me happy.

Nina I'll use some of the music we've heard here.

Hugh There's something about this country – I'm falling in love again.

Nina I didn't know you'd fallen out of love – you were very polite about it. Why didn't you say?

Hugh Isn't that when you can't talk? At least, men can't.

Eva and Mihail come on.

Eva We cannot do it.

Nina What's wrong now?

Mihail Please, Eva, sit. Good evening, Hugh and Nina, you are well? Perhaps we have some coffee and chocolate cake, yes?

Hugh What's happened?

Mihail We are very worried about the child.

Nina So am I. She needs to get out of that home.

Eva She is very ill. Mihail, he is communist, but he has honour, he will not give you very ill child.

Nina She is not very ill.

Hugh We understood your laws would only allow us to have a child who was ill.

Mihail That is the law. It is a good law if the child is a little ill, but if she is very ill it is bad and we cannot do it.

Eva Your heart breaks, Nina, I am mother, I have experience.

Nina I know I can make her well.

Mihail You would not forgive us later

Eva She is so weak.

Nina Of course she is. She needs a home, love, good food.

Hugh You told us originally she had been taken to hospital with gastro-enteritis, and that it was not very serious.

Mihail That is what we thought.

Hugh Well?

Mihail The director of the home thinks she is more ill. I do not understand.

Eva She is losing weight, any mother can see that.

Nina So would any child with that brew they feed her. Hugh, let's call Jamie right now and get him over here to examine her.

Mihail Nina, Nina, patience, we have good doctors here.

Nina Call a doctor in, then. Now.

Hugh Let's get the consultant who looked after her in hospital.

Mihail If I arrange that, and the consultant says she is very ill, you must promise you will not insist.

Nina I don't care how ill she is. I can cope.

Eva No, Nina, you cannot, you are a Nervous.

Mihail Hugh, I must warn you, if she is ill I will not help you. Forgive me.

Nina Then we'll manage without you.

Hugh Nina!

Nina I didn't mean that. Actually, I did. I can't let her go. (*She bursts into tears.*)

Mihail You have promise of happiness and we snatch it away, but you have other promises, Nina.

Eva We find other child, with something tiny wrong.

Hugh *and* **Nina** No!

Eva She smiles when she sees Hugh, she likes men. I cry. Nina, do you have handkerchief?

Nina No! I don't.

London. Robert, Tess.

Robert Today, I tried playing Vershinin as a pompous dreamer. It didn't work. What's difficult is to find that belief in the future, it's the most dated part of the play.

Pause. Tess doesn't respond.

Chekhov knew things were going badly. It must have been his act of courage to keep faith with humanity – most of us don't have that faith. (*Pause.*) The director wondered how much evidence you needed to stop being a humanist – you're not interested.

Tess You never used to talk about rehearsals.

Robert I didn't need to.

Tess What does that mean?

Robert You used to come home full of the people you'd met, articles you'd commissioned.

Silence.

Robert When are you going back to work?

Tess I'm not supposed to have any stress.

Robert You have to work.

Tess Why?

Robert Partly to pay the mortgage and partly to come home and tell me what you did all day.

Tess I can tell you what I do every single day. I walk down the street and leer at women. Which one has the good eggs? There's an exhausted twenty-year-old with three brutalised children. Shall I tell her I'll get her out of her rut in exchange for her eggs – but what kind of genes does she have? I spot a young mother in a book store,

74

perfect: brainy eggs. She goes to the feminist section, she'll wonder why my only identity is motherhood. There's a foreign student. I fantasise about kidnapping her. I wouldn't have pity. I sit on a park bench like a flasher. Women used to be my sisters. Now they're objects: egg vessels..

Robert Tess . . .

Tess I will find somebody.

Robert If you don't?

Tess I can't stop now.

Robert The agents called today, they want us to drop the price of the house again.

Tess It won't be worth selling.

Robert Then we have to stop. .

Tess If you'd only taken that television – that was so irresponsible.

Robert To what? Your madness?

Tess It's mad to do theatre these days, you've said it yourself.

Robert It's what I love. I've even got my confidence back, in it, in myself, in the worth of it all.

Tess It's not very significant, is it?

Robert What does that mean?

Tess Putting your life on hold for a few hundred people a night.

Robert That is my life.

Tess So you wreck ours.

Robert I'm not wrecking it, you have. I don't recognise you, it's like living with a junkie. Always waiting for the next fix, of hormones, of hope. What do you think it's like?

Tess What do you think it was like living with you last year when you were unemployed and despising everything? I tried to feel it with you –

Robert It wasn't a situation of my making.

Tess Nor is this. Don't you want a child?

Robert Not that badly, no. I want you –

Tess You mean my earning capacity?

Robert I want to go out with you, I want to make love to you for the pleasure of it, I can't even remember what that's like.

Tess Is that all you can think about?

Robert It used to be something you enjoyed.

Tess turns away. Pause.

I have to go over my lines.

Tess Are there any young actresses in the company?

Robert The one playing Irina. Would you like to meet the company? They'd love to see you.

Tess You could ask her – you could ask her if she would like to donate her eggs.

Robert I can't believe this.

Tess What's wrong? Why shouldn't she? She could do it when she's not working. Ask her.

Robert These hormones are wrecking your brain.

Tess What a disgusting thing to say.

Robert Well, I must be a shit.

Tess If it weren't for your sperm, I'd leave you.

Robert Perhaps that would be best.

Tess What are you saying?

Robert Look, I have to go over the lines, some of the speeches are rather convoluted.

Tess Repeat what you said just now – repeat those lines.

Robert shakes his head.

Dr Attanasov, Mihail, Eva, Hugh, Nina.

Dr Attanasov She was admitted to this hospital with a very high fever and severe dehydration caused by gastro-enteritis. She was also suffering from anaemia and a general failure to thrive. We diagnosed a lactose intolerance, and recommended a diet without milk. I have checked the records and spoken to my colleagues: there was no internal damage. There is no reason why the child should not be perfectly healthy.

Hugh and Nina embrace.

I will write a report to the Ministry of Health.

Hugh No, don't do that.

Beat.

Mihail Is there not a possibility that this condition will recur? She could have a high fever again? I am not a doctor . . . Dehydration, that is terrible . . .

Dr Attanasov She will be healthy. Keep her on a diet without milk.

Mihail A correct diet, that is very difficult in a home. We do not know what will happen with the economic situation.

Dr Attanasov The medical standards of our homes are excellent.

Hugh She is losing weight.

Eva She is thin, thin, thin, every day more.

Dr Attanasov I have her graph, yes, she is under the normal, but I have seen much worse.

Nina Doctor, you diagnosed a general failure to thrive, what causes that?

Dr Attanasov It could be sadness.

Nina And the love of two parents could cure that?

Dr Attanasov Yes, but that is not a medical fact.

Nina Isn't it?

Mihail Doctor, these kind people came here because they heard this child was ill.

Dr Attanasov Yes . . .

Mihail Doctor, the law will only allow this child out on humanitarian grounds – a small word in the law, but in the heart a large one.

Dr Attanasov I understand, but I cannot write a false report.

Mihail Of course, we would not ask that.

Hugh We love this child.

Nina Doctor, I think we can guarantee she will thrive.

Pause.

Dr Attanasov I can say she was brought to hospital in a critical condition and that we suspected pancreatic insufficiency or some form of immuno-deficiency. If no one asks me further questions, I will not have to answer them.

Nina Thank you, doctor.

Dr Attanasov Please understand that if I am asked, I will have to give the results of our tests. But next week, I am not much at my desk. Goodbye. I count on you to make this child happy.

He leaves. Statelov, an old lawyer, comes on. He kisses Nina's hand and clicks his heels at Hugh. He and Mihail embrace.

Statelov I take you into Ministry of Justice. I am supervisor of files. Very important position. Everyone knows Mr Statelov. I have friends in the courts too. Do you know Dunhill pipes? I have three. Maybe you send me more? I also have Great Dane. His name is Free Market.

Mihail I thought his name was Collective.

Statelov That was many years ago, terrible name.

Mihail Is it?

Statelov History, my friend, moves and we move with it. History moves very fast in Eastern Europe. Government will fall any day. Then who knows who rises, Turks, gypsies, worse: Jews. Poor Mihail, he move too slowly and now no one likes him. Only Statelov can get you the letter you need. Madame, you are most attractive.

Nina Thank you. It's so kind of you to help us.

Statelov kisses Nina's hand again and leaves.

Hugh Do we have to deal with him?

Mihail (*angry*) Do you know what this costs me?

Eva He was much in love with me, I think he still feels.

Robert and Tess. Robert brings a suitcase. A silence.

Robert You could still come.

Tess What for?

Robert Because it's East Germany and it's interesting. Look out there, there's a world, remember? You used to be part of it. (*He stops himself.*) What's the point?

 Pause.

I don't know where I'll stay when I come back, but you have the touring schedule. I'll call.

Tess You don't have to.

Robert What a way to end.

Tess Isn't it.

 Pause.

I remember at the beginning I'd wait up for you, and you'd walk in still quite high after a performance and I'd think, He's mine, my man. I'd pretend to have done something else all evening. Really, I'd been waiting for you.

Robert What happened?

Tess It wasn't every evening. I was very busy.

Robert Come back to me. Come back to yourself.

Tess This is myself. You don't like it.

Robert No, I'm sorry, I hate it.

Pause.

I'm sorry.

Tess There we are.

Robert Yes.

Tess You're going to miss your plane.

Robert turns away.

Robert I don't know what to say to you.

Tess There's nothing to say.

Statelov, Nina, Hugh, Eva, Mihail.

Statelov My friends, I work so hard, charming madame. I have done well.

Mihail You have the letter from the Minister of Justice?

Statelov Ah no, not the letter. I am sorry, that is impossible.

Hugh That's what we need!

Statelov I have the promise of the letter. But my friend wants letter from Minister of Health first.

Mihail We cannot get it, you know that. It is the Deputy Minister of Health who insisted on this law that makes adoption nearly impossible. But we do not need a letter from her, only from Ministry of Justice. Without that, we cannot bring the case to court. I explained all this.

Statelov I have the promise of the letter from Minister of Justice.

Nina Isn't that enough?

Hugh Promises don't hold water in a courtroom.

Statelov I work very hard, here is my bill.

Mihail looks at it.

Mihail This is criminal.

Statelov Western prices. I am lawyer.

Mihail This is communist country!

Statelov I was never communist.

Mihail You worked for the government.

Statelov I was not communist in my heart, like you. You would not speak to me in the street. Now I help.

Mihail These people do not have that kind of money.

Statelov I take some off if you send Dunhill pipes.

Mihail I am a Marxist, but now I want to go pray. I am a tired man. I have failed my country. I have failed you.

Nina I'm staying in the country. I'll go to the home every day.

Eva You cannot: they will become suspicious.

Hugh Surely everyone knows what we are doing by now. It's above board, isn't it?

Mihail Above board, that means – Ah, I understand. It is legal, I assure you, but nothing in our country is above board. (*He leaves.*)

Statelov These communists, they fail the world.

Pause.

Eva Nina, I think to myself, this Deputy Minister, Dr Romnova, she is woman, you are woman.

Nina ignores her.

And you, Hugh, are gentleman, women like that.

Statelov I look much like English gentleman when I smoke my Dunhill pipe.

Eva Mr Statelov, are you afraid of the Ministry of Health?

Statelov Statelov knows no fear.

Eva All my life I apologise to Mihail, to communists. He is unfaithful too. I am for personalism. I say, politics, enough. I am ideologist of heart. You all follow me. I say: let us storm the barricades.

The Ministry of Health. Dr Romanova comes in. Eva bars Romanova's way.

Eva Dr Romanova, we throw ourselves down before your feet: we cry pity for the poor mother. (*She gets down on her knees.*) You are a woman, you understand woman's pain. Listen and your great heart has been moved. Nina: speak. Sing!

Eva tries to drag Nina down on her knees.

Statelov Allow me to introduce myself. Mr Statelov. I am inspector of files for Ministry of Justice. Also, my wife's sister is a friend of your husband's brother's wife. They went to school –

Eva shoves Statelov aside.

Eva They love the little girl so much. Every night, Madame Sehn falls into tears, how they flow, if you seen, you who have mother's heart will also have flow. I have flow.

Hugh Dr Romanova, we are trying to adopt a child in this country. She has been ill. We want to give her a home.

Nina All our love.

Statelov The Ministry of Justice where I am inspector will hand over letter, but they need one from you. They say I may soon be transferred to Ministry of Health. I am very thorough.

Dr Romanova looks at him coldly.

Dr Romanova You know the law. We do not allow children under one year to leave the country and even then –

Hugh In this case, there are humanitarian grounds.

Eva Look how humanitarian these parents are. And the English gentleman. A saint. He gives up work, career, he is famous musician, how many woman have husband, father like that? I cry.

Nina We love this child, she will be well looked after, as happy as we can make her –

Eva And Nina sings so beautiful, like this – (*She begins to sing.*) Nina, sing.

Dr Romanova That is not necessary. The pressure against adoption, you must know, comes from abroad.

Eva She is ill, she has terrible cough like this. (*She coughs.*)

Nina Dr Romanova, I believe it is necessary for us to take this child back to England without delay. I am not a doctor, but I feel, I know, she will give up, just give up, from lack of love, you must understand.

Dr Romanova Yes –

Eva Pity for the mother and child in this world full of pain. Pity for –

Dr Romanova Enough, please. (*Beat.*) I will write the letter.

Eva embraces Dr Romanova's skirt.

Eva You are sage.

Dr Romanova Please do not tell people in England it is easy to adopt in this country.

Hugh It would not be possible to say that. Thank you.

Nina I promise we will do all we can for her.

Nina bursts into tears. Eva cries too.

Dr Romanova Come back at two.

Statelov Today.

Dr Romanova Tomorrow.

Statelov But if the government falls today –

Dr Romanova Tomorrow at two. Goodbye.

Mihail.

Mihail It is fashionable to condemn the twentieth century and make us the villains of the piece. I confess terrible things were done, in our name, and by us. And yet, we had ideals. Now I see the ideals are gone. People talk freely, but only about money. Idealism has turned on its head, everyone looks after himself in a world of chaos. I am an old man. I have known fear but now I see people suffer the greatest fear of all: fear of the future. I loved the future, even if I feared the present, with its sudden disgraces. I refuse to recant. I still believe in history. Now, it will be in the hands of the children, possibly most of all, these cross-border children I have helped to get out. Born in one country, loved and raised in another, I hope they will not descend into narrow ethnic identification, but that they will be wilfully international, part of a great European community. I hope they will carry on history with broad minds and warm hearts. They have the complexity from their childhood: change, migration, indifference and uncertainty came to them early. Now, cherished, secure, educated. Is it unfair of me to place the responsibility of history onto them? We must not go into the next century with no ideal but selfishness.

The courthouse. Everyone wrapped in coats. Mihail, Statelov, Boian, Eva, Hugh, Nina.

Nina Now I understand Dickens. We've been waiting five hours.

Mihail Ours must be the last case.

Boian We are lucky to have letters. The government will announce resignation at three o'clock this afternoon. There will be new ministers.

Statelov Only because of me do we get this hearing.

Hugh We could leave tomorrow.

Mihail Not tomorrow, Hugh. The judgment must be lodged in the court for a week to allow for an appeal.

Nina What appeal? From whom?

Mihail That is the law.

Hugh Ask the judge to waive the mandatory week, explain the situation.

Boian I will represent Ministry of Health, I will confirm urgency.

Nina Boian, how can we thank you?

Boian Tell your child a gypsy help you. One day when my children need connection, they find your child or grandchild and call on ethnic friendship.

Mihail Anyway, you have to apply for passport for the child. That takes three weeks.

Hugh I'll get it in a day.

Mihail Even in America you do not have passport in a day.

Eva You cannot even be sure the court rules in our favour.

Hugh We have the letters, the papers are in order.

Eva Mihail does not think so.

Hugh What do you mean? Mihail?

Eva Mihail, do you have ear attack?

Mihail I did not want to worry you, Hugh, but I could not go to official translators. So the court could refuse to accept papers.

Nina No.

Hugh Why didn't you use the official translators?

Mihail They require a stamp from our embassy back in England, but that would take six months, a year.

Hugh You mean our papers are illegal?

Mihail They are legal. They are not official.

Statelov They're calling us.

Eva I pray to God to help us.

Nina So do I.

Eva crosses herself and, after a moment, so does Nina.

Hugh.

Hugh The court case, solemn, brief, was almost an anti-climax. Our petition was read out. We were asked if we understood what we were doing. Whether the prosecutor noticed or chose to ignore the irregularity of the papers, we'll never know. I was beginning to discover that once you had people on your side, the law was upheld but happily twisted. We were given our child. (*Pause.*) The prosecutor agreed to waive the mandatory week. The next day was the last working day before the holidays began and everything closed for six weeks. At ten o'clock we picked up the judgment and ran to the court cashier to pay for use of the photocopying machine. Suddenly, she disappeared. A long queue was forming.

Where's the cashier?

Mihail Maybe in the bathroom, maybe at lunch. It is festival season.

Hugh I'm going to check out the bathrooms and pull her out.

Mihail You cannot.

Hugh Let's get this copied somewhere else.

Mihail Where? I am embarrassed for my country, it is because of people like her we are in such a mess. We all have important business, she does not care.

Hugh I'm going to use the photocopier without paying.

Mihail That is against the law.

The Woman comes on, a bottle of wine in her hands.

Please, we are very grateful if we can copy these papers.

Hugh We've been waiting an hour!

The Woman just stares and slowly focuses.

Woman How many pages?

Mihail Twelve.

The Woman counts them, very slowly.

Hugh We told you: twelve!

Woman I make sure. You are English? It is very wet in your country.

Hugh We photocopied the judgment. We took a taxi to the notary. He stamped every page. We now had to get a new birth certificate.

A Man comes on with papers.

Man I cannot issue a new birth certificate.

Hugh But –

Man The child was not born in the capital. You must go to the town where she was born.

Mihail The holidays begin tomorrow.

The Man nods. A Clerk approaches and looks at the papers and a small photograph.

Clerk (*to Hugh*) This is your baby?

Hugh nods. The two men look, others approach, the picture is passed round.

Very beautiful.

Nods all round.

You take her to England?

Hugh I'm trying.

Woman This is good thing you do.

Hugh What are we going to do without a birth certificate?

Clerk You are sure she wasn't born in capital?

Hugh Of course I'm sure. Look, it says here.

Clerk People make mistakes.

Man I do not remember where my children born. Too much brandy.

Mihail Do you know, I remember now this child was born in my house. That is in the capital. Here is my address.

Clerk I knew there was mistake.

Man You will swear to that?

Mihail Yes. How could I forget such a thing?

Man Then we can proceed.

Hugh We arrived at the passport office twenty minutes before it closed for the holidays.

Man I need the birth certificate, good, and then you must sign here and your wife signs here.

Hugh My wife isn't here.

Pause.

Man Are you sure? This is a big room. Perhaps she is leaning behind that pillar.

Hugh No, she – oh.

Mihail (*over him*) Yes, she is not feeling well and she is leaning behind a pillar.

Man That will explain why her handwriting is a little different. Now I will go out of this room to get a glass of water for your wife and you will ask her to sign, yes?

Hugh I forged Nina's signature and we were given our daughter's passport as the bells rang for evening mass.

Eva and Nina come on, singing.

Mihail Nowhere in the world do you get a passport in a day. I am proud of my country.

Hugh All the flights are booked because of the skiing holidays. I said it was a humanitarian emergency and they agreed to bump off two skiers. I hope they don't mind.

Eva No, they are German.

Nina You are a hero.

Nina and Hugh embrace.

Hugh Without you, Mihail –

Mihail I climbed the hills, but Eva conquered the mountain.

They embrace Eva.

Mihail Hugh, I have not told you –

Nina Then don't.

Mihail When you arrive at Heathrow, you may be arrested. Sadly, England does not recognise our laws.

Hugh I can't believe it, after all this?

Mihail You will have the child with you. You will deal with England.

Nina I will deal with them.

Eva Before you were poor bird, now you are lioness, true mother. But Nina, no more peace, always thoughts of your child, now you truly suffer.

Nina As long as she is happy.

Eva So many worries. And look out the window: the snows come. Maybe you cannot leave at all.

Act Three

*Six months later. A dressing room in a northern
provincial theatre. Robert is taking off his Vershinin
clothes. Tess comes in.*

Robert I didn't know you were in . . . Did you see Nina
and Hugh?

Tess They're coming . . . (*Pause.*) It's your last night –

Robert It's gone fast. (*Pause.*) How are you?

Tess As well as can be expected . . . You?

Robert shrugs.

You were very good. I understand why it's been so
important. What will you do now?

Robert Wait until I'm offered something else I really
want to do. That could be a long wait.

Tess I've put the flat on the market.

Robert You haven't gone back to work?

Tess shakes her head.

Tess . . .

Tess Nick is here, I want to speak to him. I've written to
Marisa. She's had a baby boy.

Robert Ah –

Tess She hasn't answered: I've asked if she would donate
her eggs. I know I was horrible to her, but that was a
year ago, I'm sure she'll understand.

Robert Tess –

Tess I'll try it once more, no, three times. Then I'll stop.

Pause.

Robert If you want me to come and give you – you know, sperm, no strings attached.

Tess Part of the problem was your sperm. I'm going to use a donor, it's younger, the clinic is very selective.

Robert I see.

Pause.

Tess Well . . .

Robert Why don't you stay the night?

Tess No.

Robert I miss you. Don't you ever feel – we could go back? Accept what has happened, go on, maybe not be completely happy, but – I don't know – live –

Tess That's fine for the three sisters, they come to terms with their lives, but this is the twentieth century. I won't accept defeat.

Nick comes on.

Nick That was – well, they're all a bit desperate, aren't they, those sisters? And Marisa wouldn't approve of you. She said to say hello, she's at home with the baby, he's got a cold.

Tess How is she?

Nick She's finding it hard –

Tess Did she get my letter?

Nick I got it, I read it. She's been too busy to open her post and she was a little depressed after the baby. I thought it was going to be a good-wishes letter.

Tess Did you show it to her?

Nick No. I wouldn't let her do it.

Tess Isn't that up to her?

Nick She's the mother of my child. You say it's safe, but those drugs haven't been around that long and we feel she should breastfeed for at least two years anyway. Don't you think you should forget about all that? Your letter sounded – well – desperate.

Tess (*shouts*) Don't judge me! (*more quietly*) I see myself.

Nick I've got to get back, I don't like to leave Marisa on her own. I'm sorry.

Tess Please give her the letter. Please.

Robert Tess –

Tess Don't –

Nina and Hugh crowd on, followed by Victor, the social worker, and then April and Jamie.

Nina You were wonderful.

Hugh It's our first evening out together.

Robert (*to Hugh and Nina*) How's the baby?

Hugh She's with our tenth nanny. Nina says it's because I've bullied her into recording too soon.

Nina After all we've been through, I hardly see her.

Hugh But we're writing a song called 'How I Killed the Nannies'. That's off the record, Victor.

Nina This is Victor, our social worker, he's been coming for six months to see if I'm a fit mother, now he wants to meet our friends.

Victor I liked the play. I would have preferred a happy end.

April (*to Tess*) You look – ravaged. What's happened?

Tess *La condition féminine* – life.

Nina (*to Victor*) What are you writing?

Victor That your friends are multilingual and that's good for a transracial adoption.

Jamie Isn't she from Eastern Europe?

Victor We don't have many categories for adoption – she wasn't born here.

Robert (*to Nina*) I wish Tess and I had done what you've done.

Tess It's too late.

Nina I'd help you –

Tess turns away.

Robert (*to Jamie*) How's the hospital?

Jamie Closed.

Robert Completely?

Jamie We fought. We lost. I've been offered another place, but that was my home. I may leave medicine altogether. My heart isn't in it.

Hugh (*to April*) How is Sappho?

Jamie I forgot to ask you.

April It's been rather popular.

Hugh And you're well?

April I live alone. I work. I have my students and my friends.

Nina Sounds like bliss.

April Yes, there's nothing to curtain me from the world the way a marriage, children, even a romance does. It makes me very clear-sighted.

Hugh And interesting.

April I think so, but no one talks about women like me. Particularly not in your magazines, Tess.

Tess I'd change that, but –

April We may not consume much, but we contribute a lot. We work. I think I live with dignity and some grace. I try to behave with decency. I feel lonely sometimes –

Nick I do too, but for different reasons

April But I keep going. My life is full. I want you to write a song about that, Nina, I want you to write a song about me.

Jamie I'd like a requiem for my hospital. For England.

Nina I've brought my child to this country, I have to believe in it.

Nick Victor, why are you wearing slippers?

Victor I wear them in the office, it's warmer and it saves on shoes. I had to leave in a hurry to get here, someone must have hidden my shoes. I'm sorry.

Robert It's the longest day. The sun rises so early up here. I don't want to stay by myself. Let's wait for the dawn, let's talk.

Nick I don't know. Marisa –

April It's only a few hours.

Nina I want to get back to my child, but I also want to stay.

97

Hugh That's how it's always going to be.

Tess I'll stay.

Nina (*to Victor*) What are you writing now?

Victor That your child is going to be brought up in a very intellectual environment, but that it's not necessarily a negative point.

Tess We only want to try and understand what we've done.

Robert You could even say that's hopeful.

Fade.

AFTER DARWIN

For J.

After Darwin was first performed at the Hampstead Theatre, London, on 8 July 1998 with the following cast:

Charles Darwin / Tom Jason Watkins
Robert FitzRoy / Ian Michael Feast
Millie Ingeborga Dapkunaite
Lawrence Colin Salmon

Director Lindsay Posner
Set Designer Joanna Parker
Lighting Designer Peter Mumford
Sound John A. Leonard
Assistant Director Adam Rush

Characters

Robert FitzRoy
Charles Darwin
Millie
Ian
Tom
Lawrence

Act One

30 April 1865. 7 a.m.
A room that is elegant and spare. On a large table,
a washing bowl, a cut-throat razor.
Robert FitzRoy wears full navy uniform minus the
jacket, which hangs. Charles Darwin, in rumpled
clothes, sits on a chair to the side.
FitzRoy holds a Bible in his hand and brandishes it.

FitzRoy This is the truth. 'Woe unto thee, blind guide . . .'
Natural selection? We cannot survive without The Book.
You want a grim future, without purpose, mockery of
all that is sacred, no moral light. 'It had been better
for that man if he had not been born.' I harboured you
in my cabin. I, FitzRoy of *The Beagle,* have brought
destruction on the world – 'Woe unto that man by whom
the offence cometh.' That nose, that nose, why did I tear
up the letter? (*Pause.*) I only ever wanted to do what was
right. I understood it, it was my inheritance – but perhaps
there is no right, no good. Forgive me, God, for what I
have done, for what I am about to do – if you are there.

He brandishes the razor at Darwin, who does not react.

You were the mediocrity, I had the destiny – you scrambled
my destiny, and the world. (*He turns away.*) Perhaps God
never looked. The fittest, so-called, grimacing their success.
Thousands like you in this world sodden with vulgarity.
No more like me. They laugh at me. No more now.
I leave nothing behind. (*to Darwin*) But you never saw
the pain of extinction. (*He draws the razor up to his
throat to slit it.*)

SCENE TWO: 'HOPE'

4 September 1831.
    The Beagle.
    Captain Robert FitzRoy in full Navy uniform,
dazzling. Charles Darwin in rumpled travelling clothes.
    The presence of wealth and elegance, very spare and
neat. Chronometers.

FitzRoy Tenerife, the Cape de Verde Islands, Rio de Janeiro, the Straits of Magellan, the Falkland Islands, the Galapagos Islands, do these names mean anything to you, Mr Darwin?

Darwin I've read about Tenerife, Captain FitzRoy, I've dreamt of Rio.

FitzRoy We do not know the exact longitude of Rio. If *The Beagle* can chart these waters and coasts accurately, she will change the history of the world. I have twenty-two chronometers on board.

Darwin Twenty-two!

FitzRoy The Admiralty provided four, I bought the rest. No more shipwrecks, think of the lives saved . . .

Darwin Yes!

FitzRoy And then the souls . . . In Tierra del Fuego I encountered the most miserable and savage creatures. I captured four and had them educated in England.

Darwin Indeed, Captain FitzRoy . . . I heard of York Minster, Jemmy Button and Fuegia – euh –

FitzRoy Basket. The fourth, Boat Memory, died of the smallpox. I am particularly pleased with Jemmy Button, who seems naturally disposed to civilisation – I am bringing all three back with a young missionary who will establish a settlement on that wild coast. I have an artist on board to record the flora, fauna, most remarkable in these parts.

Darwin Yes.

FitzRoy There lacks only a gentleman savant.

Darwin Yes!

FitzRoy To pursue researches in natural history, collecting, observing, noting . . . A companion as well: the coast of South America is bleak. The previous captain of *The Beagle* shot himself, you heard?

Darwin No, I deeply regret –

FitzRoy When I took command of the ship, the crew were near mutiny . . . (*Pause. He studies Darwin.*) Mr Darwin, I regret I was not able to get a message to you in time, but the post of naturalist on *The Beagle* has already been filled . . .

Darwin Ah! Oh, no . . .

FitzRoy I have only now written the letter confirming my decision. I hope you are not too disappointed?

Darwin Bitterly! Forgive me, Captain, if it is too late, I must now . . . I won't take any more of your time. Ah! . . .

FitzRoy I was not under the impression you were so keen.

Darwin I came as soon as I could! (*Pause.*) My father opposed the idea. I could do nothing without his approval.

FitzRoy He fears for your safety?

Darwin He thinks I'm wayward.

FitzRoy So.

Darwin But Uncle Jos – that's my uncle Josiah Wedgwood – thought it would be a capital thing to do and convinced my father. My father wants me to take Holy Orders, but the pursuit of Natural History is very suitable to a clergyman and it would only be a delay . . . We answered all of his objections and my father agreed.

FitzRoy Your father is an excellent doctor. He once treated an aunt of mine and she lived until she was ninety-five.

Darwin He is most shrewd, yes – that is, he used to take me on his rounds, he wanted me to follow him into medicine.

FitzRoy And you did not feel compelled to obey his wishes?

Darwin I hate the sight of blood.

FitzRoy I could not have guaranteed your safety in South America, Mr Darwin.

Darwin It's not my own blood I'm afraid of spilling, Captain FitzRoy, it's dissection. I shoot accurately, I assure you. I'm not very good at taxidermy though – and the lectures were so tedious! My father fears I have no application . . . (*He stops himself.*)

FitzRoy You have eminent friends at Cambridge.

Darwin I'm frightfully clever at catching beetles, Captain. Perhaps it's just as well for the Coleoptera of South America I'm not coming.

FitzRoy Professor John Henslow – his father was master of the royal dockyards at Chatham –

Darwin He's taught me everything I know about Botany –

FitzRoy Adam Sedgwick – they say his geology lectures are always full . . . What made you so wish to come?

Darwin Alexander von Humboldt.

FitzRoy You've read him?

Darwin Everything. You too?

FitzRoy At naval college. (*Recites.*) 'From my earliest youth I felt an ardent desire to travel into distant regions seldom visited by Europeans . . .' So did I.

Darwin It was Humboldt's description of Tenerife that first made me –

FitzRoy Yes! Climbing that volcano.

Darwin And then the Orinoco . . .

FitzRoy I lived on that canoe. We shall be far south of Humboldt's Venezuela, but there are great rivers in Brazil, Mr Darwin – (*Pause.*) And do you admire Jane Austen?

Darwin I have not read her – yet.

FitzRoy I have all of her books on board.

Darwin I did read Coldstream and Foggo when I heard I might come on this voyage, I studied astronomy – I believe I can follow calculations for longitude and latitude, I even plunged into fearful descriptions of storms at sea . . .

FitzRoy I have fitted *The Beagle* with a lightning conductor, making her the safest vessel in the Navy. The perils of ship life are more internal, Mr Darwin: bad temper in the sailors, melancholy in ourselves . . . the soul of a man may seem to die. You seem to have a cheerful temperament. It must make you a pleasant companion. Your family are Whigs, are they not?

Darwin Especially the Wedgwoods.

FitzRoy The FitzRoys have always been Tories. We are opposing your reforms, Mr Darwin, this dangerous tide of liberalism . . .

Darwin I find beetles and rocks occupy my thoughts. I am singularly ignorant of politics.

FitzRoy That is because you are still young. One grows fast in the Navy. I went to sea at fourteen.

Darwin I lost my mother when I was seven and was perhaps spoiled by my sisters. I kept running away from school to be back with them.

FitzRoy My mother died when I was five. (*Embarrassed pause.*) I did invite a friend of mine on board, Mr Darwin – I want a companion as much as a man of science, you understand – but he refused this morning. This letter is to another friend, a Tory – but he hasn't read Humboldt. (*He tears up the letter.*) I shall write to the Admiralty and ask them to agree to your joining *The Beagle*.

Darwin Captain! I am – overcome! *Gloria in excelsis.* Beetles of South America, here I come! Forgive me . . .

FitzRoy You may find your spirits constrained by the lack of space, but I shall do all in my power to make you comfortable. Come to the ship tomorrow. You'll need a good pair of pistols, I shall help you choose them, books, although you'll find my library extensive, I'll give you a list of clothes –

Darwin I shall follow your guidance in all matters . . . I have never been at sea before!

FitzRoy stiffens and studies Darwin for a moment.

FitzRoy Mr Darwin, forgive me for the apparent impertinence of my question, but does your father have your nose?

Darwin I believe he does ... Mine is somewhat smaller ...

FitzRoy According to the laws of physiognomy, it indicates a certain weakness of temperament. Nothing I hear about your father confirms this.

Darwin No, my father is not weak. (*Pause.*) I've always hated my nose.

FitzRoy No matter. I have great faith in your friends and I myself am no mean judge of character. I shall be delighted to have you on *The Beagle* and you shall help me fulfil another purpose. William Buckland, as you know, has found conclusive evidence of the Flood in England.

Darwin Not quite conclusive –

FitzRoy We could establish such a proof in South America. Your mentor Henslow is a deeply religious man, I understand.

Darwin Deeply.

FitzRoy Do we not live in a great age? Our natural philosophers trace God's signature on Earth as our English ships mark the contours of the world. I shall prevent shipwrecks by mapping the coasts, but together, Mr Darwin, we shall prevent spiritual shipwreck by mapping God's work.

Darwin I shall do all I can to be of help, Captain FitzRoy.

SCENE THREE: 'EMOTION'

The present.
  Tom (Darwin) and Ian (FitzRoy). Millie comes on.
She has been watching.

Millie Embrace!

Nobody moves.

Embrace: hug tight. You are both so happy, so full of hope and love for each other, you embrace.

Ian Englishmen don't embrace, Millie, particularly not these Englishmen.

Millie I don't mean homosexual, I mean emotion.

Ian Emotion –

Millie This great, this beautiful emotion of friendship, it's so obvious you embrace, isn't it, Tom?

Tom It's just that – you see – we – I mean, they – may have trouble expressing – you know: English, all that – maybe we could just move towards each other –

Millie Charles Darwin is young, enthusiastic, surely you want to embrace your *beau idéal* of a captain.

Tom Whatever.

Ian I have read everything there is about FitzRoy, which isn't much, I admit, but I can assure you he would not embrace or be embraced – he would never show what he feels.

Millie Ian, you are creating him.

Ian He is an historical character, I am finding him.

Millie You say yourself he is unknown. He will evolve into what we make him here.

Ian Why make him a fool? The phrenology business is bad enough, can't we get rid of it?

Millie It's a famous anecdote.

Ian I don't like it.

Millie You don't like anything.

Tom Ian likes the lines, Millie, he gets so angry when I get them wrong.

Millie I see emotion in these lines.

Ian You interpret.

Millie I see two men who embrace.

Ian Maybe in Bulgaria.

Millie In Bulgaria, they would take a knife to their arms and mingle their blood. And they would not be young men on an exciting voyage around the world, they would be fighting in caves and forests against the Turks. So there would be fear and also anger against the oppressor and perhaps both would be tortured, mangled – dead!

Ian And now that you've once again shamed us with the excitement of your history, you expect us to do as you want?

Millie It is not my history any more, this is my history.

Ian Then you should learn to understand repression. It may not be as romantic as oppression but it works.

Millie I do not want some gloomy English Chekhov here, Ian, I want light and tenderness. It is thought tenderness gave mammals an evolutionary advantage.

Tom It did? I have tenderness – I think.

Ian It is 1831. I am a captain in His Majesty's Navy, I am an aristocrat and I am English, I am not playing an evolving mammal!

Millie FitzRoy is religious, he knows tenderness.

Ian Not in the Church of England.

Millie I do not see how we go on. (*She throws herself down at Ian's feet.*) I beg you, I entreat you, I supplicate, I fall on my knees before you – to express emotion.

Ian This is no way to direct.

Millie It is in Moscow.

Tom I like this tenderness thing. Ian, we can try a little tenderness, can't we, repressed even, yeah?

SCENE FOUR: 'TENDERNESS'

January 1832.
The Bay of Biscay. FitzRoy's cabin. A storm. The ship rolls.
Darwin stands, sways, very seasick.
FitzRoy arranges a hammock.

FitzRoy Try this, Darwin, it may help.

Darwin tries to get into the hammock. He has trouble. FitzRoy holds it for him. Darwin reels.

You must believe me when I say this is the worst storm I have encountered in the Bay of Biscay.

Darwin I fear I shall prove useless on this voyage.

FitzRoy We have not been at sea very long.

Darwin I was sick as soon as we left the Channel. Even the Fuegians laugh at me. Have you seen Jemmy Button mimicking my sickness?

FitzRoy He doesn't mean it unkindly. They're better mimics than our London actors.

Darwin holds down a retch.

Perhaps if you lay down on my divan.

FitzRoy gently leads Darwin to the divan. Darwin collapses.

Darwin This is intolerable.

FitzRoy Lieutenant Wickham tells me you are considering leaving *The Beagle*.

Darwin I cannot be much of a companion in this state, Captain, I might stay in Tenerife and then find a ship to take me home.

FitzRoy I heard in Portsmouth there is a quarantine in Tenerife. We may have to remain aboard.

Darwin I had so hoped to see it!

FitzRoy I am sorry to disappoint you, Darwin, but you will find much to see in the Cape de Verde Islands. My officers would be sorry to see their dear Philosopher go. You have made yourself well liked. I should be sorry, too. Very sorry.

Darwin wrestles with a bout of seasickness. FitzRoy gently adjusts a pillow.

Let me read you the next chapter of *Persuasion*.

SCENE FIVE: 'FRIENDSHIP'

Tom and Ian, as before, but very relaxed.

Tom I really admire you, I saw you a few years ago. Yeah, I thought, yeah. I hope I'm not letting you down.

Ian Not at all.

Tom It's a lot of lines.

Ian You'll get them.

Tom I remember them, I just don't know what they mean – and then, words . . . They shift about.

Ian That's the pleasure.

Tom In a film, you're there for ever. Fixed.

Ian And people eat popcorn while they watch.

Tom I went to read for this film.

Ian When?

Tom I know, I'm not supposed to. They're looking for Germans, I mean, English with German accents, real Germans are too expensive or too real or something. What do you think?

Ian About Germans?

Tom Would you do a film?

Ian I'm not asked. Listen, we have a lot of words coming up.

Tom Yeah, sure, words. Will you help me? You know, hints.

Ian Concentrate.

Tom Concentrate.

Ian You don't really need my help.

Tom I know, but I like it.

SCENE SIX: 'DOUBT'

Darwin and FitzRoy.
  A month later, off *the coast of South America.*
  It is hot. Darwin reads with enthusiasm.

Darwin '– The next morning we saw the sun rise behind the outline of the Grand Canary island and suddenly illumine the peak of Tenerife, whilst the lower parts were veiled in fleecy clouds.'

FitzRoy Fleecy?

Darwin 'On the sixteenth of January we anchored at Porto Praya.'

FitzRoy You've gone from Devonport to the Cape de Verde Islands in one paragraph?

Darwin I was rather seasick.

FitzRoy Go on.

Darwin 'February twenty-ninth: the day has passed delightfully. Delight itself, however, is a weak term to express the feelings –'

FitzRoy Feelings.

Darwin '– feelings of a naturalist who, for the first time, has wandered by himself in a Brazilian forest. The elegance of the grasses –'

FitzRoy Elegance? Is that a size?

Darwin 'The novelty of the parasitical plants, the beauty of the flowers –'

FitzRoy Vague, Darwin, vague . . .

Darwin 'The glossy green of the foliage – A most paradoxical mixture of sound and silence pervades the shady parts of the wood.'

FitzRoy Which is it?

Darwin I explain the noise from the insects is loud but there is a deep silence in the forest. 'To a person fond of natural history, such a day as this brings with it a deeper pleasure than he can ever hope to experience again!'

FitzRoy Such enthusiasm. So few facts. (*Pause.*) Of course, you don't have to publish it.

Darwin No.

FitzRoy And so much of your personality. Think of Humboldt, those scientific descriptions.

Darwin It was his enthusiasm that infected me. I believed it did you.

FitzRoy Each night, Darwin, I sit here for hours and write up everything I have observed and done during the day. I had better give you my own description of our departure. (*He reads, fast, but with pride.*) 'Vessels in the offing, and distant land looming much; a few mottled, hard-edged clouds appearing in the east; streaks (mare's tails across the sky) spreading from the same quarter; a high barometer (30.3) and the smoke of chimneys rising high into the air and going westwards, were the signs which assured us of a favourable wind.' (*Brief pause.*) I've taken a whole chapter to discuss the purpose of the voyage, the Fuegians and my civilising mission, the refitting of the ship, I explain we are seventy-four on board, even you are mentioned by name, Darwin, and it is not until the end of the third chapter that I reach the Cape de Verde Islands – having discussed the possible causes of the high waves in the Atlantic, how to foresee a squall, problems of determining longitude. Nothing is omitted from my account of the voyage of *The Beagle* – I know how interested people will be in reading it. Observe and note down. Observe again. Never trust memory. I suggest you tear up your account and start again.

Darwin folds up his papers and puts them in his pocket. A pause.

Perhaps I expect too much of people.

Darwin You do not spare yourself.

FitzRoy We strive for perfection and so mirror God.

Darwin God taught forgiveness.

FitzRoy You still reproach me for the floggings?

Darwin Thirty-five lashes for a little drunkenness the day after Christmas.

FitzRoy I go on at great length about the necessity of flogging in these chapters.

Darwin I shall read them with interest.

FitzRoy Are you doubting me?

Darwin doesn't answer.

From the ship's crew I expect only obedience, but I would wish for you to understand me. When we round Cape Horn we will face storms, winds, rocks – the most dismal and dank surroundings. A captain who cannot assert discipline betrays his men, goes mad himself, mad . . . the word discipline means little to you.

Darwin I've encountered so little of it in nature.

FitzRoy Darwin, we sail into Rio tomorrow and I shall make sure we arrive at dawn as I did the first time I saw it. It is the most beautiful harbour in the world and will lift our spirits. And you can take time away from the ship to explore the interior.

Darwin Thank you, Captain FitzRoy.

FitzRoy You see I am not without sensibility – but there is so much at stake.

Darwin You work yourself very hard.

FitzRoy Too hard? Who is saying that? Wickham, Sulivan? They call me Black Coffee, don't they – when the dark mood descends –

Darwin Your lieutenants are devoted to you, Captain FitzRoy. I have only observed.

SCENE SEVEN: 'CAMOUFLAGE'

Tom and Ian, pacing around each other.

Ian No. No. No. In his autobiography, he describes himself as a simpleton who only accidentally stumbled on one of those theories that change the world. He was a good and faithful husband, adored by his children, a sound friend, brother – haven't you read anything?

Tom Millie brought me some books, I looked at the pictures. All I'm saying is, he's not nice. Nobody can be nice and that famous. You're nice, but you're not famous, I mean, you're in *Who's Who*, but you're not – like – you're not a film star.

Ian You're playing a superstar of history, Mr Millennium Man himself, you ought to work harder. He did.

Tom You want to play him . . .

Ian Everybody loves the winner, especially if he's decent.

Tom Darwin wasn't nice just now and he's horrible to FitzRoy later.

Ian Something happened on that ship, Darwin seemed to need to obliterate FitzRoy's memory.

Tom You see, not nice. It's the struggle whatchamacallit. For Darwin to go up, FitzRoy has to be pulverised. (*He makes a grinding sound.*)

Ian You can be honourable and survive.

Tom Yeah –? Before I became an actor I thought of being a soldier. You know why?

Ian It requires even less intellectual effort.

Tom Because I loved the idea of camouflage. It's a great survival tactic, you even win wars that way. Listen, it goes this way: there's this great idea, the struggle for survival.

Ian Existence. Get that right!

Tom Yeah, whatever. How was this idea going to survive in a world of FitzRoys? You use camouflage. Maybe even the idea uses camouflage, uses Darwin the nice – but not so nice – you see – in fact, ruthless –

Ian Don't tell Millie that, she's so in love with him and with you.

Tom That's because I'm nice to her. FitzRoy never learned.

Ian I can't stand all that emotion.

Tom Emotion's very fashionable now.

Ian Real passion comes from ideas.

Tom Yeah? I wouldn't know. But I'm in a muddle with this guy. He's like one of his fossils in the next scene: put the bits this way you get a giant snake, that way, a furry mammoth – you're supposed to help me – you're so experienced – so nice.

Ian I've told you: read the books.

Tom Why should I believe the books?

Ian It's called history.

Tom Yeah, but history's shifty too, I mean, isn't it supposed to be rewritten all the time? Things happened that we were told never happened, like those Yugoslavs who helped us in the war – you know – the partisans those English politicians sent back to be killed – It's in the film script. And then some things that maybe didn't happen, like the Holocaust.

Ian moves to seize Tom, quick and violent.

Ian Don't you ever say that, ever!

Tom OK, sorry. Don't get so emotional.

Ian Even your stupidity doesn't excuse a statement like that.

Tom I'm only repeating what I hear. I don't care one way or the other. (*He begins to lug bags into the middle of the cabin.*)

Ian Don't you?

Tom I wasn't there. Were you?

Ian We all carry the luggage.

Tom Not me. I live in the present. I travel light.

SCENE EIGHT: 'CHANGE'

Montevideo.
   FitzRoy's cabin.
   Darwin lugs some dusty bags. He is himself dusty,
dishevelled. The cabin is filled with dust.
   FitzRoy sits, very still, very dark.

Darwin I rode with the gauchos. They are so tall,
handsome, proud, dissolute: long hair, black moustaches,
clicking spurs and knives. So polite. (*He imitates a Spanish*
accent, rather badly.) '*Si, Signor Darwin . . .*' but offend
their dignity and – (*He imitates the slitting of a throat.*)
I watched them catch their cattle with the *lazo*. Like
this. (*He twirls an imaginary lasso.*) I tried it myself,
but I tangled my own horse's legs and we both fell.
How they laughed. Said they'd never seen a man capture
his own self before. Ha. Ha. Ha. There was I, and
the horse, both wrapped in the *lazo* like a naturalist's
parcel –

   He demonstrates. FitzRoy offers a wintry smile.

We climbed the Sierra de las Animas. I found eighty
different sorts of birds. I'll show you. All kinds of reptiles,
even a ninety-eight-pound water hog! The buck I shot
had the worst smell I've ever encountered. I used my
handkerchief on him, I think I can still smell it.

FitzRoy So can I.

Darwin We came to a salt lake of black mud, fetid. Ugh.
I brought some mud back for you but I dropped the
bottle. I'm sorry.

FitzRoy There seems to be some mud still stuck on your
shirt.

Darwin There were hundreds of flamingoes. The life, FitzRoy – on this seemingly grim and barren landscape. The flamingoes feed on worms, the worms on infusoria or confervae, all the life is totally adapted to this lake of brine, isn't it wonderful?

FitzRoy God's infinite providence.

Darwin Here's the best. (*He takes out some large and dusty fossilised bones with great care.*) I have many more coming. Wickham will be so cross with me. He can't find any more room on the ship!

FitzRoy raises his eyebrows at this. Darwin places the bones on the floor as well as some teeth and a skull. It is all very heavy.

Some of these crumble as you touch them, it's maddening.

FitzRoy Quite.

Darwin This animal was as large as a rhinoceros. The tooth could have belonged to an elephant. It's the tooth of a herbivore. And look at this: a neck like a giraffe's. (*He keeps placing and replacing bones, puzzling over the configuration.*) These animals are no longer found in South America. What happened?

FitzRoy The door of the Ark may not have been large enough to accommodate them.

Darwin Ha! Ha! Ha!

FitzRoy May I ask what amuses you so?

Darwin Surely, FitzRoy – Aren't you reading Lyell's second volume?

FitzRoy I run a ship!

Darwin Surely you agree with him that you can't explain all you find on high mountains by a catastrophic flood, but rather by a very slow – why, you said yourself –

FitzRoy I hadn't considered the consequences of such a statement. And Lyell fudges.

Darwin He proposes –

FitzRoy Waffle! Something must be one thing or another. There was a flood: the Bible tells us so.

A short silence. Darwin goes to another sack and brings out a dead mole-like creature.

Darwin They call it the tuco-tuco, because of the sound it makes. (*He makes the sound: 'tuco tuco'.*) They're very friendly. (*He brings out a dead starling.*) A kind of starling. They stand on the backs of cows and horses. Listen. (*He imitates a bird sound with a bubbly hiss.*) It seems they deposit their eggs in other nests like our cuckoos. Now listen to this. (*He emits a high-pitched sound like a peewit.*) Just like a peewit, isn't it? Now. (*He imitates a pack of dogs barking. Brings out another bird.*) Nothing like it in England. Sounds like a pack of dogs in full chase.

He does the sound again, intrigued. FitzRoy winces.

Now, where have I put it –

FitzRoy Please! Stop it!

Darwin FitzRoy? Are you unwell?

FitzRoy I am perfectly fit!

Darwin I was so delighted with my discoveries I did not think to ask –

FitzRoy That is not unusual –

Darwin You have been working very hard.

FitzRoy Yes. Mr Geographer, while you were gallivanting about the countryside, I have measured, remeasured, and measured again every inch of this coast. Back and forth, back and forth – there will no error in the charts of these waters.

Darwin Isn't that good?

FitzRoy Good, but not good enough. I have to do it again.

Darwin FitzRoy!

FitzRoy I don't expect you to understand the quest for perfection.

Darwin I am remiss for asking you to take an interest in these fossils.

FitzRoy Please to remember I was the first to notice bones embedded in the silt off Punta Alta. Had it not been for me, you wouldn't even know of these animals. (*He puts his hands to his head.*)

Darwin FitzRoy?

FitzRoy Headaches.

Pause.

Darwin I found the country as hospitable as you described it, FitzRoy, but the Spaniards do not have anything like the sophistication of our English landowners. I also felt much disturbed by their policy of killing all the Indians and sending their children into slavery.

FitzRoy I once questioned a landowner on that very subject. He called in twenty of his slaves and asked them what they thought and to a man they said slavery was a good thing.

Darwin What else could they say in front of a man who could put them to death?

FitzRoy Are you questioning my judgement?

Darwin I am surprised you believed them.

FitzRoy But then your grandfather campaigned against slavery, I had forgotten.

Darwin What is wrong with that?

FitzRoy The trouble with meddlers like Wedgwood and other Whigs is that they do not know how other countries work. I do not say we should have slavery in England, but here –

Darwin If something is unjust and inhumane, surely it is so everywhere.

FitzRoy It is a subject you do not understand.

Darwin I have travelled and I find slavery abhorrent and degrading.

FitzRoy You seem to take pleasure in contradicting me. (*He holds his bead.*)

Darwin FitzRoy, you are not well . . .

FitzRoy It is the headaches that drove my uncle to suicide, he was never mad, whatever they said at your dinner tables – dinner tables . . . yes . . . the dinner we had at the Governor's house. I said everyone was reading Jane Austen. You demurred!

Darwin I only meant there may be some who do not read her.

FitzRoy You contradicted me in public.

Darwin But many Englishmen do not know how to read!

FitzRoy Everyone one knows or cares to know reads Jane Austen, Mr Darwin.

Darwin That is not everyone.

FitzRoy Again! You will drive me mad! I wanted the company of a gentleman. I find I am messing with a man who does not even know how to tidy himself before entering the cabin of his captain.

Darwin I forgot. I am sorry.

FitzRoy From now on, Mr Darwin, I shall have to ask you to mess with the junior officers.

Darwin FitzRoy, you are out of sorts – you –

FitzRoy You will not speak to your captain in this manner! Get out of my cabin and take your disgusting specimens with you. (*He kicks a bone. It disintegrates.*)

SCENE NINE: 'FEAR'

Tom, Ian and Millie.

Millie (*to Tom*) Perfect! How do you do it? I kiss you.

Tom shrugs and takes out a computer game.

(*to Ian*) Yes, but bigger, stronger, more passionate, more desperate, more fearful, more dark.

Tom gets very absorbed in his computer game.

Tom Pchhh –

Millie 'Take your disgusting specimens with you' – symbol of everything he fears.

Ian (*icy*) Are you showing me how to say it?

Millie That bitter reference to Whigs, the Reform Bill giving all these people the vote. Darwin belongs to those upstarts now ruling England.

Ian I know all that.

Millie The Admiralty is angry with FitzRoy for buying a second ship and makes him sell it again, his world is shrinking, he's out of joint so, fear, that terrible icy fear when the climate begins to change, a long winter sets in, I've seen it, at first surprise, then disbelief, then you attack each other because there's not enough food to go around, times of betrayal, despair. And the ice advances towards you.

Ian Could you be specific?

Millie Fear, Ian, it's an English word, no? Contemporary. Daily. Why do you repress that, too?

Tom (*on his computer*) Sitting ducks.

Millie When I saw you for this, I saw that fear. I found out you hadn't worked for a long time.

Ian Through the Bulgarian Secret Police?

Millie Yes, we had to learn in Bulgaria to read a teacher's face to know whether she was teaching us something true or something she'd been told to say, so I can read faces, yes.

Ian The lines are precise, they do not describe a nuclear winter.

Millie But the writer knows social history and the struggle for existence and the world we're in. You're good at something, the climate shrinks your space, you shiver.

Ian Ask the writer to come and tell me on what line he wants me to act the fear of a species facing a cold winter. (*He begins to leave.*)

Millie He's afraid.

Ian leaves.

Tom Zap!

Millie (*to Tom*) Why don't you ever say anything? What do you believe?

Tom Nothing.

Millie In general. God, dialectical materialism, existentialism –

Tom Please, I'm English.

Millie For yourself, even: recognition, money?

Tom I wouldn't be here.

Millie The environment? That's not too mentally taxing.

Tom I like underground car parks. As a child, I loved to stand behind cars and breathe in the fumes, must have been a high.

Millie Are you saying you are cynical, selfish, stupid, immoral and want only a good life?

Tom I'm tired of everyone trying to enlist me in their ideas. I don't want to be told that this idea is the best idea that ever existed and that I have to fight for it, lose my job for it, even leaflet for it. When I see an idea floating around, about to get stuck on my jacket, I move.

Millie What about culture?

Tom Who?

Millie Here. This. I believe more in this country than you do.

Tom Yeah, that's normal, you're a foreigner. Are you going to stay?

Millie If I can. Stay and be part of it. More British than the British.

Tom You speak so well.

Millie I just get the thoughts wrong. But my accent is good?

Tom Don't lose the passion in your vowels.

Millie They may tell me to go. It depends on this. I have to prove I have something unique to contribute. I'm afraid of the post in the morning, the letter telling me to go home – I have no home.

Tom I'll marry you if you want.

Millie I thought you were –

Tom I am, I can still marry you – if it helps.

Millie What would you –?

Tom Get out of it? I don't believe in profit either.

Millie But why?

Tom There doesn't always have to be a why. When I go out at night, sometimes I take a tube into the centre, sometimes I walk in the woods. I don't know who I'm going to meet. Whether I'll come back alone or with someone; whether it'll be good or not. I could meet the love of my life, or – yeah – maybe death. If I marry you, maybe you'll give me lots of jobs, everybody wants to work with Eastern European directors, maybe they won't next year . . . The offer's open anyway.

Millie kisses Tom gently on the forehead.

Millie You know, in Eastern Europe we are very homophobic.

Tom I've noticed.

Millie I've shown it?

Tom You've shown fear.

Millie A woman's territory is already so insecure.

Tom I love women.

Millie Really?

Tom No, not really. But I do like your vowels.

Millie I can't pass for British unless I get rid of them.

Tom What a sacrifice.

Millie Not for survival.

Tom (*correcting the 'u' of survival*) Survival.

Millie Survival. I still can't believe in generosity without idealism.

Tom That's because you're homophobic. How do you think we survive?

SCENE TEN: 'IDEALISM'

1832. Tierra del Fuego, off the Straits of Magellan.
Rain. Grey. Very cold.
Several boxes are stacked in FitzRoy's cabin, making it even smaller.
FitzRoy and Darwin, cold, having been stuck at sea for a month, drink tea in irritated silence. Every slurp and swallow is self-conscious and intensely heard by the other. Darwin, seasick as usual, swallows frequently, to the annoyance of FitzRoy.
FitzRoy takes ages to put his cup down after a drink, meticulously, silently. Darwin watches, mesmerised, FitzRoy's slightly prissy gestures. Darwin's cup tends to crash a little. FitzRoy winces when that happens as when Darwin clears his throat.

At last tea is over. FitzRoy moves a tray carefully and looks at the skylight.

FitzRoy We have another hour of light.

Darwin looks up, despondent.

Darwin Will the sun never shine?

Darwin takes out some papers and spreads them. FitzRoy moves them slightly back. Darwin doesn't notice and pushes them out again.

FitzRoy In his log book, Captain Stokes described Tierra del Fuego as the dreariest landscape on earth, utterly desolate, where the soul dies – (*Pause.*) He had encountered the sorts of winds we've had, couldn't move for months. Eventually he locked himself in his cabin and shot himself. (*Pause.*) He made rather a mess of it and it took him days to die. When I took over *The Beagle*, the crew kept seeing his ghost, sometimes I think I see his shadow – just there, to your right – (*He stares and moves towards the area indicated, then stops himself.*) But I have a very cheerful task in hand. The good ladies of the Walthamstow Missionary Society entrusted these boxes to my especial care.

Darwin looks briefly and goes back to his papers.

We'll soon deposit our young missionary and the Fuegians – there are some beautiful glaciers in the channel by the way. (*He puts a box on the table, begins to unwrap it.*) I'll make a note of all the items given and the Fuegians will learn to write their own thank-you notes in good time.

Darwin I never thought to see men and women in such an abject state.

FitzRoy They are human beings.

Darwin I feel closer to these beetles.

FitzRoy They will be educated.

Darwin The nakedness, filth, ugliness, shouting, constant begging. (*He imitates.*) 'Yamaschooner, yamaschooner –' Is it true that when their women become old, they eat them?

FitzRoy Only in times of famine. I asked Jemmy Button why they didn't eat their dogs instead and he told me it was because the dogs catch otters, but the women can no longer help feed the tribe.

Darwin And you plan to educate them?

FitzRoy Not one of God's creatures is beyond salvation. Try to be a little more charitable, Darwin.

Darwin They repel me.

Darwin goes back to his papers. FitzRoy unwraps some silver-plated cutlery. He counts.

FitzRoy Thirty-six forks, thirty-six spoons, ah, thirty-six fish knives.

Darwin Surely, FitzRoy?

FitzRoy continues doggedly, writing down.

FitzRoy Four serving spoons. (*He unwraps an elegant soup tureen.*) Wedgwood! (*He now unwraps several immaculate, white, embroidered antimacassars.*)

Darwin Antimacassars!

FitzRoy Why not?

Darwin FitzRoy, they've never even seen a blanket –

FitzRoy Why should a Fuegian not sit one day, his hair cut, washed, smoothed with macassar oil, in a huge armchair reading a paper? And then his wife shall want antimacassars. Not immediately perhaps . . . agriculture must be established, basic building skills, weaving – Matthews will hold some of these back, but look how quickly Jemmy Button has learned civilised manners. My greatest ambition is to be remembered as someone who benefited mankind. Is it not yours?

Darwin I would not be in Matthews' place for the world.

FitzRoy He trusts in God.

Darwin God help him.

FitzRoy God will. (*He continues to unpack.*) Ten baby bonnets. (*He now begins to unwrap another large object.*) What can this be?

FitzRoy carefully unwraps a large, ornate, Victorian chamber pot. Darwin bursts out laughing.

SCENE ELEVEN: 'IDENTITY'

Tom, Ian, Millie and Lawrence. Lawrence is black, well dressed in a casual American way. He speaks slowly, in a well-modulated East Coast–mid-Atlantic accent.

Lawrence In November 1832, FitzRoy landed his three Fuegians with the missionary Matthews at Ponsonby Sound. Jemmy Button recognised his tribe, but could no longer speak his own language. His mother and his brothers refused to acknowledge him. The sailors erected tents and planted a vegetable garden before leaving. FitzRoy went back ten days later to find the goods stolen, the vegetable garden trampled and Matthews' life threatened. Matthews was re-embarked but Jemmy Button was left to fulfil FitzRoy's vision of a civilised

135

tribe. When FitzRoy returned to Ponsonby Sound a year later, a lone, naked savage with matted hair and painted face emerged from the mist in a dug-out canoe. With difficulty, pain, FitzRoy recognised Jemmy Button. Jemmy, embarrassed by his nakedness, refused to answer FitzRoy's questions until he had been fully clothed. English and good table manners came haltingly back to him over dinner with his beloved captain and he told a sad tale of abject treatment by his tribe and family. And yet he refused to sail with FitzRoy, insisting this was where he belonged. He undressed, lowered himself into his canoe, vanished. He had adopted Englishness with total enthusiasm, but had then readopted the customs of his tribe with equal commitment, thus becoming perhaps one of the first people to suffer the stresses of biculturalism, a condition which was to reach epidemic proportions in the late twentieth century. Jemmy Button's own tribe is now extinct.

Tom Poor Jemmy Button. I love him so.

Lawrence I've always wanted to say something in a real theatre. It's not the same as a lecture hall.

Ian Why don't you? You have a good voice.

Lawrence I wanted to, when I was at college, but I looked around and I thought, no . . . it's too crowded here, so I majored in Biology and English instead.

Tom I never imagined you'd he like this – I thought you'd be –

Lawrence (*urbane*) White?

Ian Why don't you write yourself a part: Jemmy Button?

Lawrence It's FitzRoy I'm interested in.

Tom FitzRoy!

Lawrence Playwrights are the anatomists of the failed character.

Tom Yeah . . . right.

Lawrence Not that I presume – this is my first time.

Ian Millie said you were afraid to come . . .

Lawrence I know how prejudiced you are in this country – against Americans. (*to Ian*) I saw you ten years ago. *Richard the Second*. If someone had told me then – I am a happy man! Sometimes I can't believe this is real.

Tom Yeah . . . I can't take it too seriously myself.

Lawrence It's serious all right, but I'm a teacher as well, a professor, our students have a year abroad – I make sure I'm the tutor as often as possible. Everybody wants to come to England, so I only get here every two or three years. I love it, oh, do I love it here.

Tom Why?

Lawrence Because your pavements burn with history.

Tom They do?

Millie Lawrence, do you want to watch some more? I am being very brilliant, I think.

Lawrence A few minutes, then I'm taking my students to the National Portrait Gallery – I teach a course called 'The Metaphysics of Cultural Genealogy'.

SCENE TWELVE: 'CRUELTY'

September 1835. The Galapagos.
    Change of light. Heat. Darwin and FitzRoy. Lawrence and Millie, watching.

Darwin Dismal heaps of broken lava . . . hideous lizards with the faces of ancient demons. No wonder sailors couldn't wait to get away.

FitzRoy Los Encantadas, the Enchanted Isles. The currents are so strong, the islands can vanish overnight and leave you lost in the ocean. I prefer the name Galapagos.

Darwin I see we have six live ones on board.

FitzRoy They'll keep us in meat until Tahiti.

Darwin FitzRoy . . . the Governor told me he can recognise which island a tortoise comes from by its markings . . . you know they can't swim . . .

Short pause.

FitzRoy I gather you didn't find much else of interest.

Darwin A few miserable weeds, finches, mockingbirds. Again, quite remarkable differences between them . . . I wonder . . .
    FitzRoy, I did something thoroughly foolish: I put all my finches in the same bag.

FitzRoy I labelled mine according to each island.

Darwin You are the true naturalist!

FitzRoy I'll give them to you – now you will forgive me – I have some calculations to do – I fell behind – you will forgive me – drudgery calls.

FitzRoy waits for Darwin to go, Darwin ignores him.

Darwin May I show you something?

Darwin takes out some drawings. FitzRoy takes them.

FitzRoy Finches. Quite well drawn. Mine are more precise. (*He hands the drawings back and waits for Darwin to go.*)

Darwin You see how different the beaks are.

FitzRoy Presumably they eat different foods.

Darwin Precisely.

FitzRoy Each one is perfectly adapted to its place in the world, according to the wisdom of God.

Darwin How far are we from the coast of South America?

FitzRoy Five hundred miles. Now, Darwin –

Darwin Don't some of these remind you of birds we saw in South America?

FitzRoy They look like variations, yes.

Darwin Extreme variations.

FitzRoy Perhaps. Darwin, I must ask you –

Darwin Does it not occur to you, FitzRoy, that possibly some of these variations might be so extreme as to constitute – shall we say – a species –?

FitzRoy It is sometimes hard to tell.

Darwin Suppose, only suppose that these volcanic islands emerged from the sea, as Lyell suggests, seeds drifted from South America, clung to the lava providing meagre vegetation – birds followed, settled, dropped more seeds. Suppose that in this strange, this brave new world, isolated from the rest of the continent, the islands, themselves isolated from each other – suppose there began to emerge birds so different from their forebears – look at the beaks, FitzRoy – that they must, in truth, be called a – new – species.

FitzRoy New.

Darwin New . . .

FitzRoy Stop. I see where you are going.

Darwin I do not see myself. Something is at work, but I do not know what.

FitzRoy The devil is at work, here, in this cabin! (*He brushes something away.*) This shadow . . . Darwin, I know the dark night of the soul. Doubt sweeps in like a treacherous wind and puts out God's light. I sat here for days, you heard, with this gun – (*He takes the gun and shows it to Darwin.*) – held to my head – I gave up command of the ship – you weren't here –

Darwin I didn't know. I was very ill. I would have come back.

FitzRoy Wickham saw me through. But sometimes I feel that if I turn my head this way, just a little, then all life will jangle into meaninglessness. Darwin, let me keep you from the vision of a tormented world from which God is absent. I am well now – I have sworn always to keep in sight the divine designer. You too must swear to shut out all the thoughts you have expressed here –

Darwin I don't know what my thoughts are, how can I order them?

FitzRoy Let me be their captain, let me steer us both away from madness.

FitzRoy holds out an arm to turn Darwin. Lawrence stops them.

Lawrence Something's missing.

Millie It's fine, Lawrence.

Lawrence How do you excavate the intimate moments of historical characters?

Tom What a fuss over words. What does it matter whether something's a variation or a species?

Lawrence (*picking up and studying the gun*) New. One word. 'New' species.

Millie You can be short, tall, fat, blond or brown, short-beaked or long-beaked, but if the species were not created but slowly evolved, then nothing is fixed –

Tom So.

Millie You thrive on disorder, Tom, but these two men have been living in a fixed universe. God, man, England, class. If, as Darwin suspects, it is fluid, unplanned, then it is a world without a designer, without God. Lawrence?

Lawrence (*looking at the gun*) Do you think that in a play a gun always has to go off?

Tom I know about evolution, well, sort of, but I pray to God all the time. You know: 'Please, God, don't let me catch pneumonia, please make Ian and Lawrence admire me, please make me famous.'

Millie When I was in Sofia I used to go to the Alexander Nevsky cathedral, and in the smoky hues of grey and red I could cry and find hope again, but I had left my rational mind on the steps outside. We read the Bible as metaphor.

Lawrence (*still with the gun*) Some believe access to metaphor is an evolutionary tool to stave off the grief of chaos. We need it more and more.

Tom Yeah. Right. Lawrence, you're a real help.

Ian I don't believe, I never have, but when I am working, like this, I feel what can only be described as a kind of grace.

Millie Yes, yes, it is work! It is work! We will dispel the darkness: we will work! Ian, I begin to love you!

Ian (*to Lawrence*) Is it FitzRoy's hereditary madness that's coming over me?

Lawrence There's a genetic predisposition from the family, a cultural one from Captain Stokes, and the environment is right. If you go for only one of those options you'll destroy the mystery of being human.

Tom I'm getting a headache.

Lawrence (*to Tom*) There's nothing comfortable about evolution.

Millie To suggest the words of the Bible are not literally true and no longer hold the world safe, there is the wreckage – the madness. FitzRoy sees that all sense could crumble in his mind, have you never felt that? You look outside, it's all a jumble and you hear, too – a jumble, words that belong to no language at all – FitzRoy sees – he hears – Darwin as Lucifer, defying God, jumbling the Creation. And he puts out his hand to hold Darwin back, keep him fixed. Tom, you turn away, stand there, enchanted by these islands, their possibilities – this new world that came into being so gradually, so accidentally and also – you see this already – so cruelly.

Tom I love the cruelty. Very now. Yes. Let's have more cruelty.

They stay in position. Millie watches. Lawrence toys with the gun, then hands it to Ian, who aims at Tom.

Act Two

Darwin's study. Not dissimilar to FitzRoy's cabin in feel, but much messier: a desk crammed with papers. A very comfortable rolling leather chair, books and books. Jars, skeletons.

Millie is still setting some bits up. Ian and Tom say lines quite fast to each other. Millie occasionally listens but keeps changing things on the desk, coming in and out. Ian is intense, Tom quite distracted. Lawrence comes in with a jar of barnacles.

FitzRoy 'Mr Darwin's journal is still detained, to the great regret of the scientific world, because it is to form part of a longer work including an account of the Surveys of Captains King and FitzRoy in South America . . .' And I had been led to believe that the scientific world was waiting for an account by *The Beagle*'s captain. I sent Mr Lyell my chapter on the Deluge for his comments, I am still waiting. Presumably he cannot answer. Have you read it?

Darwin I found the arguments difficult.

FitzRoy I put them succinctly.

Darwin I am a naturalist, not a theologian.

FitzRoy Your own mentor Sedgwick has repeatedly said that scientific truths are there to reveal God's intentions. I *prove* the truth of Revelation. I even use some of your finds. Indeed, Darwin, I mention you often.

Darwin I am flattered.

FitzRoy You seem to have forgotten it was by my invitation you joined *The Beagle*.

Darwin I cannot imagine my life without those five years!

FitzRoy My officers were kind to you. They could have been handsomely rewarded if they had collected their own specimens. They made room for you instead.

Darwin The specimens are even more interesting than I knew, FitzRoy!

FitzRoy Please give me their names.

Millie Please *to* give me their names. It's an interesting English construction.

FitzRoy Please to give me their names.

Darwin Many don't have names yet.

FitzRoy The names of my officers!

Darwin FitzRoy!

FitzRoy The names!

Darwin Sulivan, Usborne.

Tom What are their names?

Ian Wickham . . .! Come on, Tom.

Darwin Wickham, Stewart, need I go on?

FitzRoy You talk of sunsets, plants, generals, but never a mention of these superb officers – even I, your captain, hardly feature at all.

Darwin I shall endeavour to repair the omission.

FitzRoy nods. Pause.

FitzRoy You are getting married?

Millie I had almost forgotten! (*She goes out.*)

Darwin To my cousin Emma Wedgwood.

FitzRoy You must be patient. It takes at least six months to find happiness in marriage. Perhaps she will bring you back on to the path from which you have strayed.

Darwin No doubt she will try.

FitzRoy I am concerned by a line in your account, which you will notice I have read with great care. You propose the Galapagos Islands were originally under water, that is consistent with my chapter on the Deluge, but you then go on to say, and you will forgive me if I have not memorised it correctly: 'Hence, both in space and time, we seem to be brought a little nearer to that great fact – the mystery of mysteries – the first appearance of new beings on Earth.'

Darwin You are word-perfect, FitzRoy. Should it be 'a little nearer'?

Ian I've just said 'a little nearer'.

Tom Is it important?

Ian You say, 'Should it be "somewhat nearer"?' You've got to get this right!

Tom 'Should it be "somewhat nearer"?' Is this really important?

Millie comes in with a portrait.

Millie Your wife. Very pretty in a dull sort of English way. Do you like her? I am so excited, you are two such wonderful men.

Lawrence comes in with large jars.

And Lawrence has brought some more barnacles.

Lawrence I'll teach you to dissect them.

Millie Tom, you have terrible stomach problems. And the age, yes? And Ian, for you, it's what's called being ill at ease in your skin, it's too tight maybe – or askew . . . (*She demonstrates on Ian's arm, stares at him for a moment. She goes out.*)

FitzRoy It does not matter whether it is 'a little nearer' or 'somewhat nearer'. You agreed on the ship to abandon such thoughts.

Darwin I can think what I want on dry land. (*to Lawrence*) I don't remember Darwin agreeing to anything.

FitzRoy Not if you are a gentleman.

Lawrence Something happened between them in the Galapagos, but I haven't discovered it yet.

FitzRoy You are beginning to make a reputation for yourself, Darwin, but if you make public the thoughts you confessed to me, you will be ostracised. And I shall feel responsible for the misery you bring to yourself. I was your captain, Darwin.

Darwin That was five years ago.

FitzRoy Three. I hope I may consider myself your friend.

Lawrence I've got to go and do some more work. It's important.

Tom Is it?

Lawrence leaves.

FitzRoy I want to protect you.

A bleep goes off. Ian looks for something.

Darwin Captain FitzRoy, you will have to allow me to look after myself.

Another beep goes off. Ian takes out a tamagotchi and presses a few buttons.

Ian My daughter's tamagotchi. She comes every other weekend and I look after it the rest of the time. If something happens, she'll never trust me again.

Tom and Ian both look.

I think it wants to be fed. (*He gently hands the tamagotchi to Tom.*) A virtual baby. You get very attached.

Tom quickly hands it back.

Tom So: is it important?

The tamagotchi bleeps again. Ian looks at it.

Ian What?

Tom This . . . Darwin . . . evolution.

Ian That is rather important.

Tom They talk, that's all they do, talk. Now: if they had a shoot-out – pcchhhh.

Tom imitates a gun-fight. The tamagotchi goes off again.

Ian What do you want now? They're easily bored.

Tom Admit it, you'd love to make a film.

Ian If it was good, maybe.

Tom Even if it was bad, come on.

Ian Fifteen years ago, I was doing a good line of parts and the theatre seemed a noble, solid, even impregnable environment. This young, hot American director came to England and suddenly decided he wanted me in his film. He took me out to breakfast and laid before me the promise of stardom, wealth, power – I was dazed. As an afterthought, he gave me the script. It was about a serial murderer.

Tom Pchhh. Pchhh.

Ian His increasing skill at not getting caught. The path of such a character in Shakespeare or Ibsen would reaffirm a moral environment –

The tamagotchi goes off.

(*to the tamagotchi*) Wait. I'm talking. (*to Tom*) Not here. Nothing. I turned it down. I was sure the film wouldn't have an audience. When it came out, it was a huge success and for the first time I felt the icy trickle of fear – as if the ornate skills I was developing would soon be redundant, like the ten-foot antlers of the Irish elk which killed him when he kept getting stuck in the trees.

Tom Absolutely. No antlers for me. You can do both.

Ian You have to be very lucky or very stupid to survive in two environments at once.

Tom So my stupidity could be – what's the word? – a modern adaptation.

Ian Too many film stars give bad performances. It's not that they've lost their talent, but their sense of self.

Tom Yeah, but they're eating lots of food in the meantime.

Ian I tell myself nobody knows ahead of time which species will survive. Those first little mammals looked unpromising.

Tom You don't sound convinced. Look how pinched you are – like FitzRoy.

The tamagotchi goes off.

Ian Drink? Sleep?

Tom You see, I've been checked again.

Ian Nappy? What?

Tom For that film. Pchhh. Pchhh.

Ian *(to the tamagotchi)* Is that better?

Tom It's between me and this other guy. It would start in a week's time, so I'd have to leave this.

Ian Well, you can't

Tom Actually, I can.

The tamagotchi goes off. Ian shakes it.

Ian *(to the tamagotchi)* Let me talk to Tom! It's jealous. You're not serious.

Tom I'm hungry, Ian, I want to go where there's lots of food.

Ian You have a contract.

Tom Paper. Millie can't take me to court.

Ian One doesn't do that.

Tom You don't. I do.

Ian Tom, you cannot do this – morally.

Tom I don't understand that word, Ian.

Ian makes to seize Tom, violently.

Tom Pchhh. Pchhh. Use words, Ian, go ahead. Convince me.

Ian You're not some animal foraging for food.

Tom That's what Darwin's saying here, isn't it?

Ian You're part of a culture that nurtured you, that gives you your identity and protects you from despair. You're playing a man of extreme decency and you're taking the most superficial reading of his own words to excuse your disgusting, criminal, your tawdry –

Tom Come on, come on.

Ian You've formed relationships here, to Millie, to me, to Lawrence – how many black writers do you know? He's American, OK, but he can spawn cultural descendants here. You have an obligation and you do know what that word means because under that camouflage of idiocy is a man of talent who somewhere, however dimly, believes, believes, yes – oh my God, I don't know what to say – Give me time. Please.

The tamagotchi goes off. Ian ignores it.

Tom Sure. If you promise not to say anything to Millie, just in case it doesn't work out.

Ian Millie might just be able to find someone else – no, it wouldn't be any good. Damn you!

Tom Promise.

Ian You won't agree to anything without asking me?

Tom It's a deal.

The tamagotchi bleeps insistently.

Ian It's got a fever. They can die, you know.

SCENE TWO: 'TRUTH'

*1843. Down House, Kent. Darwin's study. Papers,
books, jars. Children's toys. FitzRoy, seemingly aged,
and Darwin.*

FitzRoy You did not answer my last letter, but I have
come down to Kent nonetheless. I've come to say
goodbye. I am being made Governor of New Zealand.

Darwin I must congratulate you.

FitzRoy There has been trouble between the settlers and
the Maoris and they want someone to calm the situation.

*Darwin looks dubiously at FitzRoy, then distracts
himself with one of his jars. FitzRoy looks around.*

You seem comfortable here. Your study reminds me a
little of my cabin.

*Darwin is increasingly absorbed by his jar. FitzRoy
eventually picks one up as well.*

Barnacles. I'm pleased to see you are homesick for *The
Beagle*.

Darwin Do you remember the new *Balanus arthrobalanus*
I found in Chile? I've decided to take on the whole genus.
Let me show you something. (*He takes out a barnacle
and dissects quickly and expertly.*) Here is a female and
what's this on her?

FitzRoy looks.

Twelve males. They have no mouth, no stomach, no
thorax, no limbs, no abdomen. They consist wholly of
reproductive organs in an envelope.

FitzRoy Fascinating.

Darwin My children find it very funny.

FitzRoy You show this to your children!

Darwin They run in and out all the time. Annie already helps me catalogue.

FitzRoy May I assume you are leaving those – other thoughts behind you?

Darwin These barnacles will take me years.

Brief pause.

FitzRoy I only ever wanted good to come to the world.

Darwin says nothing.

I am haunted by the sight of Jemmy Button. Did I fail him? I am a man of honour and integrity. How can the values I uphold have become untrue? I wanted the world to savour God through your findings. The truth cannot be as cruel as you suggested. We could not live with that truth. I failed Jemmy's tribe, don't let me fail the world, Darwin.

Darwin My little barnacles won't do much one way or the other.

FitzRoy They can show order and the beauty of the creation. (*He grabs hold of Darwin in an uncharacteristic gesture.*) Because it's there, Darwin, isn't it? It's there. (*He keeps shaking Darwin.*) It's there. It's there. It's there.

Millie comes on and gently disengages Ian.

Millie Ian . . .

Ian It's there, isn't it? Isn't it? Isn't it?

Millie (*quickly*) In the next scene, Darwin has written the most important book of the modern world. (*to Tom*) You have read it.

Tom shakes his head.

I ordered you to read it!

Tom I got put off by the pigeons. My idea of Hell is walking through the pigeons of Trafalgar Square.

Millie Go to the next chapter.

Tom I'll lose the plot. A friend is bringing me the video.

Millie Of what?

Tom Of *The Origin of Species*. It's only an hour. And it has close-ups of important words, you know, like selection, and some nice animals. I can fast-forward the pigeons.

Millie When I interviewed you, you said you were interested in evolution.

Tom I wanted the job.

Millie How dare you lie to me! And tell me only now when it is too late to get rid of you!

Tom I don't have to be Darwin to act Darwin.

Millie You have to understand every word he says.

Tom Do you?

Millie Of course, I've read all of Darwin.

Ian All of Darwin?

Millie Tom, I will sit with you every evening and read to you, you will like it.

Tom That's my body time . . .

Ian (*over*) When did you read all of Darwin? There's yards of him.

Millie (*to Tom*) It is sexy.

Ian Where?

Millie I am talking to Tom about evolution!

Ian We're both interested in your evolution. Aren't we, Tom?

Millie I do not have time to tell you. (*to Tom*) Now I will have to teach you evolution. I will start with plants. Ian, you may go.

Ian I want to learn.

Millie It's not important for you.

Ian Where did you learn about Darwin?

Millie In the Bulgarian theatre, we are very intelligent.

Ian They teach evolution in drama school?

Millie Yes.

Tom Wow.

Millie Why not? The essence of drama is conflict, no? Struggle: evolution.

Ian And it's taught to opera singers as well, ballet dancers . . . makes them leap higher?

Millie All right. I learned about Darwin in high school. Now Tom –

Ian Clearly you were a brilliant pupil . . .

Millie I wanted to come to England and study science.

Tom Wow.

Ian Wouldn't that have been better?

Tom A lot of intelligent people go into the theatre, there's nothing wrong with that.

Ian It can be the wrong choice.

Millie Evolution does not explain the suicidal gesture.

Ian That's a good definition of going into the theatre. It still doesn't explain you.

Tom You've been lying to us . . . about Moscow . . .

Pause.

Millie In the 1960s Zhivkov decreed that members of the Communist Party must be pure Bulgarians. So my family, which had had a Turkish name since the Middle Ages, changed it to a Bulgarian one. They also found a monk in Rila monastery who was willing, for a fee, to become a close cousin – so I was born into a respected medical family of pure and ancient Bulgarian origin. In my last year of high school, I stumbled on the truth, and I don't know why, I really don't know why, I decided to proclaim my Turkish identity. It was just when they were confiscating the property of anyone with a Turkish name, so I was immediately expelled – my parents went into hiding. I had never been political, I did not have the dissident's art of survival. I drifted to the capital, I found a job at the theatre.

Ian As a director?

Millie As a cleaner. When the communists fell, I took back my Bulgarian name, but it was too late to go to university. I came here and implied I was a director who had worked as a cleaner. You were so romantic about us, no one asked questions. And also I had fallen in love – with this – maybe because – maybe it could explain my suicidal gesture. I took an English name.

Ian Millie.

Millie Amelia.

Ian Why didn't you tell us before?

Millie The truth is not a good survival tool. It makes you vulnerable . . .

Ian And so attractive . . .

Ian and Millie stare at each other for a moment.

Millie I can become good at this, I know I can become good at this, I will work and work and become good at this – and then at last I will be safe.

SCENE THREE: 'THE ORIGIN OF SPECIES'

1857. Darwin's study.
More things: nests, lots of books, portraits of several children.
The men have aged.

Darwin I am not certain: Natural Selection . . . The Struggle for Existence . . . The Origin of Species.

FitzRoy And you will say that God did not create permanent species.

Darwin I say every species multiplies at an unsustainable rate. There is not enough food, hence competition, any individual who has an advantage over another –

FitzRoy Advantage given to it by God.

Darwin More like accident. The advantage is not immediately evident, but it gives the individual a better chance of finding food, a stronger beak will crack harder berries, let us say – and the advantageous trait is inherited by the offspring and this leads gradually to the formation of a new species, especially in isolated geographical areas like the Galapagos – if you remember –

FitzRoy I remember that time better than you!

Darwin The changes take place over millions of years, like the formation of our Earth.

FitzRoy And man?

Darwin That will be another book.

FitzRoy That is what everyone will want to know.

Darwin He too evolved.

FitzRoy That is not possible.

Darwin I believe it is the truth.

FitzRoy You do not have to publish your misguided beliefs.

Darwin I was sent a paper by a young man called Alfred Russel Wallace: all my ideas are there, FitzRoy.

FitzRoy Never heard of him. No one will listen to what he says, but you are respected in the best circles – let this Wallace publish.

Darwin It came to him in a three-day fever –

FitzRoy Quite –

Darwin I have spent twenty years working it out. I would have to let another man . . . another man . . .

FitzRoy Are you saying you are publishing out of the vilest personal ambition?

Millie comes on.

Millie I do not believe you are desperate enough to publish this book!

Tom I understand exactly how he feels. It would be like letting someone else have a film part, even if it's going to hurt people. Even nice Mr Darwin wants fame. It's natural. So I was right to do it.

Ian You've accepted? You promised!

Tom I was afraid you'd convince me, so I acted first.

Millie (*over them*) Tom, you must read *The Origin*, or the audience will know you are stupid.

Ian He's not stupid, just duplicitous.

Tom Yeah, my dad was like that.

Millie Here's Lawrence, maybe he can convince you.

Tom Lawrence, oh God.

    Lawrence comes on with pages.

Lawrence You know that gun?

Ian Tom has something to say. Find the words, Tom.

Tom Easy: I've accepted a film part, I start next week.

Millie That's when we start. (*Pause.*) You cannot do it. That would be immoral.

Tom Yeah, I know, but I have.

Ian In contemporary Britain, Millie, the moral dilemma is an overspecialised refinement that leads rapidly to extinction.

Tom (*to Lawrence*) I like Darwin, I'm sorry.

Lawrence Does that mean I can make you change your mind?

Tom No, it means, well, it doesn't mean anything, it's what you say when you feel bad; I'm used to feeling bad.

Millie It is the end of everything.

Tom You can start again.

Millie You stupid boy, who will give me the chance?
I begged, I cajoled for this, now, you know, no violence,
not much sex, history, ideas, not exactly popular, but we
found a small and secure space – and I am so very tired
and it is such a struggle –

Lawrence Millie, take it easy . . .

Millie Easy? What do you know, you American? You
have oil in your country, you grow wheat. I thought to
myself I could thrive in the West because I have something
you do not have – intellectual energy and passion, too –
but now I see it is a disadvantage and I will go home and
if I die of hunger at least I will know why. But I cannot
understand you, Tom. I come from a culture where many
of us had to do terrible things, but you do not have to
do this.

Lawrence I think I understand him. If you are in a
threatened environment, you have to be prepared to
jump.

Millie I do not understand you either, why don't you
beat him up or do something male or something? I am
an intelligent being, I do not want to go extinct, but I do.
I am going to sleep, right now.

Ian Millie, we can start again.

Millie The letter came yesterday. I am an economic
migrant. I have lived in the spare rooms of those who
found Eastern Europe exotic, but we are becoming less
fashionable and the rooms have got smaller and the
effort – even to dress well – and the round at the pub
which means no lunch, no supper –

Ian Why didn't you say?

Millie I will not have you feel sorry for me. Never! I am a Bulgarian! I only say this because I am going tomorrow. Today. Now. I need a phone. Why doesn't anybody have a mobile phone? What kind of actors are you!

Tom I could still marry you, we could even have children. I've absorbed enough about this to want to profligate – promulgate my genes – yours must be great, I mean, all that Darwin.

Ian moves quickly to Tom as if to hit him. Lawrence stops him.

Lawrence Hey, man . . .

Ian storms out. Millie lies down and curls up.

(*to Tom, gently*) It is quite possible –

Millie Quiet please, I am going extinct.

Lawrence – that human beings have come to the end of their evolution – some say we are even coming to the end of our knowledge, who knows, but, Tom, we will never come to the end of our imagination. When I see a character on stage, I think, Ah, where is he going, he's emerged from the tragic, is he a hybrid, a completely new form? And I never stop being excited by the human possibilities – that struggle for existence on this small space – (*Pause.*) I like film too. Is it a good part?

Tom Yeah, I think so.

Lawrence What do you say? Let me hear.

Tom (*with accent*) Line up. Move. Keep moving.

Pause.

Lawrence That's it?

Tom No, I'm in a lot of scenes and there's a close-up of my face and I go from frightened to excited to completely blank. My face on the whole screen. I'm interested in doing blank. You know: nothing. Like: beyond anger.

Lawrence I understand. Tom, I wasn't born into the black American middle class. It's been a long road.

Tom Lawrence –

Lawrence It's my mother who did it. She worked in one of these windowless offices in Washington for forty years. She took me out of school when I was eight – I was beginning to go wild, beyond anger as you say – and she locked me up with books, everything she could get her hands on. Here, she said to me, here's your friends, Shakespeare, Milton, *Moby Dick,* that's the only gang you're ever going to hang out with. She put in extra hours to hire tutors. No black writers. No writing on slavery. When I told her about Caliban she tore out *The Tempest* from my collected Shakespeare. I wouldn't do it to my children, but it worked, I guess.

Tom Lawrence, I don't do guilt.

Lawrence She's coming over in a couple of days. With two of her friends from the choir, they've managed to get the Church to raise the fares.

Tom I'm sorry.

Lawrence She's seventy years old, she's never been to England. So what I'm saying is, could you keep going until the end of the week, and I could at least bring her and her friends?

Millie curls up tighter. Lawrence takes out money and a piece of paper.

And she wants Millie to buy three hats – three English hats. For the occasion. She says she wants the best. And one for you. Will five hundred dollars be enough? I've got the head measurements here.

SCENE FOUR: 'SEXUAL SELECTION'

Ian and Millie.

Ian Tell me about your life in Bulgaria.

Millie We were doing very well for a while. We had expanded to the gates of Constantinople and were ruled with humanity and order by a man called Samuel. One day, an invading army filed into a narrow defile called Cimbalongus. Samuel was taken by surprise and escaped but fifteen thousand of his men were taken prisoner. All of them were blinded except for one man in a hundred who was left with one eye to lead the defeated army back to Samuel. When he saw this, Samuel died of grief and Bulgaria cracked.

Ian Was your family in that army?

Millie Perhaps. It happened in the year one thousand and fourteen. Like most Bulgarians, I feel in my blood the ardent desire for conquest combined with a terrible fear of being blinded. Tell me about being English.

Ian We think of ourselves as restrained and well behaved, and then, suddenly, our natural desires and passions break through and we act on impulse. (*He impulsively moves to Millie and kisses her.*) And then we are surprised and shocked by our actions.

Millie I do not allow this.

Ian Of course . . . and there is someone else . . .

Millie No, but I am your director. I will accept an apology and then I will buy the hats and then we will work.

Ian On what?

Millie We will rehearse and rehearse until Tom leaves us.

Ian Yes.

A pause between them.

Millie I will wait.

Ian For an apology . . .

Millie For the next scene.

SCENE FIVE: 'THE STRUGGLE FOR EXISTENCE'

*Down House. Same as previous scene. Darwin and
FitzRoy.*

Darwin My book is carefully argued. Look at my notes,
here – Even so, Wallace and I will give a joint paper and
then I will publish. The idea is out, you cannot stop it.

FitzRoy We strive for the good because of our faith.
Destroy that and we lose our moral sense and are no
better than animals.

Darwin We are no different from animals.

FitzRoy All of my life I have followed moral precepts.
It does not bring me advantage, on the contrary. I would
have been better liked in New Zealand if I had not
wanted the good. You heard.

Darwin I understand there is a book. I have not read it.

FitzRoy Vilifying me for wanting to protect the Maoris.
The settlers there are like you, Darwin, they believe only
in grabbing more land for themselves because they are
stronger. I tried to stop it. They burned my effigy.

Darwin I am sorry.

FitzRoy The noble man does not struggle for advantage. Let us remain noble.

Darwin But the truth.

FitzRoy The common man will misuse the truth, your ideas will be an excuse for every excess.

Darwin I wanted to give up twenty years ago when I first saw – the idea would not let go.

FitzRoy I only ask you not to publish.

Darwin Copernicus and Galileo did not destroy God. Indeed, the notion of God seems to recover quite easily from us men of science.

FitzRoy It does not matter whether the Earth revolves around the Sun or the Sun around the Earth, there is still order and harmony. This is struggle, disorder, despair, horror, chaos. (*He takes out a small Bible from his pocket.*) *This* is beauty and security. I would have thought that the death of your dear daughter would have brought back your faith.

Darwin (*very dark*) Quite the opposite!

FitzRoy And you want to drag us all into Hell. (*Pause.*) I know what it looks like. Don't think I do not understand your theory. Even see how it could – but I will not allow it to exist. (*He takes out a pistol.*)

Darwin FitzRoy, we have been here before.

FitzRoy I will do it this time.

Darwin The book is already with the publishers.

Millie and Lawrence come on.

Millie Lawrence says we have to go back to the Galapagos.

Ian Not the Galapagos!

Lawrence Those pages I gave you. I've discovered what happened.

Tom How about FitzRoy is really gay and declares his love for Darwin?

Millie Yes, but it would be repressed. (*to Ian*) You see how I adapt? Now to the Galapagos.

Tom I feel seasick, can't we just go on –

Millie No. Lawrence believes this is what must have happened at that crucial moment on the ship. It explains Darwin's later antagonism towards FitzRoy. Take off your ages, the bitterness and fatigue of life, go back to the light and heat, to FitzRoy's cabin, to the Galapagos –

Tom Millie –

Millie Silence! Be grateful for the chance –

The tamagotchi goes off.

I said silence! Give it to me, I'll keep it quiet.

Ian You know about them?

Millie I have one. I do a time share.

SCENE SIX: 'NATURAL SELECTION'

Darwin and FitzRoy. Light. Same positions as at end of Act One. Lawrence and Millie watch.

Darwin Dismal heaps of broken lava . . . hideous lizards with the faces of ancient demons.

FitzRoy Los Encantadas. I prefer the name Galapagos.

Darwin FitzRoy . . . the Governor told me he can recognise which island a tortoise comes from by its markings . . . you know they can't swim . . .

FitzRoy I gather you didn't find much else of interest.

Darwin A few miserable weeds, finches, mockingbirds. Again, quite remarkable differences between them . . . I wonder . . . FitzRoy, may I show you something?

Darwin takes out some drawings. FitzRoy takes them.

FitzRoy Finches. Quite well drawn. Mine are more precise.

Darwin Don't some of these remind you of birds we saw in South America?

FitzRoy They look like variations, yes.

Darwin Extreme variations.

FitzRoy Perhaps. Darwin, I must ask you –

Darwin FitzRoy: suppose, only suppose that these volcanic islands emerged from the sea, as Lyell suggests, seeds drifted from South America, clung to the lava – birds followed, dropped more seeds. Suppose that in this strange, this brave new world, isolated from the rest of the continent, the islands, themselves isolated from each other – suppose there began to emerge birds so different from their forebears – look at the beaks, FitzRoy – that they must, in truth, be called a – new – species.

FitzRoy New.

Darwin New . . .

FitzRoy Stop. I see where you are going.

Darwin I do not see myself. Something is at work, but I do not know what.

FitzRoy The devil is at work, here, in this cabin!

Darwin See the face of nature so bright with gladness, FitzRoy, but we do not see – we forget – that the birds which are singing around us live on insects or seeds and are thus destroying life – and we forget how these birds, or their nestlings or their eggs, are constantly eaten by beasts of prey – it is a cruel world, beak against beak – food is scarce, the one with a tiny advantage – strength maybe or a better disguise, that one will survive – the misfit must perish –

FitzRoy Swear to me you will abandon all such thoughts.

Darwin What if the truth is here?

FitzRoy takes the gun from the table.

FitzRoy I know the dark night of the soul, Darwin. I turned this on myself in my mind's darkness –

Darwin FitzRoy, it would explain all the animals which have disappeared, all those bones I found. The struggle is fierce –

FitzRoy turns the gun on Darwin.

FitzRoy You are the darkness.

Darwin Don't be foolish, FitzRoy, I am only thinking.

FitzRoy Now you will swear to stop.

Darwin Ideas multiply in my mind, they have me in their grip, they eat my rest –

FitzRoy clicks the gun.

FitzRoy Darwin, I will do it.

Darwin sees FitzRoy is serious and goes still.

Darwin FitzRoy, you have not been well.

FitzRoy I felt the brush of the devil. It was you. (*He aims carefully.*)

Darwin You cannot shoot an unarmed man. It is – dishonourable.

FitzRoy Men sacrifice their lives – I can damn my soul to save humanity. Swear.

Darwin FitzRoy!

FitzRoy Swear!

Darwin I cannot swear!

FitzRoy Swear.

Darwin I cannot.

FitzRoy On your honour, on the Bible and before God. You will go down on your knees, Darwin, and you will swear never again to think the thoughts you have expressed here. If you cannot, I, who stand here to represent God as the captain of this ship, I will have to kill you.

Darwin hesitates. The gun is aimed. Darwin goes down on his knees.

Darwin I swear.

Pause. Lawrence comes on with Millie.

Lawrence It is a modern play, the gun does not have to go off, but FitzRoy breaks his code by threatening an unarmed man. Darwin is a Victorian gentleman, he swears on the Bible, later he loses his favourite daughter . . .

Tom I had to stay alive. The idea is like a South American virus, it takes over, digs its claws, multiplies, feeds. It does anything to survive and that makes Darwin do anything to survive. Yeah. Great. Can we do it my way now? Could you be in love with me?

FitzRoy/Ian You will thank me one day . . . (*He comes close to Darwin and takes him into a very tender embrace.*) I have wanted your good, I have loved you and admired you. Will you forgive me?

Tom I like that.

Ian I meant it. I am asking your forgiveness.

Millie We are coming to FitzRoy's suicide, which is seen as an act of madness.

Ian If I could have this gun rather than a razor it would be more tragic.

Lawrence You cannot be tragic after Darwin.

Ian FitzRoy has disappeared from history because he is on the side of the losers, but I see him as a good man who gets it wrong, that is tragic –

Lawrence A new species of modern sadness, perhaps . . .

Tom Yeah, because I'm the hero, I get it right and my idea survives, great. Pchhh. I get to be famous too. I'm sorry, I'm not doing this for much longer.

Ian You are.

Tom Yeah, for the Baptist Church Choir coming from America.

Lawrence Catholic.

Tom Right – and then L.A.!

Ian (*over all this*) Just a chance, I thought – so I broke my code, like FitzRoy . . . I walked around the streets, there are so many business centres, computers, the internet, e-mail, the rapid breeding of communication.

Millie Ian . . .

Ian So I went into a computer shop –

Millie This is not interesting right now.

Ian (*over*) I found Tom's film company on the internet and I e-mailed it. I said I was Tom's lover, that I was HIV positive and that I believed Tom was, too.

Tom But that's a lie.

Brief pause.

Ian Even when I was married I told the truth, and yet – it was so easy. Words . . . I elaborated on how you'd recently been unwell . . .

Tom You've just ruined my film career.

Ian (*imitating Tom*) Pchhh. I saw a great actor when I was a child. When I met him years later I went over to him and hugged him. You're my father, I said to him, you put me into this world. I never hugged my real father. I want spiritual sons. I'll do what I have to to get them. I don't want another two years without work. I want to survive, I want Millie to survive, I want this to survive.

Tom You've destroyed my life!

Millie It's only a delay, Tom, and maybe someone will see you here –

Tom Not with that e-mail. That's it. I don't exist. No one will risk the insurance.

Ian All you have to do is send the results of a recent test.

Tom I've never had a test.

Ian I would have thought –

Tom What would you have thought, Ian? I don't want to know. It's bad enough every time I get the flu, people ring you up, you know, they wait, they don't quite ask –

Lawrence Aren't you putting others at risk?

Tom The only person who's ever at risk is myself, Lawrence.

Ian Oh, my God.

Tom My father died of a heart attack when he was forty, I had a lover who died of AIDS, my best friend was murdered. I'm a modern boy, death lurks around the corner. I'm used to that, the only question is when and what it's going to look like.

Millie But the film . . . you might have ended up on the cutting-room floor.

Tom My life's there anyway. In his terms, Darwin's, I would have left my face behind.

Millie Only great films survive.

Tom You get the video, somebody, sometime, would switch me on, even if only to say, He's good looking, where is he now?

Ian (*to Tom*) I so hated what you did.

Tom Maybe you should learn some humanity.

Ian bows his head and shrinks into himself.

Millie People have so little attention to give these days we're like animals fighting over a dwindling food supply, and so we do terrible things to survive. I am sorry, Tom, but now there is even more need to go on.

Lawrence No.

Millie We have to.

Lawrence I cannot accept Ian's gesture.

Millie Ian's not asking for your admiration.

Lawrence I would be colluding.

Millie You want to survive, don't you!

Lawrence I had a student in a creative-writing class once, one of these arrogant, very rich, East Coast kids. First day, he said to me, Teach me to write like Kafka. Find the man's moral calibre, I said, assume it, and then come back to me. He dropped out of the course. I am responsible for my own integrity.

Millie Your mother's here. Aren't you doing this for her?

Lawrence If there's one thing a black American woman from Washington D.C. knows, it's the difference between right and wrong.

Millie Tom has nothing else now. He has to do it.

Lawrence I wouldn't allow him after what Ian's done. I'm surprised at you, Millie, aren't you ashamed?

Millie I've done a lot of shameful things to get here, Lawrence, but we're almost there. I lost hope once, I'm not losing it again and I'm not going to let you destroy me now..

Lawrence You'll destroy my happiness instead.

Millie Your happiness is of no interest to any of us, Lawrence. You're a writer, you should be miserable.

Lawrence Human beings have evolved a moral sense, we don't know why, but they have. Lose that – lose what makes you human and able to do this. (*He gestures at the papers.*)

Millie But this (*gestures at the papers, the actors*) also needs to survive. Don't you want it to?

Lawrence More than anything.

Millie Well? There's a lot of competition out there.

Lawrence Don't make me betray my moral code.

Millie Ian's broken his, Tom never had one, what makes you think you can survive without getting your hands dirty?

Lawrence It's what I hold onto, Millie, it's what makes me hold my head high. It's where my work comes from. Please don't try to break me.

Tom I don't understand you, Lawrence, the person I felt most bothered about when I accepted the film was you. I thought you'd be desperate, beat me up even.

Lawrence Do you have any idea how often a man like me has to resist that impulse? This isn't my first disappointment. I'll recover. (*to Ian*) I admired you so much.

Ian (*bows his head*) Think of me as another failed character.

Lawrence shakes his head.

Millie Your own FitzRoy betrays his moral precepts to try to make his view of the world survive. Darwin does the same. It's the ideas that fight it out in their own battle for survival, Lawrence, the human beings are secondary and just have to feel bad. Stop being so rigid and let's bring your characters to life.

Lawrence (*hesitates for a moment*) I can't change. I'm – afraid of the chaos. I'm sorry . . . Give me back my work.

Millie It's not yours any more. It's ours.

Lawrence Millie, I'm an American, I know my legal rights.

Millie Lawrence, you are beginning to drive me crazy, I am about to go completely crazy, and now I am going to start screaming. One, two . . .

Lawrence begins to collect the papers.

Three . . .

Millie emits a high scream as Lawrence continues to collect the scripts.

Tom (*over*) Hey, I'm the victim here. I've lost my future in Hollywood. Glamour, wealth, even a little security – it wasn't that much to ask for, was it, Ian?

Ian bows his head. Pause.

Maybe it's shock, but I don't seem to care. Maybe I don't care about anything. It's your Darwin, Lawrence, he's scrambled my brain. He's turned Ian into moral puss. But I've been feeling this virus, gripping me. Maybe I'll be remembered as Darwin. Maybe I really want to do this, or rather, maybe it wants to use me to do itself. And I don't mind. Yeah. And then, even you couldn't say no, Lawrence, could you? I need a walk.

Lawrence I'll come with you.

Tom and Lawrence go off. Silence. Ian sits with his head in his hands, eyes closed. Millie moves very close to him.

Ian Viking, North Utsire, South Utsire, Forties. Did you know FitzRoy originated the shipping forecast?

Millie nods her head.

He was reviled at the time for believing the weather could be predicted. Now we have weather channels. Cromarty, Forth, Tyne, Dogger. They'll come back, won't they? They'll have to.

Millie shrugs.

That's all he has left, but it's not bad, is it? And then he looks fine. Fisher, German Bight, Humber, Thames,

Dover, Wight. I play the one who gets it wrong. Means
well. Does ill. Always. Tragic.

Millie smiles.

Portland, Plymouth, Biscay, Finisterre. Sole, Lundy,
Fastnet. Most of these names are FitzRoy's. Can I make
you love him?

Millie holds out her hands.

When you confessed to the absurd gesture, you became –
desirable. FitzRoy was full of absurd gestures. Irish Sea,
Shannon, Rockall, Malin, Hebrides, Bailey. The absurd
gesture is widespread but its evolutionary purpose
remains a mystery. Fair Isle, Faroes . . . unless . . . Love.
Love makes you ambitious and culture uses you to
multiply. My question is: could you love me?

*Millie gently takes Ian's head in her hands. Then she
looks up, gestures, as she sees Lawrence and Tom
offstage. Ian follows her look.*

Millie I think it's time for you to commit suicide.

Ian and Millie leave.

SCENE SEVEN: 'EVOLUTION'

*Darwin's study as it is now in Down House, some of it
cordoned off. Darwin comes on, an old man, with a
cane and beard, arranges some papers, eventually sits
in his chair. FitzRoy comes on with his razor, in full
admiral's jacket. Millie and Lawrence come on, dressed
for the outside. They look around, like tourists, taking
in some stuffed birds. Millie looks at books and reads
off their various titles.*

Darwin When on board H.M.S. *Beagle,* as naturalist, I was much struck with certain facts in the distribution of inhabitants of South America –

FitzRoy And the earth brought forth grass, and herb yielding seed after his kind –

Darwin – and in the geological relations of the present to the past inhabitants of that continent.

FitzRoy – and the tree yielding fruit, whose seed was in itself after his kind.

Darwin These facts seemed to me to throw some light on the origin of species –

Millie 'Ever since Darwin.'

FitzRoy And God saw that it was good.

Darwin – that mystery of mysteries.

Millie 'The Blind Watchmaker.'

FitzRoy leaves his biblical tone and stance and speaks to the audience.

FitzRoy I left nothing behind.

Lawrence turns toward FitzRoy and stares at him for a moment.

Darwin In considering the Origin of Species, it is quite conceivable that a naturalist, reflecting on the mutual affinities of organic beings –

Millie 'The Beak of the Finch.'

FitzRoy A light foam of ridicule and irritation.

Millie 'The Making of Memory.'

FitzRoy A puff of weather.

Darwin – their geographical distribution, geological succession, and other such facts, might come to the conclusion that each species had not been independently created –

Millie 'Darwin's Dangerous Idea . . .'

FitzRoy (*indicates Darwin, briefly*) The dark side of his light.

Millie 'The Mismeasure of Man . . .'

Lawrence Blind kings, barren women, runaway children, and castaways peopled my childhood –

FitzRoy But if you can bring me back. (*He turns towards Lawrence as if speaking to him.*)

Darwin – but had descended, like varieties, from other species.

Millie 'The Selfish Gene . . .'

FitzRoy Give me substance.

Lawrence – they became my ancestors, these loved figures carved from the crooked timber of humanity –

FitzRoy Tolerance.

Millie 'Life's Grandeur . . .'

Lawrence – lining the shelves of my memory – a parallel evolution, where imagination multiplies . . .

Darwin From that day to the present, I have steadily pursued the same object.

Lawrence Their legacy: empathy, complexity . . .

Millie 'The Origins of Virtue.'

FitzRoy (*to Lawrence*) If you can find me and give me room –

Lawrence turns to FitzRoy, acknowledges him.

Lawrence (*to FitzRoy*) The failed characters we are and create –

Millie 'The Language Instinct.'

Lawrence And pity –

FitzRoy Then I become part of this too.

Millie 'Reinventing Darwin . . .'

Darwin My work is now nearly finished . . .

FitzRoy (*to Darwin*) Both of us.

They all look at one another and out towards the audience.

FitzRoy All of us.

Fade.

CREDIBLE WITNESS

For John

Credible Witness was first performed in the Royal Court Jerwood Theatre Upstairs, London, on 8 February 2001. The cast in order of appearance was as follows:

Alexander Karagy Adam Kotz
Petra Karagy Olympia Dukakis
Paul Paul Bhattacharjee
Anna Tea Agbaba
Ali Yusuf Altin
Henry Benjamin Boateng
Aziz Anthony Barclay
Ameena Leona Ekembe
Shivan Vincent Ebrahim
Leon Roland John-Leopoldie
Simon Clive Merrison

Director Sacha Wares
Designer Es Devlin
Lighting Designer Paule Constable
Sound Designer Fergus O'Hare for Aura
Composer Adrian Lee
Company Voice Work Patsy Rodenburg

Characters

in order of appearance

Alexander Karagy
Petra Karagy
Paul
Anna
Ali
Henry
Aziz
Ameena
Shivan
Leon
Simon

Then thus I turn me from my country's light,
To dwell in solemn shades of endless night.

Shakespeare, *Richard II*, I, iii

PROLOGUE

A small archaeological dig in Northern Greece. Alexander
Karagy guides a group of children.

Alexander *Ke tora,* children, tell me this: *pos*
anakalyptoume tyn istoria? How do you find history?
Look at these walls: dug up a few years ago. Before
then, a field of wheat in Northern Greece. Now:
five thousand years of Macedonian history. See here:
we have an Iron Age layer, but above, on exactly the
same alignment, a street from the Bronze Age. A new
history built on top of old histories.Then, a devastating
fire. Later, maybe here, a house belonging to a
Macedonian general, where Alexander the Great stayed,
planning the Persian campaign. That house too was
buried and the land criss-crossed by Romans, Byzantines,
Turks collecting taxes, Englishmen planting cotton.
A school was built here to teach Bulgarian, burnt, then
another school to teach Greek. Macedonians killed
Germans here, a Communist killed a Royalist cousin.
A wedding group sang, a family danced here before
fleeing abroad. Our Macedonian history is like this
ancient dig: hidden, dangerous and covered up by a
Greek field of wheat.

   Now I want you to go into your villages and discover
other layers. No, not by digging up your gardens –
uncover the bands of your history through the witnesses.
Go to your grandmothers who have hoarded memories,
kept words hidden in the folds of their clothes. Go to the
old man muttering in the café. Greek? He remembers
other languages, suppressed songs. The layers are well

covered, because every generation has thugs who want to bury the past and level the ground. I send you on an uneasy quest, dangerous, but if you lose your history you will be poor, and flat. (*He stops abruptly. Listens.*) What was that? (*Shouts.*) *Pios ine*? (*Waits.*) Shh. We're being followed. Go out that way. Don't make any noise. Don't wait for me. Quickly! Run! *Grigora, pedia, figete.* Run!

Shadows approach. Alexander holds up his arms to avert the blows.

SCENE ONE

Heathrow Airport.
  Petra Karagy. Paul.
  Petra holds up a photograph of Alexander.

Petra Where is he?

Paul Passport control is this way.

Petra Where?

Paul Go through passport control, pick up your luggage, follow the green arrow through the doors: he'll be waiting for you.

Petra You've seen him?

Paul Heathrow's a busy airport.

Petra You could not miss my son, he is noble-looking, even with the bruises. He looks like Alexander the Great. We are descendants. You know Alexander the Great?

Paul Sikander the Great, Sikandra Bhasha, we have temples to him, he's an Indian god.

Petra Alexander the Great was Macedonian. He conquered India. What have you done with my son?

Paul Is this your passport? (*He studies it.*)

Petra It's good, no?

Paul Amateurs. You'll have to come with me.

Petra I want to see my son.

Paul It's against the rules to say this, but I'm a kind man and you look tired.

Petra I am tired of waiting for my son. I have been waiting for three years.

Paul Listen carefully: when the officer looks at your passport and tells you it's not valid, tell him you are seeking political asylum.

Petra I do not want an asylum. I am looking for my son.

Paul If you don't do it now, you'll be in trouble later. Repeat after me: I am claiming –

Petra I do not need to be taught English words. My great-grandfather was English. When he came to Macedonia, he was received, lavish hospitality was proffered. He left a child and a pride. We have always spoken English. My son is best. Do you recognise him?

Paul I see thousands come through, looking like that, from places I've never even heard of.

Petra Everyone knows about Macedonia.

Paul This job is one big geography lesson: every day I hear of a new country. Come with me.

Petra You have disappeared my son and now you try to disappear my country. I do not believe you do not know Macedonia. I am looking for my son Alexander of Macedonia and I do not move until you produce him before me.

187

SCENE TWO

A dilapidated community centre in England. Alexander, Ali, Henry and Anna.

Alexander What is an exile, children?

The children do not answer.

An exile has lost his house, her village, his country. An exile is a guest in a new country.

Ali and Anna snigger.

We are guests in England.

Henry spits.

An exile learns to love and respect his new country.

More sniggers.

But this will not happen until the exile has lamented his loss, that grim accident of history that chased her out.

More sniggers. Alexander ignores this and the children begin to subside.

Today, we cry for Ali, even though his name is not Ali. Ali came to England two years ago with the name Michel Jeune. That wasn't his name either, but it is easier to get into England with a French name than an Algerian one. When it became clear Michel Jeune didn't even speak French he was put in a detention centre and there he was called Gene because no one could pronounce Jeune. He was only fourteen so he was sent to a hostel where they called him John and then to school where someone decided he was Michael Young. Now Ali answers to any name, Mike, John, Nigel, Young, Old, Hey, You. We call him Ali because at least Ali is an Algerian name.

One day Ali will remember his home, his friends, the food he liked, the good times, because history is also the good times.

Ali is very still.

That day, Ali will remember his name. Until then we will cry for Ali. We cry for Ali.

Alexander intones the name, both Henry and Anna get into this.

Anna Ali.

Alexander/Anna Ali.

Henry Ali.

Alexander turns quickly to Henry.

Alexander Henry does remember his name, but he won't tell it to us. Henry's secret name is all he has left.

Henry remembers his country, Eritrea. He remembers his school. Henry remembers one day at school, he cannot forget that day, he tells us about it again and again and now we are going to lament that day.

It was late afternoon, it was hot.

The children have done this before, they go for it.

Anna Very hot.

Alexander There had been trouble in the town.

Ali There is trouble every night.

Alexander As he started walking home from school, Henry saw four men. He thought of running away.

Ali There's nowhere to run.

Anna The men walk down the road with him.

Alexander No one says a word.

Ali Henry whistles to show he isn't afraid.

The children all whistle.

Anna The men smile.

Henry They walk me round the corner to my house. (*He looks.*)

Anna On the front of the house.

Henry From the low roof.

The children stop, hesitate.

Alexander Hang four bodies, naked, mutilated. The body of Henry's father.

Anna Henry's mother.

Ali Henry's older brother.

Henry (*looking*) Uncle!

Alexander The men speak for the first time.

Ali 'That's your punishment.'

Anna/Ali 'That's your punishment.'

Alexander They say.

Anna They walk away.

Alexander Henry doesn't know what he did to deserve such a punishment. Now Henry is afraid to do anything in case he gets punished again. Whenever Henry starts a drawing, a game, he hears the men say:

Ali 'That's your punishment.'

Alexander And he stops.

Henry 'That's your punishment. That's your punishment.'

Alexander These words have paralysed Henry like the venom of a deadly snake. We'll cry for Henry, for the frozen memory, and maybe one day those words will ooze out, the wound heal, and Henry will tell us his secret name.

Henry is very still. Alexander moves quickly to Anna.

Alexander Anna.

Anna No one cries for Anna!

Alexander No one cries for Anna and no one laughs at Anna.

When Anna hears someone laugh, she gets angry, she kicks, she bites, she throws things. Anna speaks beautiful English, she is good in maths. When she came here two years ago, the teachers said she was a wonderful girl. Now they say she's bad. She doesn't listen. I think Anna doesn't listen because she is afraid she will hear the laughter of the men who came for her mother.

Anna clenches her fists. Alexander sees this.

Anna wants to be the only one who laughs. Catch a little girl, sit on top of her, hear her beg for mercy, then laugh. Knock down a small boy. Anna comes from an inflamed part of Europe where laughter belongs to the strong who sit on top of history. We will not cry for Anna, but we will cry for her country where screams for mercy dripped down the walls, but the neighbours laughed, we will cry for her mother who didn't have time to cry for herself, we will cry, and maybe instead of hitting us, Anna will take pity on us and dry our tears.

Alexander leans his face close to Anna. She clenches her fists, raises them, unclenches them and moves her hand to his face.

SCENE THREE

Barbed wire. A grey space.
  Several figures huddled over themselves, isolated.
  It could be a refugee camp anywhere in the world, but
in fact, it is a detention centre in England.
  Petra, Aziz, Ameena, Leon and Shivan.
  Petra holds up photographs. Nothing happens. She
moves to Aziz, shows him the photos.

Petra You have seen him?

  Aziz, very spaced out, looks, nods.

Yes? You have seen him!

Aziz I have seen him?

Petra Maybe he has a beard now.

  Aziz looks. Nods.

Aziz More handsome with a beard.

  Petra thrusts another photograph.

Petra This is older, but close up.

  Aziz pushes it away.

Aziz Please: never the head not attached.

Petra Maybe he's thinner now.

Aziz Hungry.

Petra You've seen him then? Alexander.

Aziz Alexander . . .

Petra Like Alexander the Great.

Aziz Al Skender al Adeen. Alexandria. I know
Alexander the Great.

Petra Where is he?

Aziz Alexander the Great? You're looking for Alexander the Great?

Petra My son!

Aziz Alexander the Great is your son? Ah. (*He nods. Then nods off.*)

Petra You don't look well. Are you eating enough fruit?

Aziz laughs.

Aziz *Les oranges. Les oranges d'Alger. Je les mangerais ...* If only I will keep my head.

Petra gives up, goes to Ameena.

Petra Women have better memories for faces.

Petra shows her the photos. Ameena shudders.

Please . . . you have seen him?

Ameena starts shaking.

A young man, handsome too.

Ameena (*shaking*) Sorry. Sorry. Sorry.

Ameena rocks herself. Her clothes fall loose from her shoulders. Petra covers them.

Petra You should not behave like that in front of men. It is not seemly.

Aziz laughs.

Ameena Sorry. Sorry . . .

She starts crying. Tries to take Petra's hand. Petra moves away, goes to Leon.
Leon is carving a flute. He does not shift concentration. Petra sees this and gives up. She goes to Shivan, who is reading. She waits.

Petra I always let my son finish the page.

Shivan closes the book.

Shivan Milton.

Petra English.

Shivan Very.

Petra That's good.

Shivan holds out his hand for the photographs. He studies them carefully.

Shivan Sensitive. Even passionate. An artist? No. Actor? I have it: a teacher.

Petra You've seen him!

Shivan I'm good at faces.

Petra He came to Heathrow. They said if I came here, they would help me find him.

Shivan They said that.

Petra You do not need to fear to say anything to a descendant of Macedonian warriors. (*Pause.*) He was killed at Heathrow . . . ?

Shivan This is England.

Petra I know about England and its ancient Parliament, but my son has disappeared. What happened at Heathrow?

Shivan Same as me. He will have been questioned.

Petra Tortured?

Shivan Not physically, no.
Then he was probably sent to a hostel.

Petra A hospital?

Shivan A B-and-B. A hotel.

Petra I hope it is clean. Where is it?

Shivan There are many all over the country.

Petra I will go to the hotels. I will search every street of every village and town and ask. In the civil war, Mr – Mr –

Shivan Doctor Rajagopal . . . Shivan.

Petra I walked twenty kilometres every night to feed my uncles. They hid in the marshes and I walked in mud and water to leave no footprints. I still know how to walk. Which is the way out?

Shivan Mrs –

Petra Karagy. Petra Karagy.

Shivan Mrs Karagy, it's night time. The doors are locked.

Petra Where is the person with the keys?

Shivan Mrs Karagy, may I explain –

Petra Olla, eh – olla! Open the doors.

Shivan Mrs Karagy, no one will come.

Petra Olla! Open up!

Shivan Mrs Karagy, we are locked in.

Petra Locked. Why?

Shivan Did you ask for asylum at Heathrow?

Petra The guard said I must. I am not mad, Dr Rajagopal!

Shivan No, Mrs Karagy, you are not mad. And this is not an asylum.

Petra Have they locked me in prison then? Is my son here too?

Shivan This is not a prison, but you are locked up, Mrs Karagy, you are in a British detention centre.

Aziz laughs. Leon concentrates.

Ameena Sorry. Mama . . . Sorry.

SCENE FOUR

Alexander. The children. A silence, then slowly:

Alexander Life to death, peace to war, home to exile. In my country, we sing, but we often also dance the grief of loss. Today, we will lament a name, the name Alexander Karagy.

It was a name given to a child in baptism in a village that was then in Yugoslavia but is now in a country the Greeks refuse to call Macedonia. The child grew up in what is now the very north of Greece, but is also called Macedonia. The child became a teacher who himself respected the emotive force of names, the way history reverberates in a few letters, and he spent many years teaching the meaning of that complex, bitterly fought-over name: Macedonia. But some people in his country didn't like this, and six months ago the teacher was forced to flee to England, which he could only do by borrowing someone else's name. He believed it would not take him long to get his true name back. While waiting for his papers, he has worked with you, trying to help you find your own names. He has loved this work.

But today, your teacher has been told the name Alexander Karagy does not exist, never existed. It seems the name is in no records, nowhere – and there will be no papers giving your teacher back the name Alexander Karagy. And because you can't have a no-name – an impostor – teaching vulnerable children, he has been told – very politely – he has until five o'clock this afternoon to leave. It is nearly five o'clock. The name Alexander Karagy will now dance out of this room into silence and disappear. Let us cry for the name Alexander Karagy. We cry for the name Alexander Karagy – Alexander Karagy. Alexander Karagy. Alexander Karagy.

Alexander slowly dances himself out of the room. The children wait, astonished, then leave.

SCENE FIVE

The detention centre, some weeks later. Simon Le Britten, Petra Karagy, and Leon, carving.

Simon We have no record of an Alexander Karagy entering this country.

Petra He fled to England for protection.

Simon If he had applied for political asylum, he would be on our files.

Petra Maybe a different name.

Simon What name?

Petra I refused to learn it. I sold two of my best fields of wheat and my great-grandmother's English necklace and they couldn't even give him his right name. What do you expect? They're Albanians.

Simon Who?

Petra He had to use the name already there, only change the picture. All this money and they couldn't even give him his name.

Simon You're telling me you bought a false passport for your son.

Petra When they beat him, they took his identity card.

Simon Who beat him?

Petra If I knew I would kill them.

Simon Why would 'they' do this?

Petra History.

Simon Did your son have a history of drugs?

Petra He had a history of history, the history he taught.

Simon There are a lot of drugs moving through that part of Greece, Mrs Karagy.

Petra We call it Macedonia, Mr England.

Simon Le Britten. Your village is Greek.

Petra It is now inside the Greek border. When I was born it was inside the Bulgarian border, its history is Macedonian, that is what my son was teaching. They didn't like it.

Simon The mysterious men?

Petra People in the village and the other villages too. My son could have taught in a big city. He chose to come back to the village, to the children. My son is possessed by history, Mr Britain. It's Alexander the Great's intelligence he inherited. And stubbornness. They would have killed him.

Simon For teaching in a village school? Greece is a democracy, it's part of the EU.

Petra In Greece you cannot teach unless you swear allegiance.

Simon If he was beaten, he could have gone to the police.

Petra He believed it was the police who beat him up.

Simon For teaching history!

Petra Do you know Greece?

Simon Mrs Karagy, I have been in this job for eight years. You wouldn't believe the stories I hear. The challenge of this job is to find the truth of a story and it's a challenge I relish. I'm like a historian myself, sifting the evidence. Now I'll tell you the facts of this case.

Petra You know them!

Simon Your son was in trouble over drugs. You would be last to know.

Petra I knew even my son's dreams in the night.

Simon Whether your son was in trouble with the police or a gang, I don't know. But he knew that when he came here, he wouldn't get away with claiming political asylum for long – assuming he did that under his false name – and so he did what other illegal immigrants of his ilk do, he slipped quietly through the net. He vanished, like some twenty thousand – maybe forty, even fifty thousand now – other illegal entries into this country. They have no records, no papers, they find sustenance in their communities, we only catch up with them when they die or get caught in a raid. Until then, they are invisible, disappeared.

Petra I said he had been disappeared. I want you to find him!

Simon Many young men become pimps. I have listened to you and observed you, Mrs Karagy, I am convinced you are an honest woman, that's why I'm taking so much troubles.
My advice to you is to go quietly back to your village and one day your son will come back to you, probably in a Mercedes, smoking a cigar, some tart on his arm –

Petra You are dishonouring my name, in my country that could get you killed!

Simon Fortunately, we are in England. I believe your son is dishonouring himself.

Petra We are not gypsy beggars, we own land. A pimp! My son who caressed books as a child.

Simon Maybe he only wanted to better himself. I can put myself in his place. When I was his age, I wanted to emigrate to Australia, but they wanted builders not people with management skills.

Petra Many people from our villages emigrated to Australia.

Simon There you are, they got in. I didn't. The difference between me and your son is that I accepted the situation. I didn't try to cheat my way in.

Petra My son never cheated. The mayor's son tried to buy his marks.

Simon He came to this country with a false passport.

Petra What else could he do?

Simon You love your son, you defend him. I admire you for that, but you're going to be disappointed in him. I have a hunch he's disappointed in himself. You say he hasn't been in touch for three years. Why? People come here thinking life will be easy. It's hard enough for us. I was a middle manager in the Post Office. I loved my job. There were redundancies. I was very bitter at first, but I'm glad to have this job at my age. I don't need to tell a woman of your experience that life is full of grey.

Petra Never grey. When my mother came out of the camps in 1950, she didn't talk, she only painted. She gave me a painting of a flag: red, white and black. She called it the flag of history and labelled it red for blood, black for grief, white for hope. I measured the colours. They were all the same. Except white looks bigger.

Simon smiles.

Simon Hope. I understand. I wish I could do more. I'll arrange a flight home for you next week.

Petra Mr Great Britain.

Simon Le Britten – it's a Norman name, I believe: from *Le Breton.*

Petra rummages in her clothes. She takes out a small bag from which she takes out a rolled handkerchief which she unfolds carefully. She hands a small coin to Simon.

Petra The head of Alexander. Very antique. Gold.

Simon looks at it. Hands it back.

Simon It's beautiful.

Petra For you. To keep.
I wait until you bring me my son.

Simon We don't take bribes in England, Mrs Karagy.

Simon hands back the coin.

Simon I can't help you further.

Petra Mr Le Britten – my great-grandmother was from a North Macedonian village where they spoke Bulgarian. She married a Greek from Asia Minor who had a mill in Assiros. Her sister married his brother. Bulgarian women were beautiful and the Greek men rich. After the wedding feasts, my great-grandmother and great-aunt rode with the two bridegrooms to Assiros. The villagers gathered in the market place to greet them. It's a big market place, it's always been a wealthy village. The couples dismounted and the bridegrooms asked the two women to salute the mill which would shower their children with riches. This they did. Then the bridegrooms asked the women to kneel and swear never to speak Bulgarian again because now they were Greeks and their children would be Greek. My great-grandmother's sister knelt. My great-grandmother, even though she was only sixteen, remained standing and shook her head.

Her husband asked her again, slowly. She shook her head again. He hit her. He beat her more. She still refused to kneel. From that day, we became known as the women who refuse to kneel. Because we still speak Bulgarian and we never kneel to anything or to anyone, except to God and sometimes not even that. Look: I am getting down on my knees. Let Alexander the Great and my great-grandmother and my mother forgive me, I beg you, I clasp your knees to bring me back my son.

SCENE SIX

The street. Alexander, Henry.

Alexander sweeps the pavement. Henry comes with various imaginary weapons and their corresponding sounds. Henry starts by aiming a sniper rifle at Alexander then recognises him.

Alexander Henry.

Henry Teacher!

Alexander shakes his head, shows his broom and orange overcoat.

Henry (*nodding*) Minesweeper. (*Henry points to himself.*) Freedom fighter. (*He takes a few grenades and throws them.*) Kill them all.

Alexander All?

Henry now holds a Kalashnikov – imaginary.

Henry Look at that one on his knees. Coward! (*Henry shoots.*) That's your punishment. All dead.

Alexander Who'll be left to run the village?

Henry Me! (*He dances over imaginary corpses.*)

Alexander Tell me about your village, Henry.

Henry My village is big. When you want to go somewhere and there's a house in front of you, you walk through the house. If someone is cooking, they feed you, if they are talking, they talk with you, or maybe they offer you water.
　Here, even in the street, no one talks to you, no one opens their doors, no one gives you water. Here, everything is locked.
　I kicked this boy today. Headmaster said I do it again he throws me out of school for good.

Alexander Why not try to make a life here?

Henry Rubbish-dump place.

Alexander Think of yourself as a very important guest. You wouldn't insult a house that welcomed you.

Henry They don't do welcome here.

Alexander Maybe they express it differently.

Henry Like: get out! Filthy bogey scum.

Alexander bends on himself. Henry studies him for a moment, offers him a packet of crisps.

Henry Teacher?

Alexander Eat them yourself, Henry.

Maybe you can find one thing you like here, and like that one thing a lot.

Henry One thing.
Maybe one day I tell you my name.

Alexander I'd like that very much.

Henry Why aren't you fighting for your country?

Alexander It was never a country, Henry, it's a name, a feeling – I've buried it for a while.

Henry picks his way out.

Henry Freedom fighter never surrenders. Careful over here. The mines are very hidden.

He leaves. Alexander stares out in hunger and solitude.

SCENE SEVEN

The detention centre. Ameena, Shivan, Aziz, Leon and Petra sit in the grey light of morning. Only Shivan is reading. Paul comes on.

Paul Good morning, ladies and gentlemen. Time for your pills. No cheating, no hoarding, no trading.

He gives pills to Leon and Ameena, who swallow them silently. He goes to Aziz.

Paul And two for Aziz Amani.

Aziz Doctor said four.

Paul He writes two here.

Aziz I need four. I'm going crazy!

Paul Ask the doctor next time.

Aziz Next week! I'm going crazy today.

Paul I'm not a doctor.

Aziz (*pointing to Shivan*) Ask him.

Shivan (*looking up from his book*) I am a doctor . . .

    Paul ignores this and goes over to Petra.

Paul Four for you.

Shivan That's too many.

Aziz They're mine. Doctor got mixed up.

Paul He writes 'For the Greek woman'. Are you the Greek woman?

Aziz The government said I was a woman for not joining the army to fight the Islamists and they will shoot me. The Islamists said if I didn't join them I was no better than a woman and they will rip my balls out. Other Islamists said the first Islamists were not real Islamists but were working for the government: we were old women for believing them and they'll slit our throats if we don't join them in the mountains. How do you know I'm not a woman? Give me those pills.

Petra I'm not 'the Greek woman'. He can have them.

Paul I'm trying to help, the doc says you need them badly.

Shivan The doctor saw her for five minutes. He didn't even check her heart.

Paul I do what the doctor says.

Shivan I am a doctor.

Paul At Heathrow I had three different people tell me they were deposed emperors.

Shivan Are you doubting I am a doctor?

Paul I was moved here because I believed too many stories.

Shivan I was a consultant in Sri Lanka.

Paul (*to Petra*) Take them, they make your head feel better.

Petra I don't have a headache.

Shivan The guard we had before you believed me.

Paul They make your head happy.

Petra How can my head be happy when my eyes don't find my son?

Shivan I am a doctor.

Aziz (*over*) I keep seeing my head somewhere. Sometimes, it's on the side of the road, looking up at me. Then in my mother's lap and there's blood dripping down her arms. Afterwards, on a balcony, all by itself, and the eyes blink in the sunset. Yesterday I dream they send me back to Algeria and there's my head rolling down the airplane steps, bump, bump, bump.

Paul (*to Petra*) Come on, love, please take them.

Aziz (*speedy*) When I came here I told them I was running away because my head was going to be torn off. We don't accept fear of the future, they tell me, only what happened: were you officially threatened? Officially? There's a civil war in Algeria, I say. It' s not officially a civil war, they say. If I don't have more pills my head will come off: officially.

Petra Give him the pills to keep him quiet.

Aziz You're the one always talking about history, old woman. You think you're the only one with history? My grandmother died planting a bomb against the French. But we still learn French. I can't even speak good Arabic. I like American. The Wild West, that's good history. Algerian history is making my head come off. French history says it's my grandmother's fault and English history says Algerian history doesn't exist. I need pills to keep my head straight.

Petra (*to Paul*) Give me those pills.

Shivan The guard before you took my advice.

Paul (*to Petra*) I have to watch you swallow them.

Petra You're doubting the word of a Macedonian?

Shivan You're doubting my word I'm a doctor!

Aziz You doubt I'm crazy!

Paul Please, all of you, don't make trouble or I'll have to report you.

Shivan I only ask that you believe I am a doctor.

Paul I've been told to watch for any trouble before it's too late. It's because of those troublemakers we had up north. First they rioted, then they went on a hunger strike. They were sent to prison but it was too late for one of them. I saw the photo, I haven't seen a face so thin since my childhood.

Petra Who is so thin – where is the picture? What did he look like?

Paul It's not your son, he was from somewhere else. Imagine starving yourself to death to get what you want. What kind of behaviour is that for a foreigner? It's not as if you're English or even Irish, with rights and things. You're not even supposed to be here. You can't refuse to eat perfectly decent food which is costing the taxpayer all this money, especially when you were probably starving in your own country.

Shivan I am here because I am a doctor.

Petra Did they get what they wanted, the hunger strikers?

Paul They got a lot of attention and our security group was blamed. You know, when we came over, and we were invited after all, we never behaved like that. We did everything to fit in. We worked hard, we kept our heads down, we put up with a lot. I can't make my son understand that, he's always in trouble, but he says he's British.

Petra No one can force you to eat?

Paul They can only force-feed you in prison. We had a Jamaican woman who said she'd go on hunger strike but she kept eating sweets. She was a big woman, it took three of us to get her on the plane, she was throwing her head about, she almost started a riot.

Aziz My head is out there, throwing itself against the wire. The wire's red with blood. I'm going to start a riot if I don't get my pills. (*Aziz starts banging.*)

Paul Quiet! (*to Petra*) I talk too much. Wearing a uniform is a lonely business.

Shivan There have been ten different guards in the months I've been here and they all believed me. They took my advice. Why don't you believe me?

Aziz, banging more loudly, is joined rhythmically by Leon.

Paul Quiet, I said. What's wrong with you people that if someone is friendly you take advantage?

Shivan What kind of a doctor comes to this centre? In another country, he would be measuring the pain threshold of torture victims. Here, he keeps us as quiet as he can without killing us. He doesn't even do that very well.

Aziz gets wilder, moves towards Ameena.

Aziz If I would keep my head on, I dance with a girl.

Ameena trembles, cowers.

Paul Stop that now!

Leon and Aziz start a more frantic beat.

Shivan (*to Paul*) I have been patient for months, polite. I remind myself I can help people anywhere. I am reading *Paradise Lost* for the third time to help endure the humiliation and also to share the power of this language.

Aziz moves back to Ameena.

Aziz If I knew my head doesn't fall off, I dance with a beautiful girl.

Ameena begins to sob.

Paul (*to Aziz*) Leave her alone!

Shivan If we don't share the truth of language, what then? You don't believe I'm a doctor, why should I believe you're a guard? If language disintegrates, there's nothing left. He needs help, you deny him, he riots. You deny me. I know why you deny me. You think, yes, Sri Lanka, that's a Tamil. You look at me with your North Indian superiority and you don't listen. If I'm not Doctor Rajagopal, who am I? Wherefore this forbearance? You won't let me be doctor in this hell? Very well: then shall I be Lucifer, rebel, rioter.

Shivan begins to clap rhythmically. And declaims:

> Hail horrors, hail
> Infernal world and thou profoundest hell
> Receive thy new possessor –

Paul Quiet! (*to Petra*) I'm going to lose this job too. I'm the one who helped you at the airport, that's why they sent me here, they say I'm not good at authority. If I have to call out there for help, they'll get rid of me.

Shivan
> No light, but rather darkness visible
> Served only to discover sights of woe,

Aziz now tries to get Ameena to dance.

Ameena No! No! No!

Paul Stop!

Shivan
> Regions of sorrow, doleful shades –
> Where peace and rest can never dwell,
> Hope never come

Aziz (*over*) She screams because she sees the blood from my neck!

Shivan
> Our prison strong, this huge convex of fire
> Outrageous to devour, immures us round –

Paul (*to Shivan*) I have pills for you too.

Shivan knocks them out of Paul's hand. Aziz makes a dive for the pills.

Shivan And gates of burning adamant . . .

Ameena sees Aziz diving towards her.

Ameena (*screams*) No! No !No!

Paul Help! Riot! Riot!

Shivan Prohibit all egress –

Ameena No! No! No!

She rocks hysterically, yelps. Shivan sees this and stops.

Paul Help! I need help!

Paul moves towards her.

Shivan Not a man. Mrs Karagy, quick, hold her! Only you.

Petra What's wrong with her?

Shivan You're a woman! Can't you see! Help her!

Petra stares at Ameena.

Petra Oh, child.

Then quickly moves to hold her

Ameena . . .

Ameena subsides. Sobs continuously.

We can't behave like this, it is not dignified. Nobody needs to riot here because I have decided. I will bring back my son. I will make visible the disappeared, not just him, you – you. Paul has told me how to do it: as of now, I, Petra Karagy of Macedon, I am going to hunger strike. To the death or to the appearance of my son. Great Alexander, stand by me now and help me remember who I am.

She folds her arms, sits. The others go still.

SCENE EIGHT

Alexander, Anna, Ali. Alexander is handing out leaflets. Ali takes one and recognises Alexander.

Ali Teacher.

Alexander Ali, Anna.

Anna (*with reproach*) 'Highlights, lowlights, cut, blow dry – manicure included –'

Alexander (*apologetic*) You need a permit with a name to sell *The Big Issue*.

Anna Listen to this: William the Conqueror – 1066 to 1087; William Two, also known as Rufus – 1087 to 1100; Henry One – 1100 to 1135; Stephen – 1135 to 1154; Henry Two – 1154 to 1189; Richard One, the Lion Hearted – I like him – 1189 to 1199: I know them better than anyone.

Alexander Why?

Anna It's English history.

Alexander What about your own history?

Anna (*spits*) Ask me anything about the Tudors.

Alexander Why aren't you in school?

Anna I threw a chair across the classroom. But they think my exam results will be astonishing. John – 1199 to 1216; Henry Three – 1216 to 1272 –

Alexander Don't forget your own history, Anna: have the courage to be complicated.

Anna You're not my teacher!

Alexander I should be.

Anna You walked out. We thought we'd done something.

Alexander I explained I'd lost my name. Didn't you understand?

Anna We never understood anything you said, did we, Ali? But we liked you. We believed you liked us.

Alexander Anna, Ali, I do like you.

Anna Then why did you desert us? Why are you handing out rubbish hairdressing leaflets! (*She crumples the leaflets and throws them in his face.*)

SCENE NINE

The detention centre. Petra, Simon. It is a private conversation in a public space. Leon is carving. Ameena sits very still, watching Petra.

Simon I'm on your son's trail.

Petra Where is he?

Simon He did not claim asylum at Heathrow, only later – that always makes me suspicious. He worked with refugee children in one of those dramarama self-expression type groups they so love in North London, but he was asked to leave when Greece denied all knowledge of him.

Petra Greece denied Alexander?

Simon They have no record of his birth.

Petra His father wanted him to have a Slav name as well as Alexander. The Greek priest wouldn't baptise children with Slav names. We went to his mother's village across the border.

Simon You said he was born in Greece.

Petra The birth is recorded by the Church. Try Yugoslavia.

Simon That is impossible now, Mrs Karagy. When your son was told he would have to leave Britain, he vanished, as I suspected. A year ago, someone of his description was cleaning the streets –

Petra My son is an intellectual. He does not know how to clean!

Simon We have postmen who don't know how to read. There's a thriving black economy in this country, Mrs Karagy. It makes me so angry – all these people cheating. I'm determined to find your son, even if I have to look for him myself: I came to tell you to stop your hunger strike.

Petra I stop when you produce his body.

Simon I had a call from a newspaper today. If this gets out, we'll get it both ways: we'll be accused of cruelty and we'll be accused of incompetence, we're always caught in the middle. I'm trying to do a decent job, can't you understand that?

Petra Let me look for my son myself.

Simon How would you find him?

Petra I'm a mother, I would smell him.

Simon It's a big city out there.

Petra I have been to Athens.

Simon Mrs Karagy, we're already an overpopulated island. We have Russians, gypsies, Columbians, Asians, all pressing against our doors, hiding in the wheels of airplanes. The newspapers write heartrending stories

because they arrive dead of exposure, but we have to
bury them. Do you know how much that costs? And
they learn fast. Last month a man parachuted into a
pack of hounds in Dorset. They thought it was a hunt
saboteur and attacked him. Now he has a lawyer
claiming damages. I'm afraid to turn on the news
because every time one of those countries erupts on
television, thousands more files pile on my desk. I'm
short-staffed, we have antiquated office equipment, but
still I do not send people back to be killed and tortured.
I feel sorry for those going back to hunger and disease,
believe me, but I have to see the marks of torture before
I let anyone in. Genuine. Deep. Or the real fear of death.
It's easier than you think. There were no torture marks
on your son.

Petra He was beaten.

Simon Bar-room brawl.

Petra There is only one bar in our village, I own it.

Simon Young men will fight. Maybe a girl.

Petra He told me he was beaten by the police.

Simon He lied.

 Petra gets up and slaps Simon.

Petra No one calls my son a liar. (*Pause.*) What have I
done? I have not eaten. I love my son. And I have such
pride for him. Your mother would be the same if you
disappeared. She would seek you with this cold fear in
her stomach. Is she alive, your mother?
 She is not alive? I am sorry.

Simon She is alive – but she would not understand.

Petra A mother's heart shivers day and night . . .

Simon I went away to school, to a boarding school – do you understand?

Petra nods.

A minor public school.

When I was fourteen, I was accused of stealing the housemaster's money box. I hadn't, but two boys said they'd seen me. And my marks weren't that good. I was expelled.

When my mother came to get me, she listened to the housemaster in silence. She took me home in silence. She let me go to bed in silence.

Your son does not deserve you as his mother, Mrs Karagy. I would have been a different man if my mother had slapped that housemaster.

SCENE TEN

Same as before. Leon has finished his flute and starts playing. Aziz joins in, singing, drumming on chairs. The music is jazzy, Afro-Algerian Rai. The singing is for Petra and Ameena, who holds herself next to Petra but can't help drumming the beat. Paul comes on.

Paul There's someone who says he knows your son. (*He listens to the music for a moment.*) You're not supposed to play in here. (*He listens.*) Not bad. Try this. (*He claps a rhythmic variation. Stops himself. To Petra*) We're only supposed to allow close relatives, so be quick. (*to the musicians*) Don't make too much noise or people will think you're having a good time. I'll lose my job.

Why am I so nice?

Alexander comes in. All stare at him and then file out.
Petra devours Alexander with her eyes, but doesn't move.

Petra Alexander . . .

Alexander Mamou.

Silence. They stare at each other.

Petra Alexander . . .

Alexander *Ti kaneis, Mamoube?*

Silence. Petra moves towards him, then stops.

Mamou?

Silence.

Mamou, it's me. Alexander.

Petra looks intently.

Petra Take off your shirt.

Alexander Mamou!

Petra I'm not afraid.
Take off your shirt.

Alexander does so reluctantly.

Turn around.

Alexander What are you looking for, Mamou?

Petra Let me see your legs.

Alexander That's enough, Mamou, it's me.

Petra And here? (*She points to her crotch.*) Did they do
anything – there?

Alexander I haven't been tortured, Mamou!
I read about you in the newspapers.

Petra They're threatening you?

Alexander I'm safe. You must stop this hunger strike.

Petra Three years.

Silence.

One thousand and one hundred nights.

Alexander You told me not to write.

Petra I told you not to write the first six months. I was afraid they would follow your trail. After – I told you to write to the name Xenia Xenakis, *Poste Restante*, Athens. You forgot the name.

Alexander slowly shakes his head.

The first time, I took five different buses to Athens in case I was followed. I waited in line hours in the heat with German and American students. The man looked at me strangely, no honest Greek gets letters *poste restante*. There was nothing for Xenia Xenakis. I went back six months later, only two buses this time. Six months again. Last time, I took the airplane.

Every time I saw a tourist in the village I thought maybe you'd sent a message. I gave a lot of English people coffee and water. What did they do to you?

Alexander Nothing.

Petra *Tipota. Nishto.*

Alexander Nothing. Nothing. Nothing. You wouldn't understand.

Petra I have always understood my son.

Alexander I could have written in the first six months. I taught children, you would have been proud of me. I helped them lament.

Petra Lamenting is for women. What did they do for you?

Alexander You must eat, Mamou.

Petra What happened?

Alexander I don't know . . . They didn't believe me. They called in someone from the Greek Embassy. He was my age, he was wearing a suit. He told the official my Greek wasn't very good and I was probably Albanian.

Petra Albanian!

Alexander I had only the false passport. I'd pretended I didn't know any English because I was nervous and I thought an interpreter would help. That was two lies – you'd told me the English don't forgive lies. The embassy man misinterpreted everything I said to the official. It made me unsure, hearing it in another language, but so different – I became confused. They didn't want to believe I was beaten by the police, they asked how many, details. I couldn't say for sure. Two – three – When no one believes you, you begin to doubt yourself. I tried to say why they were against my history of Macedonia, but the embassy man laughed and said since when had the Greeks been afraid of history? Then in Greek he asked who I was working for. I became angry. He told the official I seemed hysterical, I remember the word, hysterical – I thought I was going to be sent back then, I was wet with fear, but the official referred the case and I started crying. I was humiliated.

Pause.

I brought you some grapes.

Pause.

I'm all right now.

Petra You teach?

Alexander I've done different things . . . cleaning streets . . .

Petra You wash the streets?

Alexander I pick up leaves, papers – there are a lot of dogs in the city.

Petra Alexander Karagy, descendant of Alexander the Great and the Bulgarian women who refuse to kneel, is cleaning the English streets of dogs?

Alexander Not dogs. Dog – eh.

Petra My son who was too proud to teach in a Greek university, who insisted he would teach our true history to all Macedonian children?

Alexander I came here puffed with my history, Mamou, do you know what I found? Everyone who comes here has a rich and bloody history on their shoulders. I look at people in the tube, all these histories raging in their heads.

Petra I sent you here to make allies of the English.

Alexander I spent months writing our history for my case. From memory: dates, massacres, the shifting of borders, the Macedonian Uprising, First Balkan War, Second Balkan War. I read it to the immigration officer. I had come to 1913: the Treaty of Bucharest giving Southern Macedonia to Greece – when he stopped me. He had seven hundred and fifty cases after me. They've only had one civil war in England, and an endless parade of kings and queens, they speak one language, they don't even use the word history, they call it heritage.

Petra I said to go to the young people.

Alexander History for them is the childhood of their pop stars.

Petra Students love to demonstrate against injustice.

Alexander From here, it's only some obscure and convoluted corner of the world. Even for me – the more I wrote – translating all those certainties into English made them crumble –

Petra It's your history.

Alexander There is a wider world.

Petra You come from Macedonia.

Alexander Macedonia. Macedonia. Macedonia.

Petra Macedonia was your passion.

Alexander Because of you. You put me to bed with stories of Macedonian heroism. You sang me lullabies of blood and hatred.

Petra I had to make a man out of you. You couldn't get enough of the stories.

Alexander Sometimes, from here, it looks like madness this obsession with Macedonia. Here, I've felt light, free.

Petra Light, free! (*Pause.*) It's never easy to be called by the history of your land, Alexander, there are bad moments . . . When I was twenty-five, I was working for the radar station on Mount Hortiatis. I fell in love –

Alexander You don't have to tell me –

Petra – with an American officer. That was light, free. It went on many years. I didn't tell my family because the Americans had supported the other side in the civil war, but people always know. And the Colonels' Junta was forming. They had lists of all the Macedonian

names. My uncle was arrested. When he came out
months later, he showed me the torture marks: back,
legs – and – (*She points.*) He said the equipment was too
sophisticated for Greeks, he insisted it was American.

I married a pure Macedonian from Florina, a man
who only cherished his land and his hatreds. My uncle
led the wedding dance, all the village joined. Then –
April 21, 1967 – the coup. They came to arrest your
father – he died on the border, you know that – but
I never told you that even as I mourned your father by
day, at night I still dreamt of the soft skin of my
American lover.

Alexander Please – Mamou –

Petra I had a son, conceived without pleasure.

Alexander Mamou – stop –

Petra But a Macedonian son and I suckled you on the
pride of your family and of your land. My history
became your history, that's how it goes.

Alexander It doesn't have to.

Petra You're nothing without your history.

Alexander When I came here it began to lose its hold.

Petra I have understood that, Alexander. And I have
decided we will have to go back.

Alexander Back?

Petra We have no choice.

Alexander Mamou – I can make a life here –

Petra It's worse than the body, they've broken your mind.
You don't know who you are any more.

Alexander It'll take time, but I'll go on a computer course.

Petra No one can confuse you in Macedonia. Your mind will clear.

Alexander I can write something from here.

Petra You're too far from your history here. There used to be a light in your face when I said Macedonia.

Alexander Mamou – I was beaten!

Petra I will guard you better.

Alexander They said they will kill me.

Pause.

Petra What kind of a life is there when you're a nobody, without a past, without a name, without a heart, a man who doesn't even cast a shadow, when maybe you're not even a man any more?

Alexander You would risk my life? Mamou!

Petra I live for you: you're my only son.

Alexander I had the courage to die then – you didn't want me to. Now I don't want to – I'm not sure of anything any more. I want to stay here – think more carefully –

Petra If you stay here, you will lose your land, and with Macedonia you will lose everything.

Alexander We have an English ancestor.

Petra That was fertiliser. You are Macedonian.

Alexander Why should I die for your obsessions? You dripped them into my food, the water I drank. You called it history, maybe it's only your anger.

Petra History is full of anger.

Alexander Because of mothers like you.

Petra I sacrificed everything so you could have your inheritance.

Alexander I may not want it.

Petra You don't know what you're saying.

Alexander I'm trying to tell the truth – it's hard with you, Mamou –

Petra You don't want to be Macedonian.

Alexander I can't be what I was three years ago..

Petra You don't want to be my son.

Alexander I don't always have to do what you say.

Petra Sons obey their mothers.

Alexander Not in this country . . .

Petra We have nothing to do with this country – we are not part of its history.

Alexander It's interesting here.

Petra You are nobody here. Nobody!

Alexander What was I before? A link in the chain of a bloody history.

Petra They've washed out your heart, turned your liver to milk, they've ripped off your balls in this country. Alexander, come home before you disappear to mist.

Alexander It's my life, Mamou –

Petra I gave you your life! I nourished your life – never to be a washed-up wreck on the English shores.

Alexander It's still my life.

Petra It may be your life, but it's not the life of my son. I brought you up to be a Macedonian. I don't know who you are any more, but I know this: you are not my son.

Alexander Mamou, you're tired, you haven't eaten.

Petra You don't even have the face of my son.

Alexander I'll come back tomorrow.

Petra Stranger –

Alexander You will understand – rest now.

Petra I curse you.

Alexander Mamou, don't do this. Take it back.

Petra Paul!

Alexander Mamou! Please!

Paul comes.

Petra Take this man out. Don't ever let him come back. He doesn't know anything about my son. How could he? This man is not even a Macedonian.

SCENE ELEVEN

Same as before. Night. Cold. Petra, much weaker, and Shivan.
He kneels beside her.

Shivan If you don't eat, you will die.

Petra Last night, I heard the flutes of a procession. It was Alexander the Great with a garland of leaves on his head. He moved through the rooms, came down here and then went out, through the barbed wire, onto the streets. And as the procession grew fainter and fainter

I knew Alexander the Great was abandoning me the way the god abandoned Antony. You know the story?

Shivan Antony and Cleopatra. The next day Antony loses the war.

Petra My son was at the back of the procession, dancing like a girl.

Shivan You love your son.

Petra I cursed him, Shivan.

Shivan He'll come back.

Petra When we give birth to our sons, we hold them more tightly than our daughters, we tremble when they're sick, we would die to protect them, but then we ask them to be men.Our history tells us to make sons that will fight – if that's not right, what have we been doing for hundreds of years? I came here with Macedonia clutched tight in my heart to find my son, but he wasn't any more the one I was looking for, the son I raised for my pride – now I have nothing in my heart.

Shivan Try to rest.

Petra I wouldn't open my arms to the person in front of me, maybe if I had, my son would have come back –

Shivan Rest –

Petra I had to be mother and father to him, maybe a father would have understood.

Shivan I don't think so.

Petra I cursed my only son because he would not stay inside his history, but what is Macedonia to me without my son?

Shivan Try to sleep.

Petra Nothing's solid any more.

Shivan You're dizzy from lack of food.

Petra When the god abandons you, Shivan, you must die.

Shivan I am a doctor, Petra. I take death very personally.

Petra Try not to be offended.

Paul comes on, laden with bags.

Paul I've walked the city looking for this stuff. I shouldn't be doing it. It's not professional to be nice. I bought these as well.

He puts the bags on the floor and takes out some decorations, which he begins to hang across the room.

My New Year's resolution is to become tough.

Shivan looks through the bags. Ameena comes on, Shivan hands her a bag.

Ameena Cardamom. Flour. Sugar. Bananas. Coconut.

Paul I even found a mortar and pestle. Is that what you were asking for?

Ameena Paul, you are good.

Paul Being good doesn't help you get on.

Ameena begins to grind the cardamom pods.

I didn't have enough money for some of these things. When I told the shopkeepers what it was for, they gave me stuff.

I don't understand this country. One day they threaten to beat you up, next day – all this.

Shivan picks up a bag and leaves.

Shivan It is to do with the sense of fair play.

Ameena (*to Petra*) The smells of my country. (*She holds the bowl to Petra.*) Don't leave us . . . Please . . . don't leave me.

227

Aziz comes on, takes a bag.

Aziz Olives. Coriander. Lemon. Garlic. Two strands of saffron! Paul, you are a good angel.

Paul I'm changing at midnight.

Aziz (*to Petra*) I sprinkle this on the olives and you taste paradise.

Leon comes in, finds three mangoes, which he juggles expertly. Everyone laughs. Shivan now appears with a steaming pot.

Shivan Pol Sambal: grated coconut, grated onions, chilli powder, lime juice. String hoppers. Also Rusam, steaming pepper water – special Tamil brew for great warriors only – even the Sinhalese can't stomach it.

A moment of festivity. Simon walks in. Silence.

Simon There are no guards on the gates.

Paul They were refused extra pay tonight, they've gone on strike.

Simon Anyone could walk in.

Paul I called the office for reinforcements, but we agreed not many people will try to get into a detention centre on New Year's Eve.

Simon I'll hold you personally responsible if anything happens. What's all this?

Paul Everyone has cooked their favourite food for Mrs Karagy to try and make her eat. It was Doctor Rajagopal's idea.

Simon You will need your strength, Mrs Karagy: we have lost all trace of your son. He was leafleting, then carrying a board – then nothing – disappeared.

My concern with finding your son is becoming unprofessional. I have a backlog of cases spilling off my desk. I can't spend any more official time on this, but I'm doing something exceptional. I'm giving you leave to remain here for six months on compassionate grounds. You're free, Mrs Karagy, you may go and look for your son.

Petra I have no son.

Simon I am certain he is alive and close.

Petra I never had a son.

Simon You're tired. I'll help you find your son in my free time, the little I have. I've found you a good hostel, I could take you there tonight.

Petra There is no son.

Simon Why are you doing this?

Petra I'm dying, I need to confess.

Simon The hunger strike was for the sake of your son.

Petra I wanted a better life, open a shop, own a little English land. But I've been disappointed in England: you have too many foreigners.

Simon What are you trying to tell me?

Petra I have to spell everything out? That's not very English, Mr Britten. I am a, what do you call it, yes, I'm an old bogus!

Simon I don't believe you.

Petra We don't always like the truth.

Simon (*shouts*) Why are you doing this to me?

Shivan Please. She's very weak.

Simon I'm never wrong!

Petra We all of us make mistakes, Mr English.

Simon Le Britten, please! It was a mistake to get too involved, I knew that. I don't know what game you're playing at. I've spent months looking for your son. I believed in you. Now you tell me I've wasted my precious time. Tonight, I was going to eat this pizza, I even brought you a piece and I was going to go out in the crowds and look for your son. I thought if you were up to it, you'd come with me – and when you got tired, I'd keep looking. I was going to ask you for the photographs.

Petra takes them out of a pocket and tears them up.

Petra I bought the pictures. You said it yourself: we're getting clever at this game.

Simon No one lasts in this job. I spend every hour of the day sifting through your lies, liars all of you, why can't you ever tell the truth!

I have news for the rest of you.

There's no way Aziz will be allowed to stay in this country. The Algerian government has assured Britain it has the country under control. There's a plane to Algiers the day after tomorrow.

Aziz When I go to sleep last night, I put my hands to my head: it wasn't there. I find it in an airport locker, smiling, but when I reach to put it back on, it's the wrong head. Please, Mr Britten – please –

Simon (*to Shivan*) Sri Lanka is at peace.

Shivan There was an attack on Tamils last week.

Simon We have hooligans in England.

Shivan I have a right to appeal.

Simon I will be at every one of your appeals.

Shivan Mr Le Britten, my wife was murdered.

Simon When there was real trouble in Sri Lanka we took in thousands of refugees. Why didn't you come in the eighties?

Shivan I was the youngest and most highly qualified Tamil doctor. I felt my expertise would keep me safe. I was also afraid Tamils would not get proper treatment from the Sinhalese doctors. I treated Sinhalese bomb victims as well. I don't actually know who burned down my house.

Simon The violence in Sri Lanka is negligible now.

Shivan You only mean it's not front page news.

Simon Other countries have priority. I've looked over all your statements, you are not a credible witness, Mr Rajagopal. (*He turns to Leon.*) You're too young to be in here. Your passport says you're forty, I think you're under age, I'm moving you to a children's hostel. As for you – (*He turns to Ameena.*) your story has been garbled from the start. You're on the first plane to Somalia next week. Don't all look at me like that, you've been here long enough and we need your beds.

Happy New Year!

(*to Petra*) My one mistake was to believe you, I won't make another one.

Petra Wait. Please.

Don't leave like this.

Simon hesitates, moves close, Petra grabs his hand.

I have something to say.

Ameena, come here. (*She whispers to her.*)

Ameena recoils in terror.

Do what I ask. Quick. (*to Shivan*) Don't let her escape.

Ameena slowly begins to take off her blouse.
All turn away except for Shivan and Petra.

Simon Good try, Mrs Karagy, but entrapment doesn't work with a man like me. Goodbye.

Petra Look at her, Mr England. LOOK!

Simon looks – then turns away, shocked.

It is entrapment, but not by a pair of beautiful breasts.
Look again. Count. You can't? Let me help you.
Thirty-four cigarette burns on her front. Twenty-five on her back . . .

Shivan She's been here eight months. The doctor has given her the strongest tranquillisers he could find, but he hasn't once examined her.

Simon She screamed at the doctor, I have it on file.

Petra Did you ask why?

Simon I remember her first interview very well. The interpreter eventually got her to admit she'd been a prostitute.

Petra Where was the interpreter from?

Simon From Somalia, like her. Don't try to teach me my job.

Shivan Somalia hasn't had a government for the last eight years. There are twelve warring factions along tribal lines.

Simon I know all that!

Petra What faction was the interpreter?

Simon We're grateful to get someone from the same country, we pay a pittance!

Petra You put a young girl in front of two men, one an enemy, the other an official, and you asked her to tell you her life?

Simon All she had to do was say she was raped. It would have put her in a different category.

Petra Three words. Do you know what it means to speak those words? Ameena, tell Mr Great Britain what happened.

Silence.

Go on, Ameena, say the words.

Ameena (*struggling*) I – was – (*inaudible*) They sur-round me in the street. Take me inside – dark – at first I don't see.
    Eight. Eight men. I thought: for a beating – for names. I was prepared – for beating.

She laughs.

They don't want – names. For an hour, they shout – not at me – at each the other – who gets me first.

Petra She was a virgin, Mr Le Britten.

Ameena They even hit the other. I try to run then. Wrong.

She stops.

Then.
    Many hours. Turned – turned over. Turned.

Pause.

Turned. They stop to smoke and crush cigarettes – on –

Petra She was seventeen. Go on, Ameena. Mr Le Britten wants credible testimony. Let's give him testimony.

Ameena Crush cigarettes. On.

Some. Others – start again. They – on my knees.
Together now – they – everywhere. (*She gags slightly.*)
Then. They throw me – on the street. It is light – sun.
    My mother – No! I can't go home.
    I walk – walk – North. I know North. Sleep anywhere.
Many weeks. Into Ethiopia, trouble there too and a
priest, I don't know, says Djibouti – there's a boat, takes
me there on lorry, lots of people. I get on –

Petra I've seen women crawl into the gutter and die after
one man, but she had the strength to keep walking, get
on a lorry, keep going. She didn't lose that strength until
she got here and two men called her a whore.
    You still don't believe her? Ameena, take off your skirt.

Simon No!

Petra It's worse on her legs.

Simon Please!

Petra Do you believe her? Ameena –

Simon I believe her.

Petra Now you will swear to help her, you will get her a
permanent leave in England or she will take off her skirt,
and there's another scar on –

Simon I'll reopen her case.

Petra Come to me, child. (*She cradles Ameena.*) Words
are like medicine, they taste bad, but they help after.
With every English word, you will tell your story more.

*Petra subsides now, exhausted. Aziz is crying. Paul
tidies the food, haphazardly.
    Alexander comes in, dishevelled, unsteady.
    Simon stares.*

Simon Who are you?

Alexander (*laughing, drunk*) No one.

Simon Mrs Karagy – surely this is –

Petra (*quickly*) I don't know who this is.

Alexander Mamou . . .

Petra Now the newspapers have my story of hunger strike, all these young men come here claiming I'm their mother. Crazy, lonely young men, even English.

Alexander Mamou!

Petra (*to Alexander*) If I were you, I wouldn't come in here. You may never get out. Save yourself.

Alexander *Ne moga.*

Petra *Spasi sebesi. Maxnise.*

Alexander *Nebes tvaoita blagoslovia.*

Simon What are you saying?

Petra He's a crazy gypsy tinker, how do you ever let these people in? He thinks I'm a saint and he wants my blessing.

Paul Time to leave, son.

Alexander Mamou.

Alexander goes to Petra, kisses her hand. She makes a blessing over him and holds him for a moment.

Petra Go: live. *Givei.*

Paul escorts Alexander out.

Simon That was your son.

Petra slumps slightly.

That was your son. I have to get him arrested.

If I ask the police to chase an illegal immigrant on New Year's Eve, they'll laugh at me. Then it'll go on my file. I'm supposed to be off duty. I'm so tired. That was your son. I'm always right – (*He looks at Ameena.*) No. Not always.

I haven't eaten all day. The pizza's getting cold. It's New Year's Eve.

My daughter's a cook on someone's yacht somewhere in the middle of the ocean. I've been working so hard, my place is a mess. There are all these dishes piling up in my sink.

A pause. Leon starts playing the flute.

Shivan Why don't you join us?

Simon I can't.

Shivan You would see us as too human?

Simon I never felt for England the way others do. Even at school I wanted to travel. I did love the history, the kings and queens, Churchill. I'm not narrow-minded, but I don't recognise anything any more. I feel dizzy. There's a lot of illness about. I need to sit down.

Petra Mr Le Britten.

Simon Simon, please.

Petra You're not a bad man.

Simon I'm making too many mistakes.

Petra Me too. I've been walled, like you. History shifts, we can't hold it. Simon, when we turn to you, don't cover your eyes and think of the kings and queens of England. Look at us: we are your history now.

Petra subsides. Simon keeps hold of her hand Straight into:

EPILOGUE

Spring light. Alexander sits, wrapped in a blanket. He looks rough. Henry and Anna come on.

Henry Teacher!

Alexander starts, then bows his head as if it's not him. Anna thrusts a paper in his hand.

Anna Five A-levels. All grade A. Henry has a gardening job for the summer. The best university in England wants Anna Kadare. At the interview, I told them I wanted to be a Biological Historian with a special interest in genetics. You know that animals suffer something called tonic immobility – it is the same as what Freud calls hysterical paralysis – you freeze, can't move. Now they think it's evolutionary, because for animals it's safer not to move from the hunter. But what about humans? When the Serbs came to our village, we all froze. Hysterical paralysis. What makes people freeze at certain moments of history? Hysterical paralysis? Historical paralysis? If we understand it, can we prevent it?

You understand what I'm looking for? Not this country's history, or the one I came from, but the common mechanism –

Alexander nods, smiles.

I knew you would.

Remember your crying lessons? I pretended not to understand, but when I got back to that filthy hotel room where we all lived, I'd do hours of crying homework. And then I began to unfreeze. (*Pause.*) Ali's gone back.

We're going for a walk.

Come with us.

Alexander shakes his head.

Henry Remember, teacher, you once ask me to find something I like about this country. It is very hard, but I decide I like the parks.

Pause.

My name is Abdillahi Hassan.

Anna No one can pronounce it, so we still call him Henry.
Come on, teacher, come and walk with us in an English park.

THE ASH GIRL

For Dushka

The Ash Girl was first presented at Birmingham Repertory Theatre on 8 December 2000. The cast, in order of appearance, was as follows:

Ruth Jane Cameron
Judith Rachel Smith
Ashgirl Stephanie Pochin
Mother Vivien Parry
Princess Zehra Souad Faress
Prince Amir Justin Avoth
Paul Huss Garbiya
Slothworm Alex Jones
Angerbird Tracy Wiles
Envysnake/Owl Kenn Sabberton
Gluttontoad/Fairy Darlene Johnson
Pridefly/Spider Jonathan Bond
Greedmonkey/Otter Togo Igawa
Sadness Sarah Coomes
Lust Emma Lowndes
Man in the Forest Ken Shorter
Girlmouse Millie Coles/Natalie Smith
Boymouse Ezrah Roberts-Grey/Joseph Turner

Director Lucy Bailey
Designer Angela Davies
Lighting Designer Chahini Yavroyan
Composer Orlando Gough
Choreographer Michael Dolan

Characters

in order of appearance

Ruth
Judith
Ashgirl
Mother
Princess Zehra
Prince Amir
Paul
Slothworm
Angerbird
Envysnake
Gluttontoad
Pridefly
Greedmonkey
Sadness
Lust
Man in the Forest
Owl
Otter
Fairy in the Mirror
Girlmouse
Boymouse

The house, the palace, the forest

Act One

*The breakfast room of a dilapidated medieval-type
house. A very large hearth, thickly blanketed with ashes.
A massive sideboard, laden with foods.*

The room is dark.

*Ruth and Judy enter. As they come in, there is a
movement in the ashes, a ripple, no more.*

*The two girls skip to and from the sideboard, lifting
the heavy silver covers and helping themselves with glee.*

Ruth Chicken.

Judith Pigeon.

Ruth Casseroled pheasant.

Judith Boiled swan.

Ruth Wild boar.

Judith Pig's ears with juniper berries.

Ruth Clotted cream.

Judith And damson jam.

Ruth I feel full.

Judith I feel fat.

Ruth Mother says we must be thin.

Judith Why?

Ruth Because girls must be thin.

Judith Why?

Ruth How *do* you get thin?

Judith You stop eating.

Ruth Stop eating damson jam! Swan and sausages? Never.

Judith We could start getting thin tomorrow. Today, I want an unboring day.

Ruth We could practise our dancing.

Judith Boring. I want a good gallop over the fields.

Ruth Father took away the last horse.

Judith Took the horse and vanished.

Ruth Into thin air.

Judith Into a bear.

Ruth A thin, a hairy, a grizzly bear.

Judith Waits in his lair . . .

They burst out laughing. A movement in the ashes.

Ruth We could read a book.

Judith I'm bored with happy endings. Why can't the monster eat everyone?

Ruth What about that book on manners?

Judith We don't need manners, we never see anyone.

Ruth I'd like to paint, but Mother says it makes me look a mess.

Judith I'd like to find a worm, open it and see what's inside. Cut the legs off an ant, see if they move.
I'd need one of those glasses that make everything big.

Ruth There's one in father's study, shall we take it?

A movement in the ashes.

Judith Mother keeps the key: wait till she's asleep, steal the key, take everything out of the study. That would be very unboring.

Ruth When he finds out?

Judith He's never coming back. Never never –

Ruth Ever after . . .

Judith A grizzly bear . . .

Ruth In his lair . . .

Movement in the ashes. And now a figure emerges, grey, spectral, skeletally thin, a girl of about seventeen.

Judith Ashgirl. Eyeing us.

Ruth Spying.

Judith Look and tell.

Ashgirl I will tell Mother you're planning to steal the key.

They seize her arms.

Ruth You won't!

Judith She won't believe you.

Ashgirl I always tell the truth.

Ruth It's the way you tell it!

Judith Boring. Very boring. Lies are more interesting.

Ashgirl How can the truth be boring? Father admonished me always to tell the truth.

Ruth And where is he now?

Judith The grizzly bear . . .

Ashgirl Stop it!

The girls laugh.

Ruth Come on, Ashie, have some breakfast.

Ashgirl No thank you.

Ruth Food in this house not good enough for you?

Judith Growing girl must eat.

*Ashgirl tries to return to the ashes, but Judith takes a
sausage, hands it to Ashgirl.*

Take it!

*Ashgirl shakes her head.
Ruth takes a scone, lots of cream and jam. Proffers it.*

Ruth When your sisters offer, you accept, you say thank
you.

Ashgirl I don't want anything.

Ruth Book says: bad manners to refuse a gift. I like
books which tell other people what to do.

They wait. Ashgirl looks at the food in disgust.

Judith Eat!

Ruth She's so rude.

Judith Stuff it in her mouth.

*Ruth grinds the scone in Ashgirl's mouth. She gags,
spits, more grinding, more violent. Judith eats the
sausage, calmly.*

I could eat a fried pig's heart.

Ruth (*to Ashgirl, on the floor*) Lick the crumbs. Say sorry.

They pin her down.

248

Judith That's compulsory.

Ruth Conclusory.

Judith Persuasory.

Ruth We're waiting.

Judith Maybe another scone? Gnawed bone of swan?

Ashgirl Sorry . . .

Ruth Sorry for?

Ashgirl Sorry – for – for being – me.

They let her go. A moment.

Ruth The thing is, Ashie, if you were nicer to us, we'd be nicer to you.

The girls leave, Ashgirl sinks back into the ashes.

SCENE TWO
WHO LIVES IN THE ASHES

Ashgirl I don't remember much. It was another countryside, another country. Flowers inside. My mother loved flowers.

I don't know when she died, if she died. I was always with my father. I am your friend for ever, he said. He took me everywhere, travels, hunting, I sat under castle tables and listened to the men talk. We slept on his cloak in the woods, naming the stars.

Until we came here. First for an afternoon, then a night, then days, and finally to stay. He never told me he wanted to marry her, he didn't even ask me, his friend. And that these girls would be his daughters, call themselves my sisters. He said he loved me most, but he needed, needed – but he loved me.

He wasn't happy long. I saw lines of loneliness return to his face. I went to him, but he was strange. He told me he was not a good man, he had monsters to fight. I said I would fight them with him, but he said no, these monsters were different, they'd poisoned the blood to his heart and I must forgive him. And so my father went in search of his heart and broke mine.

And that's when I found the ashes. Ashes are warm and in the ashes no one sees you, you do no wrong. Ashes on your head, no one talks to you, ashes on your arms, no one touches you, ashes are safe. I will stay in these ashes, melt into them, shrink to their weightlessness. Cloak of crumbling grey. My ashes.

SCENE THREE
WHO GOES TO THE BALL

The Mother comes in. She is held back, neat, straight. The girls follow her. She holds a large golden scroll in her hand.

Mother I hoped it was from my husband, gifts, money. It's an invitation – addressed to all the daughters of the house.

Judith/Ruth We are the daughters of the house.

Ruth We haven't been anywhere all winter.

Mother You mustn't be seen with the wrong people.

Judith What are wrong people?

Mother When there's no father, people talk.

Ruth Let me read it.

Mother It's addressed to all the daughters of the house. (*She makes a gesture towards the ashes.*)

Ruth I'm the oldest.

Judith But I'm clever.

They both snatch at the scroll.

Mother You can have a look too, Ashgirl.

Ashgirl (*from the ashes*) I'm not interested.

Mother It is to all my daughters.

Ashgirl (*emerging from the ashes*) I'm not your daughter!

Mother Clean yourself up. You look disgusting. You've got crumbs all over your face.

Ashgirl I'll clear the breakfast.

Mother Judith and Ruth can help you.

Ashgirl I like to do it myself.

Mother You don't help yourself, Ashgirl. I've heard people whispering I'm not nice to you, but I try.

Ruth and Judith are unrolling the scroll. The decoration is ornate, golds and browns.

Ruth 'You are invited . . . '

Mother That paper is too bright.

Judith The letters are of gold.

Mother People shouldn't show off.

Judith 'To dance . . .'

Mother Is it real gold?

Ruth 'At the palace of . . . '

Mother A palace . . .

Ruth 'Princess Zehra.'

Mother A princess!

Ruth 'In honour of her son, Prince Amir's . . . '

Mother Amir?

Ruth 'Birthday on' – it's next week!

Judith We don't have any ball gowns.

Mother It's not a local name, they're foreigners.

Ruth A prince!

Mother That's always interesting. And rich. But foreign.

Judith He could be from Araby.

Mother Everyone important will be there, we have to go.

Ruth What are we going to wear?

Mother A normal responsible father would have heard of this ball and sent rich cloths, shoes of brocade. It seems we'll have to manage with some old gowns of mine.

Ashgirl I'll help alter them.

Mother I suppose you have to go.

Judith Ashgirl? She'll embarrass us.

Ashgirl I don't want to.

Mother If you're not there, people will say it's because I'm wicked.

Ashgirl No one will notice.

Mother Don't ever say I didn't ask you. I won't be called a mean stepmother. No one ever sees the other side.

Ruth When you meet a prince, what do you do?

Mother You get him to marry you. He'll provide all you want.

Judith Will he provide me with interesting and rare stones?

Ruth Salted hams dangling from a vaulted ceiling?

Mother One of you will marry the Prince, but you'll have to work at it, I'll tell you how as we look at my gowns. There's no time to lose.

They begin to sweep out.

Judith Rooms of marble . . .

Ruth Cakes . . .

Ashgirl remains alone.

Ashgirl Ashes . . .

SCENE FOUR
WHO LIVES IN THE PALACE

Princess Zehra's palace. It is nomadic and oriental in colour and feel: cushions, rugs, no hard furniture, a sense of luxury in the cloth as well as many books, scrolls, illuminated manuscripts.

Prince Amir, in his twenties. Dark, melancholic, anger simmering, reclines on cushions, reading.

Princess Zehra opens envelopes. A large pile is already thickening next to her.

Zehra Everyone has accepted.

Amir Since the miserable day we settled here, not one person has come to welcome us.

Zehra They're all coming now.

Amir No one has invited us. This country knows nothing of hospitality.

Zehra There are two sides to hospitality, Amir: our hosts are not welcoming, so we must be generous guests. Every girl in the region is coming to dance and some will be beautiful.

Amir No one is beautiful here, their skin is too white, they all look like boiled potatoes.

Zehra You must not speak like someone with a shrivelled heart.

Amir Are you denying they're all ugly?

Zehra You sometimes have to adjust your eyes to see beauty.

Amir You mean close them!

Zehra We haven't yet learned to find beauty in this country, we will.

Amir Never!
   Grey. Rain. Small hills. A forest with trees packed in so tight you can't even canter.
   I loved my gallops on the plains, the stars at night lancing the desert sky.

Zehra We'll become part of this country and learn to love it.

Amir I'm going back.

Zehra There's nothing to go back to.

Amir I'll find my father. If he is a prisoner, I'll free him. If he is dead, I'll avenge him and take back our pastures.

Zehra You'll find no trace of him or of our land. You will marry here and that will root you in this country. It's not the first time our family has moved to a new land.

Amir Always as conquerors.

Zehra We can still impress.

Amir I don't want to marry now.

Zehra looks at what Amir is reading.

Zehra Why do you read poetry if you don't want to fall in love?

Amir I could not love a girl who loved this grey.

Zehra There are many ways of being a foreigner in a country: you can be exiled like us, or you can be badly treated in your own land and feel a stranger. I have seen many people here with the forlorn look of foreigners.

Amir No one here has that depth of feeling.

Zehra Beware too much homesickness my son, it's a worm that eats hope and gnaws at your strength.

Amir And why aren't you homesick at all? Why don't you ever grieve for my father?

Zehra How can you know what I feel!

Pause.

Zehra I am a mother. I owe my son a future.

Amir I may not want it.

Zehra So much anger. Here comes Paul. Look at him, he's relinquished his anger and he is happy.

Paul comes in, also 'Indian', but expansive, more 'western'.

Paul You're giving a ball, Princess, that is an excellent and a brilliant idea. And I have learned many of this country's dances. Look, Amir: you'll like this one.

Paul begins to demonstrate.
Zehra and even Amir laugh.

Paul It's the very latest. Come and learn it, Amir, I've watched the boys in this country and modesty and restraint are out the windows. If we want to get on, we have to show off.

Amir Never!

Paul Amir!

Zehra We're only asking you to dance.

SCENE FIVE
WHO LIVES IN THE FOREST

A dark and ancient forest. Oaks, holly, ash trees.
Stagnating water, ivy, black mud. The Monsters, well hidden at first, emerge from different places and heights.
First to appear, Slothworm, heavily and slowly ambling around the trunks of trees.

Slothworm I'm so tired. Always in a slump. Anyone I touch even slightly slows down too. Soon they feel so tired, they sink into a slovenly slurry of exhaustion. Can't do anything, muscles soft and sludgy, they slobber, say they're sick. They are sick, the Slothworm sickness. Slubberdegullions.

I'm sick of saying so much. Why was I asked to trudge my way through this sludge of mud to come here? I'm going to lie down on the soft ground and sink into sleep.

Angerbird flaps down from a tree, spitting angrily.

Angerbird Slothworm! Don't you dare do such a dirty trick.

Slothworm A little slumber while I wait, Angerbird, I'm sinking with exhaustion.

Angerbird I've had to flap about calling the meeting for Pridefly. Why do I always have to do all the work? Every other deadly monster in this forest is useless and it makes me very angry and if you dare close your eyes, I'll peck them out.

Slothworm Soft, Angerbird. Don't take it out on me, go and make some humans angry, provoke a war or something, I'm only a slug, a deeply sleepy slug.

Slothworm yawns, Angerbird flaps.

Angerbird What do I ever do but make humans angry, spitting, shouting, fighting, killing, but I can't make wars on my own. That's why we're having this meeting. I could have humans maiming, disfiguring, blinding and murdering each other right now.

Envysnake slithers in.

Envysnake They die anyway sooner or later, they sink rotting into the soil and worms slobber over them. They give you the credit, but it is I, Envysnake, who poison them with hatred, make them hate everybody who has something, something they haven't got, and they slink around, absolutely, sobbingly, slouchingly and supremely miserable. You've got the showy plumage – I have to slave and slither all day in this slippery skin, but I'm the one who snares those humans into that sickening, snarling envy that eats out their insides and smothers them.

Gluttontoad, fat and round.

Gluttontoad I'm hungry. I have no interest in anything except great gluts of glutinous food.

Slothworm I'm sleepy.

Gluttontoad Whoever called this meeting had better provide some glowing globules of gloaming honey for the voluminous, libidinous, cavernous stomach of this gluttonous Gluttontoad or I'm going. Who did call this meeting? Is it about food?

Slothworm Who cares?

Pridefly, small, dark, shiny and brisk, zooms on.

Pridefly I called this meeting. Who else? Would anything get done without me? We Prideflies have been here for eternity and have always done our duty with total distinction and now it falls upon me once again to shake the torpor from our midst.

Anyone can see we're not doing enough to destroy the humans. Some of them even seem quite happy and peaceful when our task is to torment them, destroy their souls and encourage their extermination. Since I seem to be the only one aware of this, I called you all here to remind you of your function and to lead you all into a new wave of human destruction.

Greedmonkey I torment them all the time. They want more and more and more. More money, more houses, more clothes, the children want more toys. People are very greedy around here thanks to the Greedmonkey, and I want more rewards for my hard work.

Pridefly There's not enough despair. What's the point of being a deadly sin if you can't wreck people's lives?

Where are the wars? The suicides? Murders in the night and disappearances? I want to see devastation all around and I have devised a strategy which only someone of my intelligence can think up.

Angerbird You don't need a strategy to make people angry. You and your meetings are beginning to annoy me, Pridefly.

Pridefly That's because you're too stupid to understand the importance of a concerted plan.

Slothworm Plan, concerted as well . . . sounds like such an effort . . .

Greedmonkey Is there a large reward? I wouldn't mind some loot.

Envysnake I never get what I deserve.

Pridefly There's a ball to be given in the palace of those new people, Princess Zehra and her son. The forest will be crisscrossed by humans off their guard. We must lie in wait, vigilant, active, aggressive. Some of us will make forays into the houses and report back on the weaknesses of our future victims. We can only enter humans through some fault in their being, and there always is one. No human must come through this forest without being pounced upon by one of us.

Slothworm Sorry, no way I'm pouncing, but I'll lie in wait . . .

Pridefly We are the Seven Deadly Sins, the monsters of the soul, the terrifying shadows of the forest, and we are here to rule the world.

Sadness, a very human, bedraggled figure, wanders by, slowly.

Pridefly Sadness: are you with us or not?

Sadness looks at them all and glides off, slowly.

Slothworm She makes me feel even more tired . . .

Envysnake She makes my skin shiver. Why should she be so frightening?

Pridefly She acts as if she were better than us, but she's not. It's not made clear in our ancestry books exactly where she belongs. We are the seven deadly, monstrous sins. Is Sadness the eighth? Something else? Leave her. She'll join us when it suits her.

Now: half of us will stay in the forest . . .

Slothworm I'm not moving . . .

Pridefly The rest of us will move to the houses . . .

Angerbird I'm off.

Gluttontoad (*as he goes*) I've seen plates piled with dolloping glops of gelatinous sweets in some of these houses. I could do with a mongoose mousse in couscous, followed by a Charlotte Russe and the whoosh of a bonne bouche. A spruced goose en croute infused in juiced grapefruit . . . and then . . .

Pridefly Obey all orders. No slack. Let it be said in the chronicles of the future that I led the decisive battle against the humans. All for chaos and chaos to all!

Angerbird, Gluttontoad, Greedmonkey move off, led by Pridefly. Sloth remains and falls into a coma. Lust comes out of the shadows and waits: a Man comes forward, alone. Lust curls around him.

Lust Subtle, intricate and irresistible: Lust. I am here, always here . . .

The Man tries to free himself. Lust laughs.
The Man falls on his knees, crying.

SCENE SIX
WHO WORKS IN THE KITCHEN

Heaps of materials, scraps, threads. Ashgirl measuring, draping, cutting, pinning, sewing. The Mother rummages through boxes of shoes and gloves. Ruth and Judith twirl and hop in front of the mirror.

Judith Fields of brocade.

Ruth Cascades of lace.

Judith Camelot.

Ruth Chiffon.

Judith The coolness of satin.

Ruth A drape of velvet over my shoulders.

Judith The caress of silk around my waist.

Mother Leather for the hands. Then the feet and the problem of shoes. Too many people dress with splendour and forget the shoes. I asked him to bring back gold slippers from his travels. He failed. What will people say when they see us in old shoes?

Ashgirl I can sew roses onto these shoes and add a sprig of lace entwined with gold thread.

The Mother nods.

Judith I hate shoes, they squeeze my feet.

Mother Only peasants and animals go barefoot.

Ruth Shoes make the lady.

Mother And the lady marries the Prince.

Judith I forgot about the Prince, why do we have to marry him?

Mother Have you forgotten what he'll give you? The palaces, the clothes, shoes, furs, jewels, all yours.

Greedmonkey enters and watches.

Judith Pools of coloured stones.

Ruth Banquets.

Judith What if he doesn't want to marry us?

Mother Life will be grim if one of you doesn't marry the Prince.

Ruth Ashgirl can't marry the Prince. Ashhead.

Judith Cinderwinders, swinderbottoms, ha ha.

Mother Don't use crude language, the Prince will find you vulgar. (*to Ashgirl*) If you can make yourself a dress in time and find some shoes you can come.

Ruth You can come as our servant.

Ashgirl I don't want to go to the ball.

Ruth She doesn't want to go to the ball.

Judith She can't make the effort.

Ruth It's hard work being a girl.

Judith A marriageable daughter.

Ruth Making yourself pretty.

Judith To catch a prince's fancy.

Ruth All so you can marry.

Judith And live richly.

Ruth Ever after.

Mother These dresses don't look like anything.

Ashgirl I'll stay up through the night to make them beautiful.

Mother If your father had kept his promise and looked after us, you wouldn't have to sew the dresses.

Ashgirl I'm happy to.

Ruth Happily she sews.

Judith For ever and ever.

Ruth While we marry the Prince.

Mother I see you wrapped in furs, covered in jewels, heads held high: you take your seats at the high table.

Greedmonkey joins them.

Ruth Fry an ortolan, stuff it in a pigeon, pigeon in a chicken, chicken in a goose, goose in a swan . . . I could enjoy marriage.

Judith Topaz, emeralds, pearls, rubies, sapphires, jasper, malachite and chalcedony . . . yes, I could enjoy marriage too.

The Mother throws a pair of shoes angrily at Ashgirl.

Mother I'll have to wear these old shoes!

They go.

SCENE SEVEN
WHO VISITS THE HOUSE

Silence. A movement towards darkness.
Ashgirl remains alone.
A shadow falls suddenly across the walls. Sadness enters, moves and tests the room for a dominant place.

Sadness The sudden hush of dusk is a good time. Animals fall silent, ready for the night, and humans feel alone . . .

(*Whispers.*) Ashgirl . . .

Behind a curtain, sometimes in the corner, I am the shadow cast against the wall.

Ashgirl . . .

It's not even a sound, it's a ripple in the air, a chill in the light, a voice they hear and do not hear.

Ashgirl . . .

Ashgirl stops working for a moment.

Young girls are easiest, but I can seep into boys too,
anyone . . . I'm the icicle in the heart, the one who
makes the world so dark you wish you weren't in it.
Sadness . . . Stretch out your hand to touch something:
all you feel is an invisible layer of cold ash covering all.
Call for help: I'll muffle your voice. Dream of relief: I'll
shrink your thoughts to dust. Don't even try to move . . .
Ashgirl . . .

Ashgirl I'll sew through the night and make these dresses
memorable.

Sadness No one will thank you.

Ashgirl The dresses will dance at the ball.

Sadness But . . . never you . . . you stay alone . . .

Ashgirl droops for a moment.

Sadness I probe, I test, study the defences and slide
through the crack. An unquieted doubt, a fear, the
unguarded thought . . .
(*to Ashgirl*) No one cares what you do, no one cares
for you . . .

Ashgirl My father was proud of my sewing, even more
proud of my writing.

Sadness He abandoned you, no one's there for you.
Ashgirl, listen . . .

Owl appears at the window.

Owl Ashgirl?

Ashgirl Owl!

Sadness I hate owls!

Owl Who were you talking to? I heard a voice I didn't
like.

Ashgirl I may have been talking to myself.

Owl There's a disturbance in the air . . .

Sadness moves away. Owl studies Ashgirl.

You're so industrious. That means you work hard.

Ashgirl I know what it means . . .

Owl It means you work too hard.

Ashgirl You can never work too hard.

Owl Is that so? Dancing is good, too.

Ashgirl Owl, you're a serious and a wise bird, why are you always urging me to have fun?

Owl Because maybe that's serious and wise advice.

Ashgirl I don't want to go to the ball, Owl, I'm shy, like you.

Owl I'm only shy of humans. I like owls.

Ashgirl I like owls too.

Owl It's my nature to hunt alone in the night, but it is not a girl's nature to slave the night through sewing dresses.

Ashgirl When they see these dresses, they'll be so happy.

Owl And you?

Ashgirl And grateful.

Owl Will they?

Ashgirl Why do you keep asking all these questions?

Owl Wisdom is the asking of a lot of questions.

Ashgirl I don't need wisdom to make these dresses perfect.

Owl Perfect dresses for your perfect sisters?

Ashgirl Owl, *I don't want to go to the ball.*

Owl Could it be you don't want to want to go to the ball?

Ashgirl I'm going to get cross.

Owl Do try!

Ashgirl Please, Owl . . .

Owl Hold one of those dresses against yourself and look in the mirror.

Ashgirl Leave me alone!

Owl No one can be happy all of the time, Ashie, but there's no harm in trying to be happy once in a while. Sometimes people don't try because they're afraid. Afraid of what? Ask yourself that. Now I must go and hunt some mice.

Ashgirl Not in this garden.

Owl I'm going to Prince Amir's garden.

Ashgirl What is he like?

Owl Why don't you see for yourself?

Ashgirl What do you think of this dress?

> *Ashgirl raises it unconsciously to herself and sees herself in the mirror. A moment.*

Owl I only understand feathers, my dear, but I can see this dress is making you want to dance.

> *Ashgirl throws the dress away from herself. Owl leaves. A shadow falls.*

SCENE EIGHT
WHO WAITS IN THE TREES

The forest. The Deadly Sins.

Pridefly Humans. Coming this way. Prepare to attack.

Angerbird Two young men: easy targets for me.

Slothworm (*waking slightly*) What's all the fuss?

Greedmonkey (*whispers*) Humans!

Amir and Paul come on. The sins melt into the trees.

Amir I've never liked this forest, why have you brought me here?

Paul Look at all these trees.

Amir So?

Pridefly That tone, the lift of those eyebrows.

Paul People in this country love heavy furniture made of dark wood, look at all this wood.
    The forest belongs to a baron who's off making wars. We could buy the forest, cut the trees and make furniture.

Greedmonkey Lots and lots of money.

Amir Why?

Paul Amir, we sell the furniture and become rich.

Greedmonkey Very rich. Then we buy more forests, cut down more trees and make more and more money.

Amir I have all the money I want. Do you need some?

Pridefly Our family didn't believe in commerce either. We were aristocrats, generals. Why do you keep company with such a vulgar-thoughted un-prided profit-grubbing mortal?

Paul Amir, we're in a new country, it's a good idea to have more money than you want. Furniture is the future.

Amir Our own country is in ruins and all you can think of is making furniture in this one.

Angerbird I've got them. I always knew I had the Prince, but now I can have both. Watch.

Paul We made war over there, that's all we ever did, even against each other.

Amir You've changed your name, you imitate the manners of the people here, you forget where you came from.

Paul What's wrong with that? Life is life. Land is land.

Amir How can you say that? The land you come from, the land where your ancestors were born, is not the same as this.

Pridefly Ancestors! Only the best of us have ancestors, most only have grandparents.

Amir What's happened to you?

Paul And what's happened to you? You brood all the time, you're always in a bad mood, you mope for the past. We're here, we have to survive.

Amir You were a fighter like me. Now you want to make furniture!

Paul We lost.

Amir My family doesn't lose wars. We retrench, we start again. Are you afraid of fighting?

Paul No one knows you here, no one bows down to your great family, maybe that's what you don't like.

Angerbird It's never difficult to get two young men into a fight.

Envysnake Goaded by envy, let me whisper a few words.

Amir Honour means nothing to you!

Paul They don't use that word much over here. It sounds ridiculous.

Pridefly The proud hate laughter.

The boys start to push each other.

Envysnake (*to Paul*) And if he dies, by accident here in this forest, his mother may adopt you and let you sprawl in his wealth.

The boys suddenly stop.

Amir No! Paul! My friend!

Angerbird I hate that word, I hate it! Friend. What kind of a stupid word is that anyway?

Envysnake (*to Paul*) You always have to do what he wants, he uses you, he decides, he spurs you on and then he spurns you.

Paul is still fighting. Amir folds his arms.

Amir What's happened to us? I've always hated this forest.

Paul (*stopping*) You've been more than a brother.

Amir I don't want anything to come between us.

Envysnake/Angerbird/Pridefly It will, we will make it . . .

SCENE NINE
WHO LEAVES THE HOUSE

The house. Ruth, Judith and the Mother in ball gowns. Ashgirl in rags, running and fetching. No one sees them, but things appear quickly.

Judith Gloves.

Ruth Purse.

Judith Sash.

Mother (*to Ashgirl*) You can still come.

Judith I find this all rather silly, I'd rather be studying rocks.

Mother Ruth's hair is wrong.

Ashgirl fixes it.

Mother (*to Ashgirl*) Blow the candles out when we've left: I don't want anyone to know we've left you behind.

The girls conclude last preparations.

Judith Bring me my cape.

Ruth Tie this on my nape.

Judith Fix the wrinkles on this drape.

Ruth Don't step on my crêpe.

Judith And try not to gape.

Ruth Ashie-agape.

Judith Cinders the ape.

Mother I don't like leaving you alone.
  Girls like you always make everyone feel bad.

They sweep out, followed by Ashgirl.

SCENE TEN
WHO COMES TO THE HOUSE

Sadness comes in. Moves about and sits. Ashgirl comes back in.

Sadness Embers dying, the wind howls, draughts filter through the floor, I've been waiting for such an evening. Ashgirl . . .

Ashgirl begins to tidy.

You can do that later. Come sit by me, Ashgirl.

Ashgirl moves around.

We're alone, everything's quiet. We need a chat, just a little chat, a few cold and dismal words sprinkled here and there, those little icy words like never, alone, no one, and then the longer, subtle ones that course through your mind and freeze it: hopeless, friendless, voiceless, useless. And also badness. Change a consonant and you get my own name: sadness . . . so like madness, mad, yes, bad . . . dad . . . add a vowel – leads to dead. I love the way letters shift about, think how close kindness is to blindness . . . and limpid to insipid . . .

A scratch at the window, a high whistle . . .
    The Otter appears, shy, furry, rather human in appearance, whiskers.

Otter Psst. Ashie. Can I come in?

Sadness Another animal spoiling my plans, why are there so many animals in the world? (*She moves away.*)

Otter Humans gone? Those girls were making so much noise I could hear them from the river. You're never noisy . . . (*He puts his head on her lap.*) Let's sit quietly together and enjoy being shy.

I love ash . . .

You're more quiet than usual, Ashie, have those humans upset you?

You're thinking. Shall we think together? I love to think. What shall we think about? What were you thinking?

Ashie?

Ashgirl About a ball.

Otter That's a thought. Shall we play ball? You know I love that game. Here, catch this stone.

Ashgirl Not a ball, Otter, The Ball.

Otter What? That noisy thing that's happening at the Palace of Prince Amir. I could hear the music under the water. That's why I came here. It's not bad music, it's quite sad music, I like that, but then it got mixed in with all that noisy human laughter. It was scaring the fish away.

Much better here . . . Shall I tell you a sad story? Would you like to hear how Uncle Slim got caught in a fishing net and died?

No?

Ashie . . .

What's that noise? I hear something outside. I'll go and see. If it's a human, I'll wait till it's gone.

Otter leaves, Sadness comes back.

Sadness Only me . . . it's an old saying: always separate your prey from its friends. And now to the close.

Sadness moves around quickly, making sure all doors are closed and all candles out.

SCENE ELEVEN
WHO LIVES IN THE MIRROR

*Same as before: darker. Ashgirl moves to the mirror,
flickering in the semi-light.
Sadness moves close.*

Sadness You do not want to go to the ball. You want to
come with me.

Ashgirl If my father were here . . .

Sadness Why would he come back to you? Come to me.

Ashgirl I'll work hard, I'll grow old, one day I'll die.

Sadness Yes. Come to the ashes and we'll have a little
look at death.

Ashgirl How could I go to a ball? Look at me.

Sadness Death is no worse than life, Ashie, and it's so
simple . . .

Ashgirl (*to herself in the mirror, with disgust*) Look at me.

Sadness And turn away in disgust.

Ashgirl Look at me . . .

*The mirror glows slightly. A voice emerges from it,
clear, throaty.*

Voice in the Mirror Look at yourself.

Ashgirl Who's that?

Voice in the Mirror I am in the mirror.

Sadness Don't look in there, that's vain, you have no
right to be vain. Let me soothe you.

Ashgirl Who are you?

Voice in the Mirror Who are you?

Ashgirl Who am I?

Ashgirl stares at herself. More light from the mirror.

Voice in the Mirror I am the one you find when you see yourself clearly.

Ashgirl I can't see you.

Sadness Here . . . over here . . .

Voice in the Mirror You will when you see yourself.

Ashgirl (*staring*) I'm ugly.

Sadness Yes.

Voice in the Mirror Look at yourself with clear eyes.

Ashgirl I look disgusting, horrible.

The light begins to fade. There is a sigh.

What's happened, where are you? (*She stares.*) I'm the wrong shape, size, I'm fat.

Darker.

Voice in the Mirror (*fading sigh*) Ashgirl . . .

Ashgirl Maybe I'm not so bad. Normal.

A little more light.

And my eyes seem very bright.

Voice in the Mirror We can't do it all by ourselves, you have to help . . . Stand up straight and look.

Ashgirl I'm so crooked.

Groan from the mirror.

Don't go, I love listening to you . . . There, I'm almost graceful, actually, I am rather pleasing, there's something about having a body, two arms, hands, legs, it's all rather harmonious . . .

Voice in the Mirror Good. Now look at the mirror, at yourself, and see what you want.

Do you want to go to the ball? Answer the truth.

Ashgirl Yes, I do want to go to the ball, I always wanted to go the ball, but I can't, and yes, I do mind that I can't and now I'm going to be even more unhappy, I don't mind, I do mind, I don't want to be unhappy, I'm tired of being unhappy, draped in my ashcloth, I do want to go to the ball, oh, go away, I'm going to cry. I'm even getting angry.

The mirror comes to full light and the voice emerges from the mirror and stretches into a beautiful silver-clad Fairy, facets sparkling in the light. She holds a small mirror in her hand, like a fan, and she lifts Ashgirl's head gently. Sadness, blinded, melts away into the shadows.

Fairy If being unhappy makes you angry, then you can be happy.

Ashgirl Who are you?

Fairy I am the Fairy in the Mirror . . .

Ashgirl You're beautiful.

Fairy I am – even as fairies go. It's my clothes. And so are you, but it's not your clothes. Now, we don't have any time to waste. (*She takes out several silver scrolls, reads.*) I have to measure you.

Ashgirl Why?

Fairy Why? I'm not sure. Wait. I think I have the wrong page and I'm doing this the wrong way round. It's a standard recipe this. Let me see –

Ah, the animals first. I need some animals. Do you have any around?

Ashgirl Owl?

Fairy You can't do anything with owls, they have too much personality. It says you can use insects too, what about an ant?

Ashgirl Otter went into the garden. I could call him.

Fairy An otter is unusual. Will he be co-operative?

Ashgirl He's a very good friend. And then there are some mice.

Fairy Definitely. It says: always have a mouse or two at hand.

Ashgirl Otter! Come quickly, Mice!

Otter appears.

Otter Ashie, are you all right? Oh! You have company. 'Bye . . .

Fairy Stay where you are!

Otter Ashie, what's all this noise? Who's this human?

Ashgirl She's not, she's the Fairy of the Mirror.

Otter Do you have any idea how dangerous fairies are? They're always changing things, turning the world topsy-turvy. You're going to change me into something, I can see it in your face.

Fairy Stand still and stop being difficult. (*She takes out a scalpel and approaches the Otter.*)

Otter You're going to turn me into a fur coat! Ashie, this is beyond cruelty.
Help!

The Fairy begins to slit the fur.

Goodbye riverside, goodbye ashes, ah the sweetness of
the shy and modest life. Ouch.

Fairy Am I hurting you?

Otter Not yet, but I'm a pessimist and we're always
prepared for the worst. Ouch! All right, it didn't hurt,
but it might have.

*She continues to scalpel, scrape, pare, as the Otter
turns into a coachman, shy, bewhiskered, sniffly, but
very well dressed.*

Otter You've turned me into a human! That's degrading!
What have I done to deserve such a punishment?

Ashgirl Otter, you look beautiful.

Otter I looked beautiful before. I'm cold.

Fairy You are the coachman, Otto. You will drive the
horses and look after Ashie at the ball.

Otter And now I have to join a lot of other noisy humans
at a noisy ball! I'm a creature of the river, Fairy, please
let me free.

Fairy What's next? Horses . . . We need horses. Quick.
Where are those mice?

*Two mice have crept in, a Girlmouse of nine and a
Boymouse of five.*

Girlmouse Here! Are you a good fairy or a bad fairy?

Fairy All fairies are good until they get cross. I'll only
get cross if you don't do as you're told.

Girlmouse That's what everybody says.
    Hello. (*to the boy*) Say hello.
    You see how polite we are. Now I'm brave and I'm
bold, I'm clever too and I know about planets and stars
and I would like an adventure, please.

Fairy I'm supposed to change you into silver ponies.

Girl I'd rather be a silver dragon.

Fairy Ah – well – we don't have to do what everyone else does. You will be a silver dragon and you will be a silver pony and you will both gallop through the forest drawing the carriage. Oh! I completely forgot about the carriage. (*She reads.*) 'You may use a pumpkin.' Have you seen a pumpkin? 'Or a melon.' It's the wrong season. 'Or anything round and carvable from the vegetable kingdom.' Round. Carvable.

Ashgirl When I was a little girl I played with the shell of a walnut and pretended it was a carriage.

Fairy You always wanted to go to balls, Ashie, but then one day you lost your dream. That's the worst kind of spell. Is a walnut a vegetable?

Ashgirl It's edible.

Girlmouse A nut is a fruit. It's a seed, it's the seed of a vegetable. You may proceed.

Fairy Thank you.

Ashgirl I even painted the shell silver. That was so stupid!

Fairy Careful, Ashie: don't make me have to leave.

Ashgirl I did keep the shell under my bed and during the day, I still keep it in my pocket. Here it is.

All crowd and admire the shell Ashgirl brings out of her pocket.

Girlmouse It shines like the moon on the river.

Boymouse There are seats inside.

Otto I say, Ashie, you painted this beautifully.

Ashgirl It's so small, how can it work?

Fairy Size is nothing to creatures of imagination.

Girlmouse Human beings think they're large, but when they look up at the stars they feel small.

The girl and boy Mice start rampaging around the room.

Fairy Size is relative, but beauty is not. I hold something beautiful in my hand. Mice, what are you doing?

Boy Practising the gallop.

Girl I mustn't get my dragon's tail caught in the trees.

Fairy Go outside, please, and wait. Where was I?
Oh you spirits of imagination, come to my help now –
Something beautiful in my hand, something beautiful in my mind – matter shifts under the power of wish, shapes itself to the image sparkling in the mind, feeds on the desire for existence and – a thing of beauty emerges in the garden.
I think I've done it!

A carriage in the garden.

Fairy Now to the most difficult item, your dress.

Ashgirl I can sew.

Fairy I can change matter, but not the cruel rush of time. The ball has started, we need the original dressmakers of the early world, we need the spiders.

The spiders begin to climb down from ropes. There are quite a few of them and Ashgirl screams.

Ashgirl But I'm afraid of them.

Fairy No magic without courage.
Let them measure you.

The spiders measure, work quickly.

Fairy They want to know what kind of a dress you want.

Ashgirl Anything . . .

Fairy A spider's web?

Ashgirl I want something beautiful, shiny, slinky, silvery, watery, glittery, dangly, jangly, tingly, glossy and fleury.

Light silver cloth, layer upon layer: Ashgirl finds herself dressed and draped in a mirrory silver dress, long, elegant, sparkling.
    The Fairy turns her to the mirror.

Fairy Now you may look at yourself.

Ashgirl It isn't me.

Fairy It is you.

Ashgirl It is.
I am here.
I am beautiful.

Fairy At last: the transformation of the heart begins.

Ashgirl Let's go, Otto, I'm ready, let's go!

Fairy Wait!

Ashgirl It was a dream . . .

Fairy Not a dream, but magic. And magic cannot last because it is a chance and chance is short and fleeting. There is another magic that might last, but it depends on you. For the moment, know that the carriage, the dragon and the pony, Otto himself and your clothes cannot move through the twelfth bell of midnight. Why? Because time buries chance and no fairy has ever diverted its ruthless rhythm. We try. Sometimes we cheat by a few years, once we managed a hundred – I was there. Where was I? Here. Now. You must return home before midnight. Otto and Owl will warn you. Do not forget – return home.

Ashgirl To my old life?

Fairy If you let chance change you, no. Now go.

Ashgirl Can you not come with me?

Fairy I breathe your reflection, I must live in the mirror. Sometimes you'll find me in water.

Ashgirl What made you come to me tonight?

Fairy Yourself. Go . . .

Ashgirl I am beautiful and I am going dancing.

Fairy A girl is always beautiful when she is going dancing.

Act Two

SCENE ONE

Zehra's palace. Reds and golds, flowers. Sense of plenty and hospitality. Zehra, Paul and Amir greet guests as they come in. Then a farandole forms, led by Paul. A dinner bell rings, and Zehra leads everyone out.

Only Amir remains behind, plucking idly at an instrument, melancholic. He sinks in the cushions and remains unseen when Ashgirl arrives.

She bursts in, resplendent in her silver dress and cloak. Otto follows, very twitchy, takes her cloak. Ashgirl centres herself in the seemingly empty room.

Ashgirl I've missed the dance!

Otto They've all gone in to supper.

Ashgirl I've missed what I most wanted.

Otto Let's go home.

Ashgirl You'll have to dance with me.

Otto I only like river music.

Ashgirl takes Otto by the hand and makes him dance. He is not happy.

We could be having such a good time in the ashes. And these human bones are aching. Dance by yourself.

Amir emerges from the cushions, smiles at Ashgirl and takes her hand. They dance easily, look at each other a little and keep dancing, unable to speak.

Ashgirl (*out*) I'd like to say: I love dancing with you –
    but I don't want him to know I've never danced with a
boy before.

Amir (*out*) I'd like to say: I love dancing with you –
    but I don't want her to know how much I'm enjoying
being with her.

Ashgirl I'd like to say: Please stay with me all evening –
    but I don't want him to think I'm too stupid to talk to
anyone else.

Amir I'd like to say: come in to dinner with me and sit
with me –
    but I don't want her to know she's the only girl I want
to talk to.

Ashgirl I'd like to say: It's so beautiful here –
    but I don't want him to know I've never been anywhere
so full of light and colour, even though it's true.

Amir I'd like to ask: Where have you come from? Why
so late? And without parents –
    but I don't want her to think I'm so interested, even
though I am.

Ashgirl Should I leave? I want to stay.

Amir Should I stop dancing? I want to go on.

Ashgirl I can't say anything: he must think I'm stupid.

Amir She must think I'm a cretin.

*They look at each other, each holds a hand out to the
other.*

Ashgirl/Amir (*over each other*) What's your name?

They laugh. Pause.

Ashgirl/Amir (*over each other*) Ashgirl. Amir.

They laugh.

Amir Where have you come from, Ashgirl?

Ashgirl (*out*) I can't tell him about now, but I could about before . . .
  (*to Amir*) I had a pony when I was little.
  (*out*) Why did I say that!

Amir There are wild ponies where I come from. Great festivals too.
  (*out*) What a stupid thing to say.

Ashgirl We had music and flowers in our house.
  (*out*) He's going to think, so what?

Amir We raced ponies over the plains.
  (*out*) Why can't I stop talking about horses!

  A pause.

Ashgirl I'm tongueless, mute, unvoiced. Fairy of the Mirror, change this silence into words.

Amir I can fight battles, I've never feared death, but I'm too afraid to say anything to her.

Ashgirl/Amir I loved dancing with you!

Amir Come in with me to have dinner.

Ashgirl Yes! I'm so hungry.

  Ashgirl starts at what she's just said then moves off with Amir. Judith and Ruth come on, food in their mouths, and collapse on the cushions.

Judith You eat, you dance, you get hot, you get bothered, you get tired, you get bored, it's such hard work marrying a prince, I'm going home.

Ruth Mother said one of us has to marry this prince.

Judith What will she do if we don't?

Ruth When Mother is disappointed I feel like I'm going to shrivel into a speck of dust.

Judith With me it's more like feeling strangled.

Ruth She loves us and wants everything for us.

Judith I don't want everything, I only want a microscope.

The Mother storms in.

Mother Why aren't you two sitting next to the Prince?

Ruth He has that girl in silver next to him and only talks to her.

Mother Move in. You only have one night to marry this prince. I'll send him this way: don't disappoint me.

Zehra comes in.

Zehra Are the young girls all right? They left the banquet.

Mother They're delicate and need a little quiet.

Zehra Shall I ask the musicians to play something soothing?

Judith No! Your music's boring.

Mother We live very quietly, grandly, very grandly, but quietly. Silence will do. My daughters work so hard at their accomplishments . . .

Zehra Indeed, and these are?

Mother Everything feminine.

Zehra Ah?

Pause.

Ruth I cook and I eat – I paint too.

Zehra So does Amir. He likes to paint scenes of our wars and of our land.

Ruth I like violence too, I paint things that rot, with flies.

Zehra Shall I send in some food?

Ruth Yes! Syrupy cakes. And a slice of marzipan from Turkistan . . .

Mother And they would so enjoy speaking to your son.

Zehra Of course. Paul, where is Amir?

Paul I keep looking for him, I am doing all the dancing, (*to the girls*) I will dance with you.

Judith Do you have a title?

Paul Yes, I have been the fastest rider and soon I will be the fastest dancer.

Mother My daughters will wait quietly for your son, Princess.

The Mother sweeps Zehra out. Paul follows.

Judith What do you do to marry a prince?

Ruth You kiss him and then you marry him. If he kisses you, he has to marry you, those are the rules.

Ashgirl and Amir come in, talking.

Amir I don't know where my father is . . .

Ashgirl Mine told me he had to leave . . .

Amir We had many enemies . . .

Ashgirl My father spoke of enemies within.

Amir Everything is so different here . . .

Ashgirl It all changed when he left.

Amir I never feel at home . . .

Ashgirl I have to tell you I'm not what I seem . . .

Amir Sometimes I'm no longer sure of who I am . . .

The sisters begin to move in.
  Owl appears at the window.

Ashgirl I have to go.

Amir Please not yet . . .

Ashgirl I want to stay . . .

Judith and Ruth close in, finger Ashgirl's dress.

Amir I want to ask you . . .

Ruth Where did you find all those little mirrors?

Judith What makes your hair sparkle so?

Ruth Can I look more closely at your shoes?

Ashgirl keeps trying to move away. Otto comes in,
flustered, shaking, Owl hoots.

Amir Tell me who –

Judith What are these precious stones on your bracelet?

The clock strikes and Owl hoots. Otto dangles
Ashgirl's cloak.

Ashgirl I have to go.

Amir Tell me where –

Owl hoots.

Judith That's strange, you have ash in your hair.

Amir Let me know who you are!

Ruth, turning towards Otto, lets out a scream.

Ruth That man is holding a giant spider's web in his hands!

Ashgirl flees, with Otto following.
Amir tries to go after her, but Judith and Ruth circle around him singing a child's game.

Judith/Ruth
Round the green gravel the grass is so green
And all the fine ladies that ever were seen
Washed in milk and dressed in silk
The last that stoops down shall be married –

Ruth picks up Ashgirl's shoe, throws it to Judith who throws it back.

Judith/Ruth
There's a lady on a mountain
Who she is I do not know –

Amir I would like that shoe.

Ruth throws it to Judith. They get frantic.

Judith/Ruth
Choose to the east, choose to the west,
And choose the one that you love best.

Amir Please have the kindness to give me that shoe.

Ruth
If they're not here to take their part
Choose another with all your heart.

Judith (*stops dancing*) I will give it to you: in return for a kiss.

Judith dangles the shoe.

Do you want the shoe or not?

Amir kisses her quickly, but she holds on to him.

Judith You kissed me and now you marry me.

Ruth Those are the rules.

They start singing again.

Judith/Ruth
She kissed him, she hugged him,
She sat upon his knee
She said, Dear Prince, won't you marry me?

Amir rushes out with the shoe.

Judith I'm not sure I want to marry him.

Ruth Then you should have let me kiss him, now you have to obey the rules.

SCENE TWO

The forest, dark and threatening. Ashgirl in torn rags and black spider threads. Tormented by what's on her.

Ashgirl Spiders in my hair. Where am I? Where was I?

A Man emerges from the trees.

Man Got you!

Ashgirl Let me go!

Man Later. Maybe.

Ashgirl What do you want?

Lust comes and joins them.

Lust (*to the Man*) All you know is that you want. Here is a chance.

Man Come with me.

Ashgirl Where?

Lust (*laughs*) Into the deepest and darkest part of the forest.

Man (*looking at Ashgirl*) You're so young!

Ashgirl I'm not afraid.

Man Please! Have pity.

Lust When have lust and pity ever mixed?

Ashgirl (*to the Man*) Who are you talking to?

Man The monster I can no longer fight!

Lust Here, everywhere, in any shape, in her shape.

Ashgirl Who are you?

Man (*laughs*) I can't remember.

Lust Late one night, a man worked hard in his study. He looked up and he saw me. He tried to read, he tried to cry.

Man She looks like –

Ashgirl (*to the Man*) Your laugh – not exactly the same.

Lust No one remains what they were when I pass through them.

Ashgirl and the Man stare at each other. The Man pushes Lust away.

Man (*to Lust*) Siren-voiced fiend. I won't let you drag me down – not to this.

The Man runs off, screaming. Lust pursues, laughing.

Lust He tried to pray, he tried to run.

Ashgirl remains still.

Ashgirl Father? Father . . . (*She calls.*) Father!

Sadness approaches. The other Monsters also begin to close in, but silently, watching Sadness at work.

He didn't recognise me.

Sadness You have no father.

Ashgirl He loved me, he protected me.

Sadness He found something better.

Ashgirl Where am I? Who am I?

Sadness Nowhere, no one . . . alone . . .

Ashgirl I was at the ball, I'm sure I was at the ball.

Sadness If you were at the ball, I was there too.

Ashgirl I danced.

Sadness I don't remember.

Ashgirl It was so beautiful. And so was I.

Sadness Look at yourself: ashes, covered in spider webs.

Ashgirl I wore silver.

Sadness Look around, Ashgirl, feel the world as it is.

Slothworm creeps up.

Slothworm Aren't you tired? Aren't your limbs feeling heavy and slow?

Ashgirl Please . . .

Sadness This is what you get from your sisters:

Angerbird You take up too much room, we don't want to see you, *shrink*!

Sadness Their mother:

Pridefly We had respect, you brought us down.

Ashgirl The Prince was at the ball, we ate together.

Gluttontoad You ate? Mounds of molten meats? Fluid rivulets of fetid fat revolving and dissolving in the oleaginous omasum of an omadhaun . . .

Sadness (*over*) You knew the world was like this, that's why you hid in the ashes. What arrogance made you want to come out?

Lust caresses Ashgirl.

Lust I wrapped myself around him . . . I threaded through the sinews of his sober heart.

Ashgirl struggles.

Ashgirl Help me!

A figure appears, wrapped in a dark cloak. Ashgirl screams.

Figure There you are at last.

Ashgirl No! No! No! Please –

Otter Ashie, what's the matter, it's me, Otto, I mean Otter. I've been looking for you, I've never been in this part of the forest – we must get to the river and then I'll know the way out –

Ashgirl There's no way out . . .

Otter Ashie, quick, I sense danger, and when I sense danger I have to run, it's instinct, I can't help it. Run with me.

Ashgirl I can't.

Otter I'm beginning to shake, that means I have to run, Ashie, take my paw.

Ashgirl Leave me here . . .

Otter Can't you feel it? I have to run, my heart is beating, my feet twitching ! Save yourself!

Otter runs off.

Ashgirl I can't move.

Slothworm There's safety in paralysis.

Gluttontoad Sweet and sticky the trickle of sugary syrup on your breath.

Owl hoots.

Ashgirl Owl?

Sadness There's no owl, it's in your mind, your mad mind.

Owl hoots.

Owl (*distant*) Ashie . . .

Ashgirl Where are you?

Owl Over here, in the moonlight, at the edge of the forest.

Sadness There's no edge, there's no moonlight, there's no way out of the forest. This is the world when screams go silent.

Ashgirl: frozen in terror, shaking.
  The two Mice scurry on.

Girlmouse Help! Ashie, help us. We're so frightened and we're lost and I'm not a dragon any more.

The children start crying and throw themselves on Ashgirl.

Boy She's cold.

Sadness Turned to stone. Leave her . . . run along.

Girlmouse Ashie, can you hear us? If you don't help us, we'll be lost for ever.

Sadness And if you don't run soon, this toad will eat you.

Girlmouse Toads don't eat mice and we're more frightened of owls. I can feel a heartbeat.

Sadness Not for long . . .

Girlmouse Ashie, we're your friends and you're our only hope.

Ashgirl makes a final effort to extricate herself.

Ashgirl Hope . . .

Sadness They're mice, Ashgirl . . . mice. Mice!

Girlmouse What's wrong with being a mouse?

Boymouse Mice are nice and have no vice.

Ashgirl laughs. The Mice take her hands. The Monsters vanish.

Owl At last, you're safe.

Otter Let me dry you with my fur.

Ashgirl Where were you all when I needed you?

Owl In the forest, dear girl, you need yourself.

SCENE THREE

The house. Ruth. Judith. Ashgirl.

Ruth We were surrounded.

Judith Admired.

Ruth We danced with the Prince.

Judith And he chose me.

Ashgirl He didn't!

Ruth Were you there?

Judith The Prince kissed me.

Ashgirl He couldn't have.

Judith Were you there?

Ruth She made the Prince kiss her.

Judith He wanted to kiss me.

Ashgirl He did not want to kiss you.

Judith Were you there?

Ashgirl Yes! No! I can imagine.

Judith Then you can imagine me kissing the Prince. He's going to marry me.

Ashgirl He isn't!

Judith You know him?

Ashgirl In my imagination.

Ruth He only wanted the shoe.

Ashgirl The shoe?

Judith There was this stupid-looking girl and she lost her shoe.

Ashgirl She was beautiful!

Ruth You were there?

Ashgirl The shoe –?

Judith Princes are shy, the shoe was an excuse.

Ashgirl It stayed as a shoe? It didn't change?

Ruth It was an ugly old shoe to begin with.

Ashgirl It was not!

Ruth Were you there?

Judith I'd have to cut off half my foot to get into that measly titchy witchy ugly shoe – it was what we call a preliminary – it began the kiss.

Ashgirl But the shoe stayed as it was?

Ruth The shoe's not part of the story. We're marrying the Prince – well – Judith is marrying him and I'm going to all the parties.

Ashgirl He'll never marry Judith.

Ruth You'll stop him?

Judith Dance with him?

Ruth Kiss him?

Ashgirl Why not! – in my imagination.

Ruth Then you can marry him – in your imagination.

Judith No! Not even in her imagination. I'm marrying him, no one else. Say: I wasn't there.

Ashgirl Leave me alone.

Ruth Say it: I wasn't there.

Ashgirl I can't do anything about my imagination.

Judith Then I'll have to open up your head and cut it out.

Ruth You had better say you were not there.

Judith In any shape, form, image or -ation.

Ruth Say it!

Ashgirl Maybe I wasn't . . .

SCENES FOUR AND FIVE

The palace and the house. Amir, Paul and Zehra in the palace. Ashgirl alone with the mirror in the other.

Zehra How do you know she was more than a spirit of the air?

Paul I made a list of all the girls who came and of their parents and of their wealth, and there is no one on this list by that name.

Amir She was there. She was human.

Zehra It's not easy to tell who is human, there are so many imitations.

Ashgirl in the hearth.

Ashgirl I wasn't there. It wasn't me.

Amir I looked at her, I knew I wanted to marry her.

Zehra You cannot marry a girl who vanishes into the night.

Ashgirl Where was I if I wasn't there?

Paul At the top of the list, I have put the five wealthiest and most beautiful girls for you, Amir. Portraits are being sent.

Zehra She must have been a serving girl with stolen clothes.

Paul What I like about the girls in this country is their hands are so soft, they are so wealthy they do nothing all day. Did you look at her hands?

Amir They were strong, that's what I liked.

Ashgirl And I'm hungry all the time. Hungry for him. Hungry.

Zehra I have to announce your choice or the whole country will be offended.

Paul They'll say you think no one is good enough for you.

Zehra You have to marry.

Amir I cannot love anyone else.

Zehra I said marry, I wouldn't pry into your heart.

Amir You're asking me to marry without love.

Zehra We all fall in love with a dream, we wake up one day anyway and find ourselves living with a stranger. Marriage is learning to live with that stranger.

Amir I touched her hands. I remember how they felt.

Ashgirl We talked, we laughed, we held hands. I remember.

Amir I have to find her.

Zehra How can you find a spark that's gone out?

Amir takes out the shoe.

Amir I have this.

Ashgirl And the shoe never changed. I was there.

Zehra studies the shoe.

Zehra Mirrors, gossamer threads finely webbed. There is beauty here, Amir, but what can you do with a shoe?

Amir I don't know . . . I don't know!

Zehra I have to advise you to be sensible. Falling in love with a shoe is not wise.

Paul I think Amir should obey his mother and marry one of the girls at the top of the list, that's what I would do.

Ashgirl The shoe didn't change, the other shoe is buried somewhere in the mud of the forest.

Paul Even if she existed, you'll never find her again.

Zehra And she won't be the one you remembered from a whirling evening.

Ashgirl What can I do? Nothing. Was I ever even there? I'm so tired . . . Time to bury the dreams . . .

Amir You've worn me down. Show me the list. Or choose yourself.

Ashgirl In the ashes.

Amir Leave me now: I have battles to plan . . .

Ashgirl and Amir both go still and listless.

Ashgirl Amir . . .

Amir Ashgirl . . .

Fairy of the Mirror Ashgirl . . .

Zehra Amir . . .

Fairy of the Mirror Ashgirl . . . don't waste time . . .

Zehra I can give you three days, no more, to find this girl and bring her to me. I will ask her questions that will make her reveal who she is.

Fairy of the Mirror The shoe didn't change, find the shoe.

Amir How am I going to find her?

Zehra That's your quest: you have a shoe.

Ashgirl In the forest! I can't go back.

Amir I can hardly ask every girl in this land to try on a shoe!

Ashgirl I'm afraid, please . . .

Fairy of the Mirror Look into yourself, find your courage.

Paul It is a very good way of meeting families, I'll come with you.

Amir I'll be laughed at.

Zehra Being laughed at is an excellent preparation for marriage.

Fairy You can't love without courage.

Ashgirl Life was so safe in the ashes.

Amir She distracts me from my plans . . .

Amir and Ashgirl stretch out their hands to each other.

Amir/Ashgirl When we touched . . .

Ashgirl I couldn't tell my fingers apart . . .

Amir My hand melted . . .

Ashgirl . . . from his.

Amir . . . into hers

The Fairy hands a silver cloak to Ashgirl.

Fairy of the Mirror Take this cloak, it will help you find your way.

Zehra wraps a coat around Amir.

Zehra This will keep you warm: beware the shadows of the forest.

SCENE SIX

The house. The sisters and their Mother. Ruth is working a piece of cardboard.
Greedmonkey explores the room.

Ruth It was even smaller.

Judith It couldn't have been smaller.

Ruth I'm an artist, I remember these things. (*She cuts.*)

Mother Put your foot on it.

Judith does so, they all stare.

Mother How did you get such big feet? I told you not to walk so much.

Ruth It's the big toe that doesn't fit.

Mother Yes. Only the big toe.

Pause.

Do you need it?

Greedmonkey becomes attentive.

Judith Need what, Mother?

Mother Your big toe. Is it of any use?

Judith It's my big toe.

Pause.

Mother Without it, the shoe would fit.

Pause. Greedmonkey whirls.

Palaces, clothes, jewels, wealth, power.

Ruth Not just you, either: your family. I could paint with gold and silver. I'd paint your portrait. Next to a big white cake.

Greedmonkey mimics.

Mother People would bow down to us as we passed. At grand feasts, we'd stand tall in our finery and all would try to catch a glimpse of us, beg for a kind word, cringe for one of our smiles.

Ruth If only you didn't have those toes.

Mother Without them, you'd be a princess!

Judith Yes, but I do have toes.

Mother At the moment.

Pause.

There's a country I know where young girls have all the bones of their feet broken to look beautiful. These are only big toes.

Judith I don't understand . . .

Ruth The shoe would fit.

Mother I've always thought toes ugly.

Judith I like them, they're mine.

Mother Especially big ones. They're just not dainty, are they?

Judith I don't even want to marry the Prince! (*to Ruth*) You marry him!

Ruth You kissed him.

Judith What are you going to do?

Mother There's a woman on the edge of the forest who knows how to add a little flesh here, take away a few bones there, all for the sake of beauty. We'll seek her advice.

Judith About what?

Mother It's all for your own good.

Judith I'm not going.

Ruth You have to! Girls don't disobey their mothers.

Mother I'll be there. Looking after you.

Judith I don't want to see an old woman who does things to the body!

Mother We'll only ask her advice.

Ruth Time to stop snivelling and act like a princess. Imagine all the things you'll have to play with in the palace.

Judith You won't let her hurt me?

Mother You won't mind anything when you feel gold run through your fingers.

Greedmonkey turns out, leading the three behind him.

Greedmonkey No human can resist a tempting picture: they look, they want. Gold for you, madam, sweets for you, my girl, what about a palace? Here's a picture of you wearing furs, silk. A slide-show of wants: Want – want – want more, and now, they follow me – Pied Piper of tempting images, playing the jaunty jingles of greed.

SCENE SEVEN

The forest. Monsters.

Angerbird A disturbance in the air. Cruelty, anger, hatreds rage through the world. Turbulence and confusion drive waves of humans hither-thither, inexorable fear in their dark minds. The humans are converging towards the forest tonight, we must seize our chance and be alert.

Slothworm Alert? I have to be alert?

Envysnake Alert. Subtle. So easy to pour the smooth poison of envy into those soft human veins. The heart seizes up, the mind splutters and spits and their spirit smothers in sourness. So: alert.

Pridefly Do you know how many famous alert flies have graced the pages of history? Poems, ballads, short stories have been written about us, even in French.

The animals, alert, try to hush the fly.
 Amir and Paul, weary and dejected.

Amir Three hundred and seventy-five feet. And when I looked up, faces convulsed in greed and giggles.

Amir sits – it happens to be on top of Slothworm.

Slothworm My motto has always been: all comes to the one who does nothing.

Envysnake (*to Paul*) You've tried three hundred and seventy-five shoes on three hundred and seventy-five feet with him and the girls never even looked at you.

Amir And not one of those girls made my heart beat faster.

Slothworm (*to Amir*) Listen: girls are a Big Effort. Not worth it.

Envysnake (*to Paul*) All your life, you've looked after him and now you're exhausting yourself running after his dream. But you're still on your own struggling to get rich.

Amir (*to Paul*) Shall we go home?

Pridefly (*to Amir*) You'll never find anyone to match you, Prince. This is a country of shopkeepers, that's one of my best sayings; you can quote me any time.

Paul (*to Amir*) If you wish.

Slothworm (*to Amir*) Much better to lie in soft cushions than trudge around the countryside.

Paul (*to Amir*) There are a few more houses on the other side of the forest.

Pridefly The wrong side of the forest.

Slothworm Why bother?

Envysnake Always helping him. Why?

Amir She was a dream . . .

Slothworm Best if she stays that way. You can dream about her and have a sleep at the same time. That's what I call romance.

Paul I believe, like your mother, she was a serving girl who tricked you.

Pridefly Mocked princes soon become tarnished objects of boredom.

Paul Princess Zehra will find you a suitable wife and you'll be content.

Amir That may be enough for you! I don't want to be content!

Paul (*angry*) Some of us would be grateful for that much. I don't have parents looking after me, worrying about my happiness, I don't have anything, but you can't stop complaining!

Amir Everything I have has been yours to share.

Paul/Envysnake I don't want to share! I want it all for myself!

Crashing through the trees, whimpering – the Mother appears with the two girls and Greedmonkey. Judith is hobbling and crying.

Mother We heard you were making your way to all the houses, but we thought it best to come and meet you: here is your wife, Prince Amir.

A moment.

Amir I do not recognise her.

Mother Men have no memories for faces. The shoe will fit.

Amir (*to Judith*) What did we talk about?

Mother How can a girl remember what a prince said to her?

Amir The girl I remember would remember.

Mother You proclaimed you would marry the girl whose foot fits the shoe. Do people in your country not keep their word?

Paul kneels down and puts Judith's foot in the shoe. She writhes in pain, but the shoe goes on.

Paul The shoe fits.

Mother The shoe fits.

Ruth The shoe fits.

Amir There is one other condition: the girl whose foot

fits the shoe must come back and answer three questions put to her by my mother.

Ruth An exam, we're good at exams! Can I come too?

Mother (*to Judith*) Go with the Prince.

Judith Now? On foot?

Mother Have you not provided a carriage for the Princess?

Amir She is not a princess yet and it is not far.

Paul She seems in pain.

Amir Perhaps the shoe does not fit?

Mother The shoe fits. Now please give her a pledge of your love.

Amir reluctantly offers a ring. Judith looks at it, dejected.

Mother Take her to the palace, Prince, and show her around her new home.

Ashgirl comes on, covered in mud. She sees Judith and the Prince. She reaches out, about to speak, but Sadness covers her mouth.
Amir, Paul and Judith go off hurriedly. Mother and Ruth leave in a different direction. The Monsters melt into the forest and watch.

SCENE EIGHT

Ashgirl He left with her. He forgot me.
I tried to call him when he passed by, mud and ashes came out of my mouth.

She holds the mud-covered shoe. Sadness stays very still, watching.

307

Ashgirl Fairy of the Mirror . . . you were never there . . .
Amir . . . Illusion.
It was all for nothing.

Lust Desire coiled around him . . . I held him fast . . .

Ashgirl Where do I go now? Mud and ashes . . .

Lust All strength worn away. Lost in the forest . . .

Ashgirl This endless forest . . .

Slothworm Endless . . .

Screams and sobbing in the distance. Ashgirl moves off, Sadness following on her heel.

SCENE NINE

The forest: the Monsters move forward, Angerbird prominent.
Darkness.
Amir and Paul drag Judith on. She is crying, hobbling, bleeding heavily. Angerbird hovers.

Amir Cheat. Liar. False.

Judith Your evil mother did this to me asking those stupid questions. I stamped my foot and this!

She shows her blood-soaked foot.

Amir You never felt love.

Judith What does love have to do with it? You're rich. I'm supposed to marry you!

Amir I despise you!

Judith You're not much to look at yourself.

Paul Why go to such extremes?

Judith My mother told me to.

Amir The cunning in your mother's eyes.

Judith She's better than yours, that witch waiting in the forest.

Amir I will not trade insults with you. Paul will take you home.

Judith Leave me here, both of you. I don't need you. (*to Paul*) That goes for you too, Footboy.

Envysnake Footboy!

Amir You make me despise women.

Judith How do you think I feel about men!

Paul leaves. Angerbird wraps Judith.

Angerbird She made you cut off your foot for an idiot. You never felt such pain. Your mother lured you, betrayed you, your sister laughed when the old woman sliced off your toe. What is there left for you now but hatred and revenge? Make someone else suffer as you have, that's the kind of anger I like, an anger that spreads like a forest fire through crackling trees. Rage, Judith, rage.

The Monsters surround Judith.

Judith I hate this world. I hate, I hate – I hate everyone. I hate everything.

SCENE TEN

Mother and Ruth come on. They see Judith.

Mother Judith!

Judith Don't ever talk to me again.

She lunges for her mother.
The Mother sees the blood.

Mother He found out!

Judith How could you do this!

Mother I wanted only what was best for you.

Judith Not this, never this! Look at me.

Mother I didn't make the world, Judith. What else could I do?

Judith Mother: I'm mutilated.

Mother It will be worse if we don't save the situation.

A pause. The Mother and Judith look at Ruth.

Ruth No! No! Please! No!

Judith Oh yes, yes, yes. Now you'll see what it feels like to help your family. Oh yes.

Mother We have to, Ruth, or we'll be disgraced, we'll be turned into beggars!

Ruth No!

Mother I never liked this harsh world, but we have to survive. There's no time to lose –

Ruth No! Help me, someone, please!

Judith Obey your mother!

Ruth tries to escape, but is caught by the Mother and Judith, who drag her off. Ashgirl comes on with Sadness at her heels. Screams in the distance. Ashgirl stands still.

Ashgirl Where are you?

Sadness Here.

Ashgirl Yes.

Sadness You're tired, aren't you?

Ashgirl Yes . . . the screams . . .

Sadness If you sleep you'll only hear my breathing.

Ashgirl So cold . . .

Sadness I'll wrap you in my arms.

Ashgirl Nowhere to go . . .

Sadness Lay your head on my shoulders.

Ashgirl Yes.

Sadness Lie down, it's so quiet here, no sounds, no memories . . .

Ashgirl Amir . . .

Sadness Who?

Ashgirl I don't know.

Sadness Turn your face towards the mud . . . down.

Ashgirl The Fairy's cloak . . .

Sadness Here's my cloak . . . I'll keep the world quiet, you'll never feel pain again . . .

Ashgirl The shoe . . .

Sadness There's such peace without memory, turn your head to the mud. Do you really need to breathe?

The Monsters approach. Sadness motions them to be quiet.

Shh. I think I have her.

Fairy's Voice Ashgirl . . .

Ashgirl What was that?

Sadness The wind in the trees. Rest now. Turn your head back down, down to the mud. You've had enough . . .

Ashgirl Yes . . .

Fairy's Voice If you fall asleep, you'll never wake up.

Sadness And so? Sadness in every breath. Ugliness. Sleep . . .

Monsters Sleep . . .

Fairy Find your courage, Ashgirl . . .

Sadness What's courage but a stupid rush into more knocks and pain? Who needs the horror of the world, Ashgirl? Sleep.

Monsters Sleep . . .

Fairy Look into yourself.

Sadness Remember the darkness that surrounds your life.

Fairy Look into your heart, Ashie, and remember your courage.

Sadness The cruelty of your sisters.

Fairy The animals who make you laugh.

Sadness Days and nights shivering in the ashes.

Fairy Dancing at the ball.

Sadness Always alone, shunned.

Fairy The warmth of shared words . . .

Sadness You caused suffering.

Fairy Find your hope . . .

Sadness Where did hope lead?

Ashgirl When we danced: ashes . . . no, when we danced, light . . . I was that girl, happy, ashes . . . no, I was hungry, happy, and I could give: suffering, no, the pleasure of my company, I looked at myself. I saw: spiderwebs, no, the glitter of possibility, what I could be, ashes . . . no, I was . . . nothing . . . no, I see: mud, no, I see light coming through the trees, illusion, don't look, no, beauty in the world . . .

Fairy In myself.

Sadness Too late, let me sleep.

Ashgirl Too late.

Sadness Too much.

Ashgirl Too sad.

Sadness Nothing.

Fairy One good memory. Maybe two.

Sadness No reaction. I have her.

Ashgirl I can remember . . .

Fairy When you travelled through the woods with your father . . .

Ashgirl I searched for words to describe the first light.

Fairy Fragile, filigreed . . .

Ashgirl I could never catch the words, but I felt . . .

Fairy/Ashgirl Joy . . . strength . . .

Dawn has filtered into the forest, rain washes the muddied cloak, Ashgirl rises covered in the cloak.

Ashgirl I know who I am and I will be what I am.

Sadness I've lost her!

Ashgirl I'm not afraid of the shadows of this forest, nor of myself, nor of the future.

Fairy I've been so frightened for you.

Ashgirl I know there is darkness, I've seen the monsters of the forest, but I'm not afraid.

Fairy I couldn't come to you until you came to yourself.

Ashgirl I will never be afraid . . .

Amir comes on. Stares at Ashgirl –

. . . of asking you to remember . . .

Amir I heard your voice . . . I sensed your presence.

Ashgirl I came looking . . .

Amir I searched the muddy pools, I held on to my memory . . .

Ashgirl For you . . .

Amir Of . . .

Ashgirl I knew despair.

Amir I lost hope. It is you?

Ashgirl Your hands . . .

They hold their hands. The Mother comes on with Ruth.

Mother Prince! Here is your bride. (*She laughs.*) My girls are like twins, they always play these tricks. It was never Judith, it's this one. The shoe fits Ruth!

Prince I have found the one I love.

The Mother sees Ashgirl.

Mother What are you doing here? Go back home at once! (*She laughs wildly.*) She's the embarrassment of the family, we take pity on her and feed her, she's full of tricks, her father's a criminal who ran away into the forest – Go. Disappear! shamed child of a shamed father. She won't deny her father's shame!

A moment. The Man emerges from the forest.

Man I'll deny it. I'll deny every word you've uttered.

Ashgirl Father . . .

Man I have been caught in the claws of a most terrible monster. I live in the forest and fight daily. I cannot free myself yet, but there are no crimes . . . I have come close – but there are no crimes.

(*to Amir*) This child is a brave child, Prince. I don't know her heart now, but I knew it well when she was little.

Ruth (*to her Mother*) You cut off my heel for nothing! It's infected! I'll never walk again!

Ruth cries out in agony. Judith limps forward.

The Man (*to the Mother*) How could you do this to your daughters?

Mother (*to the Man*) I did what I had to. Where were you when we needed you?

Fairy (*to the Mother*) These are your own daughters: where was your love and your compassion?

Mother Love? Compassion? Whoever had love and compassion for me? Keep up appearances, that's what I was taught, crave power, grasp riches, I was told. Love and compassion rotted underneath. I only ever did what was done to me.

The Mother lifts her skirts to reveal her own stumps. The father bows his head. The Fairy turns to Ashgirl.

Fairy Will you have the courage to change this circle of cruel convention?

Amir We will.

Ashgirl We will change everything.

Paul appears, stops them.

Paul Princess Zehra has sent me to tell you to do nothing until she has spoken.

Amir I know my own heart.

Paul holds a sword. The Monsters watch with interest.

Paul Amir: your mother has given me the power to make you do as I say. You will wait.

SCENE ELEVEN

Change of light. Zehra appears, regal, in full dress, very formal. She stands tall and turns to Ashgirl. The Mice come on and watch intently.

Amir Mother, this is my bride –

Zehra Not yet. (*to Ashgirl*) You will answer my questions.

Amir I know her.

Zehra But I do not.

Judith She'll never be able to answer the questions!

Mother The shoe still fits Ruth.

Amir Mother, I will not allow your questions.

Zehra You promised.

Paul You do not break promises, Amir.

Ashgirl Fairy of the Mirror, don't let me lose everything now.

Fairy Remember yourself and you will answer the questions.

Mice Good luck, Ashie.

Zehra (*to Ashgirl*) Come here. Closer.
  Why do you love my son?

  Ashgirl doesn't answer. A moment.

Amir Surely you can answer that.

  Ashgirl stays silent.

Zehra Here is my second question:
  Will you love my son for the rest of your life?

Amir That's easy.

  Ashgirl stays silent.

Ashie, please: say yes!

  Silence.

Zehra My third question is:
  Will you always be able to wear the silver shoes you wore at the ball?

  Silence.

Mother Ruth could answer all those questions.

Amir Please answer my mother!

  Ashgirl stays silent. A pause. Judith and Ruth smirk.

Zehra Come here, child. I give you my son.

Amir I don't understand.

Zehra How can you say why you love someone? A thousand reasons crisscross the heart, but at the centre – no reason at all, only the mystery of that person. If you say you love someone because they are rich or handsome or powerful, you love only a fraction. She knew this.

Will she love you for the rest of her life? It is you, Amir, who must make her love you as she will make you love her. Neglect her, treat her badly, you will kill her love. Never sit back lazily waiting for love to take care of itself, tend it, cherish it.

As for the shoes: perhaps they will fit, perhaps not. She will change. She will not want you to ask her to wear shoes that were beautiful once but no longer feel like hers. Never ever ask her to cut off her foot to fit a shoe from the past.

The questions could not be answered. Your future wife knew this.

Paul (*to Ashgirl*) I will be your brother.

Fairy My work is almost done. (*to the Mother*) I have to change you into something horrid.

Mother I followed the rules. They were the wrong rules, but I had no way of knowing that. Do what you want with me, I no longer care.

Fairy I'll change you into an ash tree under which nothing grows. You'll stay in the forest.

Paul Which I will cut down. One day, you'll be a piece of furniture.

The Mother shrugs.

Fairy (*to Ruth and Judith*) As for you, when someone, even your mother, asks you to do something stupid and harmful, have the courage to say no. It is difficult, I know, and I won't be harsh. Choose your own punishments.

Ruth I want to live alone and never see anyone again.

Fairy I'll turn you into a hermit who lives in a cave.

318

Ruth I'll paint the carcasses of dead animals.

Judith I want to stay in the forest and study rocks and leaves and map the inside of the earth, it's all I ever wanted to do.

Fairy And now to you, Ashgirl: you too will change, move, search, but first you must live this part of your story and conclude it. Come here, Ashgirl, who sought and found her heart and her courage.

The Father (*to Ashgirl*) I did not want to remember my name in the forest. And so I had forgotten yours too . . . but now I can give it back to you: your mother and I named you Sophia – because it is an ancient word for wisdom.

Lust comes on.

Lust I found him in his study –

The Father turns to go.

Ashgirl Father, I need you

Paul A father's place is here.

The Father hesitates, stays.
Zehra now wraps a beautiful cloth around Ashgirl and Amir. The Fairy helps. The Monsters begin to move and exit.

Angerbird What is it about these humans that makes them so strong?

Envysnake What do they have we can't break?

Slothworm Energy?

Lust Pity.

Pridefly Friendship swats the Prideflies every time.

319

Greedmonkey I'm leading them in my dance and suddenly, they stand still, reach out their hands and break the spell with one dazzling gesture of generosity.

Envysnake It makes my venom powerless, it is called hope.

Sadness hovers over Zehra for a moment.

Zehra (*to Sadness*) I know you, but not now . . . (*to Amir and Ashgirl*) We have stilled the forest.
It is your time now . . .

Amir and Ashgirl, wrapped in each other.

Ashgirl I was always looking for –

Amir I searched, I kept searching –

Fairy Seize now the glitter of these moments –

Ashgirl It was a ray of memory –

Amir I remembered your hand –

Fairy The never forgotten sparkle –

Ashgirl Even when I believed I'd lost you.

Amir It was never a dream, I knew you were there –

Fairy The rare flash –

Ashgirl I searched, and I found –

Amir I knew I could find –

Ashgirl You –

Amir You –

Fairy Of happiness.

DIANEIRA

Dianeira was originally broadcast on BBC Radio 3 on 28 November 1999. The cast, in order of appearance, was as follows:

Irene Olympia Dukakis
Dianeira Harriet Walter
First Chorus Jenny Quayle
Second Chorus Emily Bruni
Third Chorus Joy Richardson
Nurse Sandra Voe
Hyllos Joseph Fiennes
Heracles Alan Howard
Messenger Jonathan Tafler
Lychas David Bradley
Nessos Simon Callow

Characters

Timberlake Wertenbaker
(Introduction)

Irene
Dianeira
Chorus
Nurse
Hyllos
Heracles
Messenger
Lychas
Nessos

INTRODUCTION

Timberlake Some years ago, when I was in Athens, I heard there was a village up north where you could still find storytellers in the Kafeneions. I asked my friends to take me there and we drove up mountain roads to the village. We arrived at dusk and went to the market place, but we discovered that most of the storytellers were already well into their tales. It felt like arriving late for a movie and we were about to leave, when a café owner pointed to a woman slumped asleep over a table. We were told her name was Irene and no one had dared to wake her up, but we were strangers and could take that liberty. We shook her awake, put some bills on the plate in front of her and ordered her a coffee. She asked us to add a glass of brandy. She was grey-haired, with a slight moustache, dressed in a floppy black and white dress with a dark jacket. She could have been the widow of the local solicitor but her eyes were watery and veiled. Of course, she was blind, most story tellers are. She asked us what kind of story we wanted. I wanted one about love, but my friends said they'd heard lots of those, they wanted adventure. We settled on anger. This is what we heard.

KAFENEION

Irene I will tell you a story of anger. It took place a long time ago, any time, in Trachis, which is over there, on the other side of the mountains. But Trachis is more a state of mind than a place. You know this, you come from Athens, the seat of logic. Trachis is a plain of disappointment. Disappointment – and that's where anger puts down roots and finds its nourishment.

The three heroes of this story are Dianeira, Heracles and Hyllos. Now, even though you're students you probably won't have heard of Dianeira and that's part of her story. Heracles you'll know. Hercules, Heracles, the great man, always labouring, a model of manhood, but an unloved one. Why? I'm not sure. And their oldest son Hyllos. A young man who at the beginning of this story is not marked or mapped yet – that is to come.

Where does anger lie? Somewhere in that plain between the hopes of a life and what actually happens to it, a plain clouded over by fear and foreboding. That neutral plain of Trachis, that's where it found its breeding ground for this story. Listen to Dianeira. It is dark, she stands on a terrace looking at the night. It is time to go inside to sleep and she is surrounded by some of the women of Trachis who keep her company, a chorus, whose job is mostly to listen and occasionally to echo.

TRACHIS

Dianeira There's this saying that you cannot judge a person's life as happy or wretched until that person is dead. That's what they say, but I don't need a trip to the underworld where they'd hand me a map of my memories to understand that I was born to be unhappy. Already, as a young virgin in my father's house, it started going badly. All the other girls of Etolia were looking forward to their marriages. But who had come to my door as a suitor? I'll tell you: a river. Yes, Akilos, the river god. Even he didn't have the nerve to come to a house as running water so sometimes he presented himself as a bull, pawing, snorting; sometimes as a snake, all shivering skin, slithering coils, darting tongue; and sometimes he took on the naked body of a man, that's bad enough, but with the head of an ox, his beard spluttering jets of water. Who wants to marry a spitting fountain? I prayed to the gods to let me die rather than share a bed with *that*, but you never know if the gods hear you.

So when, at last, at long last, he came, him, he seemed like a saviour, a maiden's true hero. Heracles. He came, tall, a protrusion of muscles –

First Chorus Rippling, glistening . . .

Dianeira He came –

Second Chorus And he had his bow and arrows.

Dianeira And fought the river god. Don't ask me to describe the fight. I was crouched down on the other side of the river, with my head bowed over my knees, trembling, and cursing the beauty of my face which was bringing me nothing but suffering, more suffering. Well, as luck would have it, Zeus, the god of battles, made the outcome a good one.

Third Chorus It could have been the goddess of love, it usually is: Aphrodite.

Dianeira Heracles won, and I became the wife of the hero.

Since our marriage, my life has been one long bleak torment. Wave upon wave of fear breaks over me, that's all I ever feel, fear.

Terrors of the night.

Night, consummate artist of fear, shapes and reshapes it, colours it different shades of grim and dark. Terror turns so malleable in the night. Yes, we have children, but Heracles is like an absent landlord who visits his holdings twice a year, once to sow and once to reap. And then he goes back to work, always for someone else's benefit. Work, labour, all that strength always at the service of somebody far away. He had it predicted to him that these labours of his would eventually come to an end, but now I am more afraid than ever. Here I am, in Trachis, a stranger in the house of a stranger, waiting. But nobody seems to know where he is, this hero of mine, my husband Heracles. He's been gone for fifteen months. Ten I'm used to. Fifteen is excessive, even for him.

There are so many ways to be afraid. There's the fear that stalks you through troubled sleep, but there's a morning fear, too. Sharp as the first sliver of the sun on morning frost. And so I am afraid to go to bed and even more afraid that I will have to wake up.

Irene In that long ago time, people did not have character as we know it today, childhood was no more than the empty plain between birth and marriage and, once married, a woman always had a nurse to advise her. Obvious advice and often disastrous as obvious advice must be. The nurse – an antique version of the horoscope: 'Convince someone influential that your hidden depths could be of benefit. Stop short of flirting with danger, however.' Here is the nurse, come to wake the mournful Dianeira. She is old, bent down by humility, but the morning is new and she feels it is time to advise.

Nurse My lady Dianeira, you are always complaining about your husband's absence. And yet, you have children and you haven't sent one of them to find out where he is. Surely Hyllos, your eldest, wants to know what his father is up to. Send him to find Heracles, that is, if you don't object to the advice of a humble slave.

Irene In the pure air of that long ago time, in the stillness of the early morning and in the golden light of the sun on the rise, comes Hyllos, himself with that first golden beauty of the young male, untouched by trouble or by doubt. He is a son, a promise, hope. He carries this lightly, insouciant, open.

Dianeira Hyllos, my child. Come close to me.

Hyllos Mother.

Dianeira Closer.

Hyllos Yes, Mother.

Dianeira You've grown.

Hyllos Since yesterday?

Dianeira It happens.

Hyllos But only you see it.

Dianeira Stay with me a little. I hardly see you.

Hyllos I'm always here . . .

Dianeira Almost a man . . . No, already . . . so soon . . . Hyllos –

Hyllos What is it, mother?

Dianeira My child . . .

Hyllos What is it? I can see shadows move across your eyes. I know those shadows. Let me wave them away.
 There . . .
 You taught me to love the mornings.

Dianeira How?

Hyllos I could always find you – in the mornings.

Dianeira Hyllos, I want to ask . . .

Hyllos Do I not always tell you everything you want to know?

Dianeira Hyllos, have you never asked yourself where you father might be?

Hyllos My father. Isn't he always away on some heroic mission?

Dianeira Yes, but don't you wonder where he is?

Hyllos Does it matter? When he's triumphed, he'll come back.

Dianeira He's been away longer than usual.

Hyllos It's always long.

Dianeira That's the way with heroes.

Hyllos I keep hearing about him.

Dianeira It's hard not to hear about Heracles, but where is he now?

Hyllos I heard he was in the service of some woman in Lydia.

Dianeira In service to a woman! Heracles? Who told you that?

Hyllos But that's finished and now he's about to go on a campaign against Euboea, that's what I've heard anyway.

Dianeira Euboea . . . there were predictions . . . Euboea. He told me . . .

*

Heracles Dianeira, I went to consult the sacred oak of my father, the great God Zeus. I felt him come to me in that shady grove and I heard him say to me that in Euboea, my fate would fork. Either I would find rest at last, retire from these great labours or else, it's in Euboea, Dianeira, that I would meet my end.

Dianeira Heracles . . .

Heracles I have triumphed over so many enemies, and I
am strong: look at me. The oak leaves through which my
father spoke were whispering so softly I could only just
make out the words. Rest is what they said, what I heard,
rest. I have worked so hard, Dianeira, I would welcome
rest at last. I am sure that's what they said. Wait for me.
If I am not back by the fifteenth month, then . . .

Dianeira Heracles –

Heracles Wait for me.

*

Dianeira Then gone again . . .
    I am afraid, Hyllos.

Hyllos You always are, mother. He can look after
himself.

Dianeira The distant beat of foreboding . . . like the
crack of a branch, the cry of a migrating bird . . .
    Hyllos, you must go and find him. Go today. Bring
him back safely. We're late, but maybe not too late.
    Fear closes in.
    Quickly. Go.

Hyllos I will find him, Mother, have no fear.

Irene Hyllos will go out of the house, out of the village,
to find his father in a country not so big you can't walk
it eventually. And now, for the first time, the shadow
of destiny falls over him too, the son, as he seeks and
comes closer to his father. His father's shadow begins to
cover him, merges with his own shadow. Hyllos walks
eastward, towards Euboea.

Hyllos I'll meet someone eventually who has some news.

A shepherd, a soldier. And then I'll find him. It's not as
if I know him that well, this heroic father of mine. He
comes home weary from his labours, dives into my
mother's bed, ruffles my hair, says little, says nothing.
Now doesn't even ruffle my hair, looks at me with
surprise as I grow almost as tall as him.

Heracles You've grown, you keep growing.

Hyllos Do I detect distaste at my height? Then he goes
away again. My mother cries. Then weeks of sadness
and silence. And always his unspoken name hovers over
us. Well, someone will tell me where he is because
everybody in Greece is always talking about the great
man, my father Heracles.

Irene Dianeira does not have the relief of movement and
search. She has to stay still and wait, all movement in the
imagination. Imagination too is a breeding ground for
anger, but for the moment she and her woman friends
are content to muse about darkness, life and geography
and borrow from our poet Sophocles his sketches of the
night.

First Chorus Here comes the night, draping herself in
her sequined cloak of stars.

Second Chorus Shimmering.

Third Chorus See rather the night as a womb, heaving,
pulled apart, rent asunder, she pushes forth in terrible
pain, the sun.

First Chorus Later, enfolds him again, caressing him, she
has already forgotten the pains to come, the loving mother,
the tender night.

Third Chorus Again and again, recurrent birth pangs
and then forgiveness as she closes him into herself.

Second Chorus But only the sun can penetrate the

crannies of the earth, the hollows of the oceans, and tell us where Heracles might be.

First Chorus They say Heracles can hold back the two continents as they move towards each other, about to crash and splinter.

Second Chorus He was last seen battling the waves on the edges of the earth.

Third Chorus I heard he was storming the battlements of a rich city.

Second Chorus I call on the sun to light up the continents, search him out, and tell me where the child of Alcmene and of the lightning god Zeus is to be found.

First Chorus You tremble, Dianeira, like a bird who's lost its nest and fears finding it even more, in case it is revealed to be empty. Too many labours, you say, worse than the sea, they come one after the other, wave upon wave of works, yes, Dianeira, too many adventures, but hold on to hope, that sturdy crag face of our destiny, and then remember that in a human life nothing ever stands still.

Second Chorus Not the stars
    not misery
    not wealth
    they come, they are taken away
    someone rejoices
    yes, but someone else then cries out in pain.

Third Chorus And so, hold tight to your hopes.
    Zeus is not without care for his children.

Dianeira You mouth the banality of hope, but you understand nothing. You don't know what it is like to be me, you're too young. Youth basks in its ease and thinks there is no such thing as time, but wait until you get

335

married. Pain after pain after pain, husband, children, you'll never sleep in peace again, believe me, not for the rest of your life. I'm already the widow of his labours, I've tasted that loneliness, I don't want to swallow widowhood whole. And you see, usually when men go away, they tell you not to worry, but this time –

*

Heracles In Euboea, Dianeira, in Euboea . . . ease, at last, peace, or, well, maybe death. And yet, see. I am like a god in my strength, but I am a man too and my father Zeus wants me to know fear, and to know what it is to triumph over fear – like a man, a godly man. Wait for me. If after fifteen months I haven't returned, then . . . but until then, wait patiently, without fear.

*

Dianeira I have waited. Fifteen months. You tell me to hold on to hope.

Irene A messenger is a strange being. He has no name, he is the messenger. He comes running, always breathless, and brings news. Sometimes good, sometimes bad, but most often seemingly good but really bad. Pass the parcel and unwrap the worm. In those days, there was always a messenger or two, who came running hot off the press and dropped a bombshell. This one's no exception. He's running across the plain, through a narrow street, up to the house, onto the terrace, here he is.

Messenger I wanted to be the first person to bring you the good news, my lady, your husband is alive and well, and will soon be home.

Irene Dianeira knows better than to trust the first

appearance of words. She checks.

Dianeira What are you saying, how do you know this, where have you heard it?

Messenger The herald of your own house, Lychas, is making his way here to tell you, but he is surrounded by so many people he has to keep stopping to trumpet the good news and answer questions. So I decided to beat him to it.

Dianeira He's coming back . . . at last . . . he's safe . . . throw off this damp cloak of foreboding Dianeira, lift your face to the light
    Here comes Lychas himself to tell me more.

Irene Lychas has a name and so he is more than a messenger. Who is he? A house herald, that is a messenger attached to a particular house, who brings messages back and forth, a kind of postman. Unfortunately, he has ideas of his own, a tragic complication. How he missed Hyllos, we don't know. One took the lower route the other the higher one. Lychas is not breathless because he's made a more leisurely way to the house, talking to everyone as he came. He is covered with dust from the road but dignified, as a house herald must be.

Lychas I bring you welcome news, lady Dianeira, your husband is completing his final rites of thanks to the gods and will be home soon.

Dianeira What kept him away for so long?

Lychas He had to serve the woman called Omphale, himself dressed as a woman.

Dianeira Dressed as a woman . . . humiliating.

Lychas Yes, and that's why he took a few extra months to sack the city of the King Eurytos.

Dianeira That's in another part of the country, I don't understand.

Lychas You see, Heracles blamed Eurytos for his enslavement to a woman. He was a guest at the house of Eurytos and the king started to make fun of him, mocking his bows and arrows, saying he couldn't shoot straight, he was no hero at all, and eventually Eurytos threw him out of his house.

Irene Now I must tell you this is what you call a likely story. The rules of hospitality were so stringent in those days, even the most debauched and insane tyrant would think twice before throwing any guest out of his house, but listen and listen to a slight tremor in the tale Lychas tells.

Lychas Heracles was furious. One day he spotted one of the sons of Eurytos standing on a high cliff looking for some runaway horses. He sneaked up behind him and pushed him over the cliff. Now, Heracles had killed this man by stealth and treachery, not in open combat. Zeus became angry with the unheroic behaviour of his son and punished Heracles by making him dress as woman and become the servant of Omphale. Heracles always blamed Eurytos for making him behave badly, and as soon as he was freed from his service to Omphale he sacked the city of Eurytos, killed the King, collected the bounty and enslaved the women. He sends you this small group here, they have been following me, they are coming now, look at them. It's too bad, isn't it? Their houses have turned to ashes, their husbands to bones, and they start a life of misery, drudgery, as slaves without names. That's how it goes, my lady, but your husband is safe, and comes home to you in triumph and you must rejoice.

Dianeira Rejoice . . . your husband comes back to you . . . And yet, look at these woman making their

338

way slowly up the hill coming to stand before me now, humble and silent, who are they? They were wealthy, some of them, inhabitants of a strong and safe city, and then one day, war, ravage, rape and servitude. They had names, now nameless, refugees. Look at this one, so young, a terrible grief seems to course through her veins and make her shiver, but on her face, no expression, not a flicker, and see how beautiful that face is . . .

(*to Iole*) Tell me who you are, child, I can't help feeling you must once have had a name you bore with pride, I can see it even now, in your stillness. Don't be afraid of me. What is your name? Tell me.

Lychas, why doesn't she answer? Tell me who she is.

Lychas I don't know. She sobs sometimes but she never speaks, not a word. Perhaps we ought to respect the pride of grief and not press for answers.

Dianeira I will not add to the suffering of these wretched women.

They cast the shadows of the future. How easily it happens. Especially to women. One day, daughters of kings, wives of heroes, and the next sex or kitchen slaves. Ripped open, beaten. Fortune is unstable and the gods manic-depressive. Grim demons lurk around the corners. I am afraid . . . And yet he is on his way back, my hero, I am safe, am I not? Rejoice, and be kind, be kind.

Lychas, take these women into the house and let them be well treated.

Lychas I would have expected nothing else from a lady so gracious.

Irene You've no doubt detected that Lychas is covering something up. And so he rakes the soil and prepares it for the seeds of anger. What is worse than to feel you've been lied to? Who doesn't revile the man who goes on television and appeals for the discovery of the child he has himself killed? We feel such fury when our politicians deny all wrongdoing the day before their crimes are revealed. It never does good to cover up, but at the moment Dianeira is taken in and looks at these women with pity, and also with the fear of contagion, should this evil destiny be catching. And so she acts with compassion, but the messenger, the nameless messenger, has been listening to all this in silence and now he is angry. Why? Perhaps a mixture – the one who has the truth can't help feeling angry when he listens to blatant lies and also because his own importance as a messenger has been overshadowed by Lychas. He feels unappreciated, and in that terrain anger rises quickly.

Messenger Lady Dianeira, in all that Lychas has said to you the only true statement is that Heracles is alive and coming home.

Dianeira What do you mean?

Messenger Heracles didn't sack the city of Eurytos to revenge his dignity but to satisfy his lust. He fell in love with Iole. He wanted her. Her father, this Eurytos, would have none of this and now the city lies in ruins and Iole has been brought to your house as Heracles' new wife.

Dianeira Who told you this?

Messenger Lychas himself has been saying it to all and sundry. It's only here he's kept it hidden, thinking you would hear nothing within the walls of your house. And so it is that you are the last to know what concerns you most.

Dianeira Call Lychas here.

Messenger If he denies any of this, he will be lying.

Irene In that great story by Sophocles, *Oedipus*, two messengers argue about the facts of Oedipus' birth. One wants to reveal all, the other to cover it up. Both men

want the best, but their attitude to truth diverges. The
one who wants to cover the facts up believes that truth
is inevitably tragic and it would be better to live without
such pain. He is proved right, although we might say
that it is our search for the truth that makes us human.
However, this is not the subject of our story except for
one thing: hearing of the truth late is the worst. When
a comfortable deception is brutally cut by the truth, it
leaves a wound where rage must breed.

Dianeira And now what must I do? Here comes Lychas.
Confront him. Calmly, show nothing. She showed nothing,
walking into my house wrapped in my husband's lust.

Lychas The women are safe in your house, I will go to
Heracles and tell him of your kindness, what message
from you should I add?

Dianeira You're in a hurry to leave and yet you took
your time in coming here, we have more to say to each
other.

Lychas I'm at your disposal.

Dianeira Will you entrust me with the truth?

Lychas Yes, at least the truth of what I know.

Dianeira Who is the young woman you brought here?

Lychas She's from Eurytos. But if you're asking whose
daughter, I have no way of knowing.

Messenger Lychas, that girl you say you know nothing
about, didn't you refer to her as Iole, the daughter of
King Eurytos?

Lychas When did I say that? Find a witness who'll agree
I said it.

Messenger You shouted it all over the market place,
every Trachinian has heard as much. I was there.

341

Lychas I was only reporting hearsay. Rumour. That's not the same as facts.

Messenger But you said you were leading Iole to the house of Dianeira to be Heracles' new wife.

Lychas By God, who is this man?

Messenger Heracles was forced to dress as a woman to serve Omphale but that was just one of his labours, he took it in his stride. It was never shame that drove him to destroy the city of Eurytos, Heracles never has time for shame, it was desire. Lust. Love. The goddess. Aphrodite.

Lychas I can't keep talking to this idiot. I must go.

Dianeira But it is not an idiot woman you are dealing with, Lychas and I beg you by the gods, I beseech you to tell me the truth. I know that human beings are by nature changeable, inconstant even. I know too that love rules even the gods with its caprices. And so, who would I be to complain or to resist this power? I cannot blame my husband if he is the victim of desire nor can I be angry with this woman who does not wish me ill, I am certain. But you – you –
　If you're lying because Heracles ordered you to, you are unwise. On the other hand, if it's your own idea and you're doing it to spare me, you are making a mistake. I would rather know the truth. I'll find you out in the end, Lychas, because liars are always found out. Are you afraid? What can be bad about truth?
　It isn't as if Heracles hasn't had women before on his travels. Have you ever heard me complaining? And I won't be harsh to this girl, no matter how deeply she's sunk into her own passion for him. I only feel pity, because her beauty has destroyed her life and that's something I know about. Lives must bend to the sway

of the wind but truth is hard to flatten. Tell lies to whom
you please, but not to me.

Messenger See how reasonable she is, how superior,
human too, ready to forgive the weaknesses of men, and
you want to belittle her with your lies.

Dianeira The truth, Lychas.

Lychas The messenger speaks true: Heracles was seized
by a dreadful longing for this girl. And so he destroyed
her city and took her. He didn't ask me to hide anything
from you, I alone wanted to spare you such pain. My
mistake, but now that you know everything, I beg you
for his sake and for yours to be kind to this girl. The
strength of Heracles always bent everything before him,
but here he was laid low by his passion for this girl.

Dianeira Women of Trachis, let us go in now, and you,
Lychas, fear nothing. We'll be sensible and we'll be wise –
I won't try to fight single handed against the gods on this
matter. But you cannot go back to Heracles without one
gift when he sent you here with such an abundance, such
a crowd of people. Wait here.

First Chorus Zeus, Poseidon and Hades divide the world
between them, but one flick of her rosyplump finger and
those great gods leave the heavens, the air and the underworld and run to her, tripping foolishly over their lust.
    Megagoddess, the powerful Aphrodite.

Dianeira So. That's it. And I opened my door to the girl
like some poor benighted sailor who takes on a seemingly
light cargo, but it's the instrument of his own shipwreck
he's lugging on board. Because she must be my end.
    What will happen to the two us? Under the same roof,
ha, under the same blanket, waiting for him to take one
of us in his arms. No need to ask which. And this is my

reward for the long years of looking after him, his house, things, children.

It isn't the first time, but then he was discreet, the odd woman on his travels, but now he expects me to share his marriage, or worse. What am I supposed to do? Watch complacently as her youth blooms triumphant and I wilt to nothingness, unwanted, shrinking into invisibility. She'll blossom, take up more and more room, and I'll be squeezed into a corner, a thin and wrinkling shadow. His eye will always turn to her, moth to light, bee to flower, desire to beauty, and all I'll see of him is an evading back of the head, a quickly departing heel. And then they say it's unbecoming of a woman to be angry in such circumstances, it's so common after all, I should behave with dignity, because I'm getting old and what can I expect, bees will be bees.

First Chorus Let me part the curtain, dust down history. Remember the beautiful sad virgin, the girl Dianeira, let her come on to the empty stage of memory, crouch down. Now look, who comes on?

Second Chorus The River Akilos takes on the shape of a bull for the fight. Now comes Heracles, marching from Thebes, carrying his club, his bow and his arrows. You recognise him by muscle and height. Both after this girl, who will bed her. One has to die.

Third Chorus And now she is here, invisible, intent, the goddess of desire, Aphrodite, umpire wand in hand. She will decide. She hardly notices the girl. The girl's beauty holds no interest for the goddess, it is the men's desire she thrills to. She watches coolly as they fight.

Dianeira Look at Iole, there she stands, aloof, apart, radiates loveliness, her loss laced with pride. She will seduce him with her indifference and he'll get drunk on his guilt. And where will I be?

Second Chorus The fight: dust and groans mingle and rise from the ground. Heads butt, fists beat on bone and air, bows and hands tangle with horns as legs climb onto a beast's back and hooves clamber up a human trunk.

First Chorus I, the chorus, who was there, who am always there, can't describe it as well as I might because of the confusion of cracking foreheads and the pained groans that ooze out of the tangled mass of flesh.

Dianeira Desire. I hated being the cause of it but I fear even more not causing it. His eyes will slide over me as he searches her out through the house. What am I do? Kill her now, here, but he'll know and he'll despise me, everyone will cast me off as vile. He'll cast me off anyway. How come he gets to kill anyone who stands in his way? What other labour have I ever had but to keep his desire? Oh you gods, why have you done this? Do you expect me to sit here meekly and watch my own disappearance? Does he?

First Chorus And where was the beauty in this whirlwind of blood, groans? As far away as she could. She sits on a mound, wrapped in her loveliness, a shimmer of innocence.

She keeps her eyes shut tight, not wishing to see the brutal horror they say she causes. She sits and waits for the tap tap on her shoulder of a husband.

Second Chorus She saw nothing, but I, the chorus, the spectator of history, saw it all and I can tell you what happened, even though she, subject of this tale, cannot. She can only wait, anxious, pitiable.

Dianeira Desire. No good praying to Aphrodite. She was never a friend.

Third Chorus She waits, her face distorted by fear.

345

Dianeira Desire. Who knows about desire? What am I trying to remember? The river god, the bull, no, no, someone else, the half-horse, half-man, that monster of desire, Nessos . . . I'd forgotten, made myself forget . . . Nessos . . .

Second Chorus Suddenly, a wail, then silence. She feels a hand –

Heracles Come, Dianeira, come with me.

Third Chorus – and she is quickly –

Second Chorus – brutally –

Third Chorus – led to marriage.

First Chorus Like a calf to the slaughter.

Second Chorus Blood.

Dianeira Nessos . . .

Third Chorus Yes, now she is a woman and now she is alone.

Dianeira Only a few days after my marriage. We were crossing the river. The current was strong and the river too deep. Heracles was encumbered with all the paraphernalia of the great hero.

THE RIVER BANK

Dianeira (*shouts*) Heracles!

Heracles I have to protect my bow and arrows from the water and these clubs are cumbersome. I can't carry you myself, Dianeira.

Dianeira And then he came out of the woods, shaggy, black, gamboling friskily and made his way towards us.

Human face, long arms and torso. I'd never seen a
centaur before.

Heracles Climb onto the back of this beast, Dianeira, he
will swim you across the river.

Dianeira But – Heracles . . .

Heracles Don't be afraid of him, he's a centaur, a beast
of burden with human pretensions. Kick him if he goes
too slowly, I'll be behind you.

Dianeira What is your name?

Nessos Nessos, my lady.

Dianeira Nessos . . . But in the middle of the river . . .
with his hands, human hands, he started . . . first my
legs, then up . . . up . . . hands and water . . . I screamed.
   Heracles shot him with a poisoned arrow, from the
back . . .
   He dragged him up onto the river bank.

Heracles Beast, low mangy hairy foreign beast, not to be
trusted, uncontrolled appetite, ignoble in your actions,
and now that I've killed you, as you deserve, I have to
apologise for it and go and make a sacrifice to the gods
to purify myself.

*

Timberlake Irene stopped talking. She said that's all
we'd paid her for, she was thirsty. We argued that was
no place to stop, she hadn't given us a resolution, but
she remained silent, her mouth tightly shut, her eyes
increasingly veiled. After a while, we put more money
into her plate and ordered brandy for all of us.

Irene So: Dianeira was angry about getting old. She
hadn't known she was getting old until Heracles made

her see herself in Iole's reflection and, of course, her story isn't finished yet, although it could be. Many stories of anger finish in a blank. Now I'll tell you about the centaur Nessos. There were a lot of centaurs in those days, colonies of them, these horses with a human torso and arms, mocking eyes, in essence horses, but untamable and anarchic, and all of them with those wonderfully sensual hands. There are still some today in these parts, people say they hear them galloping through the woods at night. There were all kinds of other monsters too, like the chimera and the many-headed giant serpent Hydra but they belong to other stories although a few of them might come into this one. Well now, you know how powerful and also how heavy horses are and how terrible it is to watch them die. Heracles went off immediately to ask forgiveness of the gods for shooting him like that in a flare of anger, and Dianeira was left alone with the dying, the human monster. And this is the story of the anger of Nessos.

*

Nessos Why did he kill me like that, Dianeira? From the back too.

Dianeira I'm sorry . . . I didn't mean to cry out, I couldn't help it.

Nessos Never been touched down there before?

Dianeira Please . . .

Nessos We're good with our hands, I thought you liked it.

Dianeira I didn't understand at first, I thought it was the water.

Nessos Ha ha, he wouldn't know how to make you feel that, would he, too busy, too much in a hurry, ha ha.

Dianeira Stop it! You're disgusting! Still, I'm sorry you're dying.

Nessos I can feel the poison, look at this wound, it's oozing black. He didn't have to use poison, he could have just wounded me if he couldn't control his anger. Why didn't he carry you over himself? Because he cared more for his weapons. He didn't have to use poison . . . I'm beginning to feel the fire. It's going to be horrible, I'm going to be in terrible pain. You know, Dianeira, monsters feel pain more sharply than humans, we're not used to it.

Dianeira Can I clean the wound for you?

Nessos What's the point? The poison's inside. Your husband is a thoughtless man, Dianeira, prone to the moment, let me be blunt, he is a stupid man.

Dianeira Stop it.

Nessos And stupid men don't know how to resist temptations. He protects you now and kills anyone who wants you, but one day he'll turn away from you to follow the diaphanous drapes of youth. I know these heroes, their attention span is short.

Dianeira Stop it!

Nessos Stupid men take what they want, they don't calculate the consequences. Now I am going to do you a favour and give you a great gift, even though you have been the cause of my death. Ahh – it's coming, it's coming, burning red coals charring the inside of my flesh.

Dianeira Nessos . . .

Nessos I can't see any more. I only wanted a little fun, you humans are so absolute . . . now listen to me. Collect this blood and put it in that wooden vessel.

Do you see the very centre of my wound, don't be afraid, look, where the flesh is charred black.

Dianeira Yes . . .

Nessos The blood pouring out, more now . . . I can feel it, entwined with the black poison.

Dianeira Yes, Nessos.

Nessos Don't let it go over your hands, put the vessel here, just under there, is it filling?

Dianeira Yes . . .

Nessos Fast, eh, look how much blood we centaurs have. Now keep this a secret and when, one day, and it will happen, when the desires of Heracles wander away from you, then anoint your husband's cloth with this magic liquid and he will love you again. I promise, word of a centaur . . . And listen carefully, you must be sure this liquid is never exposed to sunlight or to heat, keep it in the dark, in the dark . . . until you need it, only then, always in the dark, secret, Dianeira, remember my words . . . Hide it from Heracles. Ahhh . . .

Scream of agony from Nessos.

Heracles I'm clean now, I've prayed to the gods, I've poured water over my hands,
    Why did you make me so angry?

Nessos Why didn't you control yourself, Heracles? You're a man. You're supposed to be rational –

Heracles How could I? Why did you provoke me?

Nessos You shot me in the back.

Heracles I ought not to have done that, but I've washed my hands and prayed. I had to take revenge.

Nessos For what, Heracles? I was only doing what I do best. A little mischief. Harmless.

Heracles You're a monstrous usurping hybrid who shouldn't be here at all.

Nessos I don't want to die. And not tortured like this. Not like this.

Heracles I can't help that. You didn't deserve to live.

Nessos I didn't deserve this torture, and it'll be slow, I know it'll be slow.

Cry of agony.

Heracles Come, Dianeira. Look, my hands are clean. Don't cry. He made me so angry. I couldn't let him get away with it. Don't keep looking at him. He's no more than a beast. Let's go.

Nessos Don't forget me, Dianeira.

Heracles Come, quickly.

TRACHIS

Dianeira I see you are ready to leave us, Lychas. Here is the gift I promised you for my husband.

Take this casket in which I have folded a robe which I wove myself during these long months of waiting. It is to be worn when he makes his sacrifices to the gods, when he needs to be seen in the full splendour of the hero, only then. Tell him to keep the robe well hidden from the sun so that its brilliance may not fade. Make haste. As for a message . . . what can I say . . . words of love might splinter against his indifference . . . no words then. Hurry.

Lychas I will move swiftly, dear lady, and do all you have asked.

Dianeira What have I done? Dreadful doubts casts their shadow.

Irene You can be angry and hit out, scream, kill. But you can also be angry in a manner so hidden even your actions seem unwilled. This invisible unfelt anger multiplies fast, undetected, unpreventable.

Dianeira What have I done . . .

Irene The anger that can't be admitted is the worse. It goes under and rots all.

Dianeira That magic, what have I done?

Irene I can't tell you if Dianeira knew what she was doing. How can I know? Anger could have paralysed her mind but made her hands more active than ever. That's not unusual in these women.

Dianeira screams.

First Chorus I hear Dianeira! Why these screams.

Second Chorus Let's go in, quickly.

Dianeira Women of Trachis, what have I done? Look, look there.

Gasps.

First Chorus Black.

Second Chorus A boiling mass.

Third Chorus Curdling.

First Chorus Black, oozing, look, it hardens.

Third Chorus Crumbles.

Second Chorus Shrinks.

First Chorus Leaving molten dust, this pulsating thing, not-thing.

Third Chorus Dust, still heaving. A mound of dust.

First Chorus Still alive . . .

Second Chorus Smouldering.

Third Chorus And the smell . . .

Chorus Ahhh.

First Chorus Putrefaction,

Dianeira That was once a square of sturdy cloth.

Third Chorus Sulphur.

First Chorus The stink of disease.

Second Chorus Look, it coils on itself . . .

First Chorus Self-consumed . . .

Third Chorus Vanishing . . .

Dianeira I used that square to anoint the robe I sent to
Heracles.

Third Chorus You anointed the robe?

Dianeira Yes, I had a magic ointment given to me long
ago by a friend, well, a centaur who . . . He told me to
keep the ointment away from the sun and from the heat
of the fire. I did this and today I applied it to the robe
under the cover of darkness and then I put the robe in
the casket, well protected, as you saw, with my
instructions to Lychas. Then I put the square of cloth
I used to impregnate the robe of Heracles on the stone
by the window and thought no more of it.

Third Chorus That?

Second Chorus Specks still moving, smoke, then nothing.

Dianeira What have I done?
  Why would that centaur do me a good turn? Heracles
shot him with a poisoned arrow. Because of me. Heracles

had steeped the arrow in the blood of the monstrous Hydra.

Third Chorus The many headed snake? *That Hydra?*

Dianeira Yes, who else? When Heracles killed the Hydra, I forget how, one of his works, he steeped some of the arrows in the monster's blood. But of course Nessos would have wanted to destroy the man who caused him such pain, treacherously too, I have to admit that, Heracles shot him in the back, that wasn't very heroic.

Second Chorus But Dianeira, I've heard that the putrid blood of the monstrous Hydra made even the gods ill when they smelled it.

Dianeira Yes . . . I'd forgotten. I wanted his desire back. The centaur told me to take his blood as it mixed with the thick black liquid from the arrow, he told me it would make Heracles burn with love for me. Burn . . . But I remember how dark, how thick, how disgusting it was, well, sometimes desire too . . . I didn't question it then, but now I believe this magic . . . I wonder . . . magic given in such anger and hatred, how can it lead to good . . .

If Heracles dies, I will die too.

I wanted desire, not the world's contempt, no, I couldn't take that.

First Chorus Softly, Dianeira. Don't let your fears run ahead of events. You don't know . . .

Dianeira I don't know . . .

Second Chorus You didn't plan to kill him.

Dianeira No, I didn't. Plan.

Third Chorus You can't be condemned for an unfortunate mistake.

Dianeira A mistake, yes, if there's no ill intent, but how do you know what intents form in a muddled and desperate heart? And fear, fear confuses intent too. What have I done? What did I mean to do? How can I know that?

First Chorus You must be quiet now, Dianeira, say nothing more. We can see Hyllos running towards the house. Here he comes. He will reassure you, or at least give us news.

Irene The last time we saw Hyllos, if you remember, he was walking through Greece looking for news of his father. And he was innocent, casting almost no shadow, a son who loved his mother and searched for his father, normal. Now his story begins, his own terrible story.

Dianeira Hyllos, my child, come to me, you look tired, pale, hurt. Let me look at you, I think you've even grown a little more, is your hair darker? Come close.

Hyllos I have only three things to say to you. I wish you had never been born. I wish, if you had to be born, you had never been my mother, and I wish you were dead.

First Chorus Hyllos, such words – to your mother!

Hyllos She is not my mother, she is disgusting, she is evil.

Dianeira Hyllos.

Hyllos Murderer!

Dianeira Hyllos! How dare you talk to me like that?

Hyllos You dared murder my father.

Dianeira Take back those words.

Hyllos As well take back what has happened. It's there, it happened, manifest, it can't be erased now, made not to have happened. Murderer! Look at what you've done.

Dianeira I don't know what I've done . . .

Hyllos I'll tell you. I won't spare you.

Here, look.

It didn't take me long to hear news of my father. I was told he was on his way back from the ravaged city of Eurytos laden with the spoils of his victory, weapons, treasures for you, hundreds of heads of cattle. He made his way to Cape Canean where there is a promontory overlooking the sea, and it was there he set out altars to pray to Zeus his father and thank him for his victory. That's where I saw him, surrounded by his army, as he was about to sacrifice some of the animals he had taken. It was there too that Lychas found him, Lychas: bearing your murderous gift, your finely woven robe.

Heracles (*delighted*) From Dianeira? Woven by her? For me?

Ah, it's magnificent.

Hyllos He put it on as you had instructed, keeping himself in the shade. And then, fit, tall and proud in the splendour of his robe, my father led twelve oxen to the altars. He seemed so happy, so glorious, and as he began his prayers his noble face was suffused with pride and with joy. I was standing in the crowd, but I was proud too, mother, that this splendid man was my father. The branches caught fire and crackled and the flames began to leap. He prayed, his face lit by the fire, maybe by the god.

Heracles God of the heavens and of all victories, Zeus, my father, I stand here to thank you for my triumph. The city razed to the ground, bounty, slaves, and for you these oxen. From you, Zeus, my strength, my purpose, and my hope. Accept these gifts, god of lightning, and stretch down the flames of your power to your mortal son, Heracles. Grant me a safe return, grant me days of peace, grant me my promised rest, grant me the time to

enjoy the fruits of my labour. Let your prophecy be
fulfilled, father, and let me rest at last.

Hyllos It was then, mother, that a sweat suddenly
glistened over his skin as the robe seemed to fold itself
around his body and cling, as if it had been glued to
his entire frame. He began to scratch himself, all over,
scratch, scratch, right in the middle of the sacrifice. It
was as if the cloth was gnawing at his bones, he couldn't
scratch hard or deep enough. He twisted himself around
and around, scratching, clawing. And now we could see
that the poison was feasting slowly on his skin the way a
snake wraps itself tightly around a limb. He began to
scream and called for Lychas to come to him and tell
him why he had plotted his ruin and decided to kill him
with this poisoned cloth. Poor Lychas tried to tell him
the gift came from you but as he spoke a new spasm of
torment coursed through the limbs of my father and he
grabbed Lychas by his heel and hurled him against a
rock. His head cracked open, brain oozed onto rock.
I had loved Lychas, Mother, it was from Lychas I learned
to be proud of my father, you never talked about him,
Lychas told me all the stories. And now, all that was left
was a white paste matted with blood dripping slowly
down the rock to the sea.

The people began to shudder in horror and to emit
a stifled shout, a cry kept subdued by fear as my father
began to throw himself on the ground, then jump up
again, writhing in agony, yanked like a yoyo by the
invisible hand of the poison. His cries clanged from the
mountains of Lochris to the rocky crag of Euboea. At
last, wearied, he fell to the ground cursing his marriage
to you, woman of evil luck, who had always harboured
his death in her heart. And as he lifted his eyes from the
smoke, he spotted me in the crowd, weeping, weeping.
And my father called out to me.

Heracles Child . . . come here. Child, don't run away from my torment. Come to me, my child.

Hyllos I ran up to him, mother, but I could not embrace him because of his pain.

Heracles Child, don't let me die here on this desolate promontory. Take me away with you. Take me to the sea.

Hyllos We did as he bid, carried him with much trouble and effort onto a ship where he bellowed his pain to the waves. Landed on the coast and now he makes his way here. Whether you will see his corpse or the living breathing wreckage of the man, I can't say, but I will make you look at what you've done. Yes Mother, clever plot, but you have been found out. All Greece will echo with your evil and I pray that the guilt and torment of all the furies of Hell will pay you back in kind for what you've done.

First Chorus Hyllos . . . This is your mother, show due respect and don't transgress the law.

Hyllos She usurps the name of mother, pollutes it with her presence.
   I hear my father, the greatest man on earth, the best of fathers, I'll make you face him, let him do what he will with you.
   I'll take you before him and if he has the strength, he'll kill you and I won't care.

First Chorus Look, Hyllos, your mother glides slowly towards the house, not a word.

Hyllos Let her slink away, slithering murderess.

Second Chorus Still your mother.

Hyllos Is there anything in her behaviour to show she ever gave birth? That crawling piece of evil flesh is not a mother.

First Chorus I can feel a lament threading its way through the house, what now?

Third Chorus A draught of misery, a trembling of walls . . .

First Chorus Let's go in, I see Dianeira's nurse.

Nurse She moves from room to room, she won't speak, I follow her. Look. First she went to all the altars in the house..

Dianeira The things I cannot say . . . Yes, I knew.

Nurse She glides through the house, touches each object, vases, her loom, a seat of stone.

Dianeira I felt no surprise. I knew it was poison, would kill him. I knew . . .

Nurse Then she went into the bedroom, sat in the middle of their bed.

Dianeira The things I cannot say: some pleasure in those screams of pain. Because of my own pain, all these years, when he first took me, when he left me, when he came back, when children came and now when he chose to discard.

Nurse She loosed both brooches from the shoulders of her robe.

Dianeira The things I cannot say: I don't feel pity, not even sorrow, not now. And yet, there must have been love. Now kneaded, pounded, pulled into the shape of anger. Why was this my life? Passive, always in the dark, waiting for the dawn, a new day, a return, a farewell, waiting.

And finally waiting to disappear burned by jealousy, well, let him burn instead.

Nurse I saw then she had a sword in her hand.

Dianeira Hyllos, that I cannot bear: to be orphaned of my child, abandoned by him and hated, no – the house empty of children and of love, no, not that.

Nurse She cried out and mourned her abandoned hearth and the ashes grown cold. She cried out and I rushed to call Hyllos to help me.

Dianeira The things I cannot say: I don't mind if I die now, I wouldn't have minded earlier, what has this life been for? There's nothing there. Let the night come down with its shimmering blanket of nothingness, let the night cover me.

Nurse And she pierced her side with the sword.

Dianeira The things I cannot say: I look for the pattern now, the diagram giving my life sense, but I see nothing. It was all a waste of breath.

Nurse How did she find so much strength in her arm, what woman kills herself with a sword?
  This is a terrible end and with her end comes mine. What life is there when you have no one to look after?

Hyllos Why are you calling me? Can't you hear the screams of my father wending their way up the hill? I must go to him. And then she will face her torment.

First Chorus She is already dead, Hyllos.

Third Chorus Killed herself.

Second Chorus With a sword, heroic act and manly.

Third Chorus Condemned by you.

Second Chorus Unheard and undefended.

Third Chorus Alone.

Second Chorus Your anger.

First Chorus She never intended to kill your father.

Second Chorus That robe was dipped in a love potion.

Third Chorus Now.

First Chorus You have no one to rail against.

Second Chorus Where will you throw your anger?

Third Chorus Where?

First Chorus Not her. Now.

Third Chorus Out of your reach.

Hyllos Mother . . .

First Chorus No good throwing yourself on the bed now.

Third Chorus Crying.

Hyllos Mother . . .

First Chorus No good kissing her hands, taking her in your arms, bathing her in tears. Her blood smeared on your hands. Too late.

Second Chorus That's the essence of death: too late.

Third Chorus She can't hear, silent herself

Second Chorus You might as well go back to your father.

First Chorus We want you away from here now.

Second Chorus Go to your father.

Hyllos My mother . . .

First Chorus Go.

First Chorus Go now. To your father.

*

Irene I can stop now. Unless you give me more brandy and a few more bills in there, eh?

Dianeira is dead, dead in anger. What kind of a life was that? Of what significance? All shadows and quiet, sometimes it makes you angry just to remember those lives. I can go on. Because now the story takes a right-angle turn. Now we have the great man, once strong and beautiful, the man of great works, ravaged and humiliated by disease and now we have his anger and the scarring of his son. Listen.

The women of Trachis laid out the body of Dianeira ready for burning and then moved slowly out of the house as they heard the heavy tread of a mournful procession winding its way up the hill.

Second Chorus I don't want to be here.

Third Chorus I don't want to see any of this.

Second Chorus Why do we always have to witness these horrors?

Third Chorus I never asked for this.

Second Chorus I think I'd rather die myself.

First Chorus Here they come. Strangers. They carry him with tenderness and care, but he may be dead.

Second Chorus That would be best, but he might only be asleep.

Third Chorus Hyllos walks at the front, head bowed.

Second Chorus I really don't want to see this.

Third Chorus I can see the body and a shudder run
through it.

First Chorus They put the litter down. They're so gentle
with him, these strangers.

Second Chorus He lifts his head.

Third Chorus Hyllos stands beside him.

Heracles Child, dear child, where are you? Take my
hand. My son . . .
  Now comes the pain, I can feel it clawing my flesh,
digs deep, deeper. Hyllos, if only you could take my
sword, and slice, slice off the pain at my neck, here, head
from neck, it's easy, do it. Oh you furies from Hell, let
my life close up now.

Second Chorus I shudder at the sight of this man. Such a
man, so much pain.

Heracles I worked so hard. All my life. Painful even in
the telling. I never stopped. I crossed swords with a
thousand men, I braved an army of giants, I mastered
the wild beasts of the earth, I purified my country of
diseases and the scourge of monsters. Look at my hands.
I throttled the ox-eating lion with them, I subdued the
hissing invincible many-headed Hydra. I tamed those
lawless horses with the heads of men, the anarchic
centaurs, and I even dragged the three-headed dog of the
underworld to the light. That was before, no after, I killed
the dragon who guarded the golden apples on the far edges
of the world. How many other labours? And I always
won. No one beat me at anything, ever. And now look
at me. Mown down by the blind sweep of misfortune.
No, not fate. Her. What neither Greek nor stuttering
Barbarian could do, she's done by wrapping this cloak
of venom around me, she, without a sword, her hatred
only, she's turned me inside out, revealed me to be no

more than a girl, a girl. Crying, begging for help, I have no strength, not even courage, I'm a girl, a girl.

Cries.

I can't bear this pain, this flaming itch. It flicks and then it grips and then it throttles every limb. Look at your father, Hyllos, look at this gangrenous puppet, limbs jerking in all directions, screeching distress, that's what she's done. No respite. Never again.

I always did my duty, followed my calling without complaint. I, son of the noble Alcmene and son also of a god, look at me now, shredded.

Screams.

Hyllos Father . . .

Heracles Bring her to me, bring her here, Hyllos. Never mind that she is your mother, that she suckled you, cradled you, bring her out and deliver her into these hands. Still strong. Quickly, Hyllos, show yourself to be a true son of mine, waste no time. And let me see whether you feel more for your father or for your mother when she lies before you mangled by my hands as she's mangled me. Go.

Hyllos Father . . .

Heracles I may be nothing now, but I can still inflict on her the same torment she's inflicted on me. Bring her to me and I'll pull out of her one by one sounds that declare Heracles always takes revenge on the wrongs done to him.

Irene Our parents are the great heroes of our mythology, our Olympian gods. To watch them fall is unbearable. Hyllos sees his great strong father cry like a girl and he can't help despising Heracles a little. Hyllos then begins to feel the most painful anger of all, anger against oneself.

Hyllos Father, you must listen to me.

Heracles The pain roars in my ears, what did you say?

Hyllos Listen.

Heracles Be quick, before the next spasm.

Hyllos My mother . . .

Heracles Why isn't she here yet? You promised to bring her, why have you disobeyed?

Hyllos Father . . . my mother . . .

Heracles It roars, it roars. I want her in my hands, why are you withholding this last pleasure from me?

Hyllos I must speak to you of her, Father, she did wrong, but not willingly.

Heracles How can you speak of her with that tone of voice when you stand in front of the father she murdered?

Hyllos You wouldn't say that if you knew –

Heracles Am I not dying? Did she not poison me? Are you in league with her? Are you going to show yourself a murderous villain and not my son?

Hyllos She is dead. Just now. Pierced by the sword.

Heracles You did this?

Hyllos She did. Alone.

Heracles She did. Coward. And so she slips from the torture of my hands. Rage.

Hyllos Your anger will subside when you learn more.

Heracles Relinquish my anger? Never!

Hyllos She knew of your unbridled lust for Iole, she wanted to apply a love charm that would turn your

365

desires back to her. She wanted to save the house from
Iole's long shadow, keep her marriage, protect the family
and me too, Father, your oldest son – if you were to
install as your wife and my mother a girl not much older
than I.

Heracles Who in Trachis is so expert in drugs?

Hyllos Nessos the centaur gave her the charm many
years ago and told her it would rekindle the dying
embers of your love.

Heracles Olololola. I see the shape of my fate now, the
man-monster galloping from Hell with his deadly revenge.
Your father is no more, Hyllos. Darkness for me now.
  Call your brothers and your sisters, call my mother,
that proud bride of Zeus. Why? What was it all for? Her
marriage, bearing me? Nothing, all in vain.
  When you are all gathered I will disclose the final
predictions concerning my fate.

Hyllos When you left for your last works, our family
scattered, Father, but I am here. Speak to me, I will assist
you as best I can.

Irene All his life Hyllos longed for the intimacy and the
confidence of his great and absent father. He feels a
moment of joy at not having to share it, being the only
one there, at last recognised and valued. So he believes.
He can't know that when parents die they behave no
differently than when they lived.

Heracles Now listen carefully, Hyllos, and prove to
me you are indeed my son and not some bastard of
your mother's. It was my own father Zeus who told
me I would never die at the hands of a human being.
I thought he was promising me immortality or at least
a heroic combat with a god. Now I see all he meant
was that the hatred and anger of a mortal being, of an

animal, would be stored cold in the jaws of hell, waiting
for me.

And Zeus said more when I went to consult his sacred
oak. I remember how the branches bent down to me and
the leaves murmured in soft tones that all my work, all
that endless effort would one day come to an end. And
I thought the branches were singing of ease to come,
retirement, rest at last, but they were only mouthing
words of death. Of course! Only in death do we rest
from our labours. Ha ha. That was the prediction! Now
it all twists together and glistens in the light. My destiny
made manifest.

What was all that work for? Nothing. Vanity. Passing.
You, my child, must now help your father. Be my
companion and my friend, do not make me repeat any
of this twice and do what I ask with joy and with due
respect for the law that orders sons always to obey their
fathers.

Hyllos These words said so solemnly frighten me, Father,
but I will obey.

Heracles Hold out your right hand, touch mine and
swear.

Hyllos Here is my hand.

Heracles Pray also for unending torment as punishment
if you fail.

Hyllos I can keep my promises, Father, but even so I ask
for punishment if I fail.

Heracles See the peak of Mount Oeta over there. You
will carry me to that peak in your own arms, my son.

Hyllos Yes, Father, I will do that.

Heracles When you reach the mountain peak, cut off the
branches of some deeply rooted oaks and add the strongest

branches of an olive tree. Then make a pyre and use the soft branches of a fir tree to light it. And on that pyre, Hyllos, you will throw my live body.

Hyllos Your body, alive –

Heracles You will throw my live body on the fire. And you will do all this without a tear, not so much as a moan or the least sign of mourning.

Hyllos You can't ask this of me.

Heracles I have told you what you must do, if not, you are someone else's son, not mine.

Hyllos You are asking me to be your killer.

Heracles I am asking for you to end this torment, to be my healer.

Hyllos How can I cure your body by burning it live?

Heracles It is mercy.

Hyllos It is killing.

Heracles Mercy-killing then. Take friends with you if you cannot bear to do this alone. Don't cross me now, Hyllos, don't make me angry.

Hyllos Father, I will carry you there, that I cannot refuse.

Heracles And you will prepare the wood for the pyre.

Hyllos Yes, I can do that, but I cannot let my hands bring on your death.

Heracles I don't care who lights the pyre.

Hyllos No one will agree to be your murderer.

Heracles I am the one in pain. It's what I want.

Hyllos I cannot kill my own father.

Heracles You understand nothing.

Hyllos My gesture, my guilt.

Heracles My pain.

Hyllos Father, please, release me.

Heracles Too late: you swore and the gods witnessed.
Now one other small favour . . .

Irene Listen to the gasp from Hyllos. This intractable
and totally self-absorbed father, asking for what now?
And where can Hyllos turn? To Zeus, his father's father,
who seems to have mocked Heracles all along?

Heracles Do you know the daughter of Eurytos?

Hyllos You mean Iole?

Heracles Yes, I mean Iole. Hyllos, she shared my bed,
I don't want an unknown stranger to lay his hands on
her when I'm gone. I have decided you will marry her.
Obey the sacred duty you owe your father and do not
confound your good behaviour by disobeying me over
this small matter.

Hyllos Father: Iole's presence caused my mother's death,
your unendurable pain now. Who would ask me to marry
her but someone whose mind was beset with poisoning
spirits or by the avenging hounds of Hell. I would rather
die than share a house, a bed with my most hated enemy.

Heracles I'm the one who is dying.

Hyllos You can't see any more, Father, but she's coming
out of the house now, as if summoned by her hated
name. And I can see from here triumph on her face.
Don't forget you killed her father, burned her city, took
her by violence.

Heracles I loved her.

Hyllos Strange manifestation of love, Father, but now you're dying, writhing in agony, and she gloats on your pain, on my mother's death. What I see is a curl of pleasure on her cold lips. Don't ask me to marry such malice.

Heracles It's what I want. It's the fulfilment of my fate.

Hyllos Is it fulfilling your fate to prevent me from living?

Heracles I've had enough of your disobedience and your doubts. If you disobey me in this, I'll call down the vengeance of the gods, and believe me they will wait for you and they will destroy you.

Hyllos Your mind is sick.

Heracles And you're arousing my pains again, I can feel them unfurling, Ah – you're doing this to me.

Heracles begins to moan, louder.

Hyllos I am lost, I don't know where to turn.

Heracles Listen to the man who gave you life.

Hyllos You're asking for the impossible, it's against every feeling.

Heracles Obey, ask no questions.

Hyllos Make an end of you with my own hands – marry in hatred.

Heracles Don't turn over your actions so much when I am the one commanding them.

Hyllos Where are the rules? All my life I loved you and trusted you.

Heracles Then trust me now. Don't arouse my pains. Take me to the mountain quickly.

Hyllos Father, how can I love my children if I loathe my wife?

Heracles Love.

Hyllos Didn't you love my mother?

Heracles I hate her now.

Hyllos Father, please, let me decide: give me back my life.

Heracles We must look to my death.

Irene It could go on, this argument, but in the end, fathers do eat their sons if they can, there is no other myth that rings so true. I know you young people like to think differently, but you give yourselves the illusion of too much power. You do what your fathers tell you in the end, one way or the other, even now, you'll die by their order. You can hear that death from here, right now, taking place up north. That's another story. A story of obedience.

And now the long arm of Heracles bows down the head of his son and turns this young man full of hope and life and possible love into a man overflowing with resentment, anger. And so it continues.

Hyllos I can't disobey you, I'll do as you say, and if what I do is wrong it's by your command, Father, and not of my own will.

Heracles I did as my own father asked . . . Laboured, laboured, never questioned, never complained. Do I reproach him now for the grim and itching end he's kept for me? Do I accuse him of falsehood when I heard promises from him that made me dream of ease? No. I bow my head to him. I accept, as a man does, as a son must. Now lift me up, gently, before a new spasm contorts my body. Carry me, child.

Hyllos Yes father.

Sob and groan from Hyllos, murmurs of women.

Heracles Now my hardened soul must clamp itself shut. No cries, no cries. And let this act you perform with such reluctance fill you with joy because it is my release, my child, long awaited. This is the end of the man I am.

Hyllos Let us carry him to the mountain, friends, and let the world grant me forgiveness for what I am about to do.

First Chorus And we will follow this procession since we have witnessed these awful sufferings. We must remember, however, that all that has happened has been the will of the god.

Hyllos The will of the god, oh yes, let us contemplate, as we carry my father Heracles to that mountain, the heedless carelessness of these gods. They call themselves our fathers, Zeus called this man his own seed, his mortal son, and yet Zeus looks on his pain unmoved, if he bothers to look at all. Here is my father enduring in anguish this god-given ruin, it brings out our human pity, horror and compassion, but what do the gods feel? Not even shame.

Irene The procession made its way slowly up the mountain. There were no more cries from Heracles. Iole and the women of Trachis watched as his wrecked body burnt down to ash. Iole never said a word. She never said a word when she married Hyllos. She never said a word to her children. What was there to say? the bitterest anger is silent. And so anger threads its way through generations. There is only one more curve to the story. One morning, some years after his marriage, Hyllos went to Iole.

Hyllos Iole . . .

Irene Naturally, she gave no answer, did not even turn to look at him.

Hyllos Iole, for years now we've lived in bitter hatred, anger . . .

Irene She turned then to look at him, bland, confirming those words.

Hyllos Iole, my life was ruined by the hatred of my parents for each other. Do you want to ruin our children?

Irene She stares at him, still with no expression.

Hyllos What if I let you go? Would you then forgive my father and my family?

Irene Hyllos watches for a flicker but there is none, maybe a slight widening of the eyes.

Hyllos You could go back to your city, rebuild it even. Leave the children here while they are young.

Irene Iole smiles now and Hyllos mistakes the smile.

Hyllos You would be free, you could rebuild your life, the city of your father, and when this is done the children could come to you and we could end this anger.

Irene But Iole's smile is the smile of refusal. She has suckled her children with her anger, she is her anger, how can she relinquish the anger that she is? Anger is her life, her identity, and even a not too unpleasant habit. She shakes her head and Hyllos feels his own anger rising again, fury at her stubbornness, and he shakes her, shakes her hard.

Moans from Iole.

Hyllos I wanted to stop this.

Irene He shakes her harder, so hard it hurts. More anger for both, another notch of hatred.

*

Iole's city was never rebuilt. The ruins are over there, you can't see much now, but you can visit them. The family had descendants but they became scattered and unimportant. And the gods looked on, indifferent, and then they changed too and were forgotten.

Eventually, people stopped telling the story, this terrible story of anger, and it too was forgotten. It happened so long ago. At least I believe it was a long time ago, but I am tired now and need to rest.

*

Timberlake We left her, nodding over her brandy and put a few more notes in the plate. Outside, in the clear night, we could hear the guns of the country north of the border, where there is always a war. And then we drove silently back to Athens.